SCIENCE, THEOLOGY, AND CONSCIOUSNESS

SCIENCE, THEOLOGY, AND CONSCIOUSNESS

The Search for Unity

JOHN BOGHOSIAN ARDEN

Westport, Connecticut
London

Library of Congress Cataloging-in-Publication Data

Arden, John Boghosian.
    Science, theology, and consciousness : the search for unity / John
Boghosian Arden.
        p. cm.
    Includes bibliographical references and index.
    ISBN 0–275–96032–3 (alk. paper)
    1. Consciousness. I. Title.
    BF311.A676 1998
    153—dc21   97–18723

British Library Cataloguing in Publication Data is available.

Library of Congress Catalog Card Number: 97–18723
ISBN: 0–275–96032–3

First published in 1998

Praeger Publishers, 88 Post Road West, Westport, CT 06881
An imprint of Greenwood Publishing Group, Inc.

Printed in the United States of America

The paper used in this book complies with the
Permanent Paper Standard issued by the National
Information Standards Organization (Z39.48–1984).

10 9 8 7 6 5 4 3 2 1

In memory of the Boghosian family,
Mesak, Louise, Marjorie, and Margaret

Contents

Illustrations

Preface

Like many people I have always been fascinated by questions such as: "How did human consciousness emerge?" and "What is consciousness?" My intense curiosity has driven me to explore a vast diversity of opinions and attempts to answer these questions. Yet I have been frustrated at being unable to find a comprehensive theory addressing the evolution and complexity of consciousness.

During the past twenty-five years my quest to understand consciousness has taken me on a journey through many schools of thought, including philosophy, evolutionary theory, physics, anthropology, theology, and psychology. Each of these fields offers a valuable part of the picture, but an incomplete explanation of who we are and how we came to be conscious beings. What we need is a coherent synthesis of the worthwhile contributions of each perspective.

Just as I have explored various fields, so have theorists from these fields attempted to construct a theory of unity and an exploration of consciousness. We have, for example, seen philosophers, computer scientists, anthropologists, physicists, biologists, and theologians all attempting to develop models of consciousness and descriptions of what it means to be human. However, for the most part what we have seen are compartmentalized approaches with little cross-fertilization between these fields.

In my own field of psychology I have advocated a multidisciplinary approach to the study of consciousness. Out of frustration I argued in my earlier book, *Consciousness, Dreams, and Self: A Transdisciplinary Approach*, that we must avoid the "theoretical clubhouse" model. Instead, we need a broad-based explanation of what it means to be conscious individuals, not just theories isolated by the field of the author.

This current book is an attempt to extend the multidisciplinary model and simultaneously reach an audience beyond the confines of academic psychology. Instead of limiting my focus on the body/brain, society/culture, and thoughts/emotions, I also address the uncanny and hard to explain area of transpersonal/spiritual experience.

This book is an attempt to make sense of a diversity of viewpoints and to synthesize conceptually useful elements of each approach into a single unified theory. To accomplish this synthesis of seemingly diverse fields requires that I throw out antiquated concepts and beliefs, however popular. Unfortunately, many of the obsolete concepts and beliefs I will question are held near and dear to the hearts of the bulk of humanity.

One of the many concepts I confront is "dualism," which is the belief that there are two or more levels of reality that have little to do with one another. I will explain how this belief has been a major obstacle to developing a coherent theory of consciousness.

The other beliefs, concepts, and methodologies that I will clarify and question include: "determinism," "linearity," "objectivity," and "reductionism." I will explain each of these terms in the next several chapters. While these terms still have some usefulness, they have limited utility within the overall "paradigm shift." I will also introduce and explain the new concepts which are consistent with the major paradigm shift occurring in the natural sciences including: "nonlinearity," "bi-directional causality," "chaos," and "interconnectiveness." This latter set of concepts provides us with the opportunity to understand much more clearly the nature and meaning of our experience in a complex evolving universe. I have also provided a glossary of terms, which readers may find helpful. The reader need not have prerequisite education in any of the areas discussed.

In this book, consciousness is described as a multidimensional process in which multidirectional causal interrelationships occur. I attempt to address the issues of nonlocal causality, free will, the mind/body connection, and transpersonal experience in one unifying and multidisciplinary theory.

Overall, if we are to understand the evolution of human consciousness, we must take into account the vast array of factors that influence consciousness. We must understand how these factors themselves coevolve with one another. In other words, we must understand consciousness to be the result of numerous factors that are interdependent and coevolve.

I cast a broad net and incorporate elements of many fields, including evolutionary theory, physics, theology, philosophy, and psychology. I have attempted to introduce and explain relevant developments in these fields in a nontechnical manner. It is my hope that after a thorough reading of this book you, the reader, will gain an appreciation for the convergent unity of consciousness and a well-balanced perspective of what it means to be a conscious human being.

ORGANIZATION OF THE BOOK

Chapter 1, "Then and Now," presents the need for an actual paradigm shift and critiques those efforts that have used the term "paradigm shift" to mask antiquated concepts that are simply tacked onto current paradigms. I trace the sociocultural and philosophical foundations of our current fragmented and compartmentalized conceptual dilemma. The concepts of linear causality, complete objectivity, reductionism, and dualism are shown to have major limitations. I then describe the emerging shift toward a process philosophy whereby the concepts of change through fluctuation and multidisciplinary perspectives widen our understanding of consciousness.

Chapter 2, "Evolution and Chaos," presents the major paradigm shifts that have occurred in evolutionary theory, thermodynamics, chaos theory, and complexity theory. This overview and discussion is important because consciousness is an evolutionary phenomenon and has to be understood as such. The concepts derived from the theories and discussed in this chapter—such as "coevolution," "autopoiesis," "far-from-equilibrium conditions," "nonlinearity," "bifurcation," and "attractors"—will be used throughout the rest of the book to describe the evolution of consciousness.

Chapter 3, "The Self System," presents the biopsychosocial and nonlinear coevolutionary process. This chapter summarizes many of the issues addressed in my earlier book *Consciousness, Dreams, and Self: A Transdisciplinary Approach*. The emergence of what I refer to as *self systems* will be described. The multidisciplinary field of psychoneuroimmunology is described to illustrate the coevolutionary nature of the biopsychosocial aspects of consciousness.

Chapter 4, "Nocturnal Consciousness: The Nature of Dreams," discusses the dream process from a multidisciplinary perspective. The phenomenon of dreams represents a beautiful example of how biophysiological, sociocultural, intrapsychic, and transpersonal dynamics coevolve. Also discussed is the relationship between psi field phenomena and the altered states that occur in dreaming. The dream state is inherent to self system dynamics. Periodically the dream state can be sensitive to dynamics that correspond to experiences that extend beyond the self—to transpersonal interconnective dynamics. An argument is made that this state is not subject to the same constraints as waking consciousness because reciprocal interaction with the environment is not necessary.

Chapter 5, "Perennial Philosophy and Sociotheological Systems," describes the emergence of "sociotheological systems" and what can be regarded as the perennial philosophy. The emergence of sociotheological systems exemplifies the nonlinear coevolution of the sociocultural, self-system, and transpersonal aspects of consciousness. During periods of far-from-equilibrium sociocultural conditions, the attractors for the major sociotheological systems emerged. The cultural conditions that existed in the Middle East, India, and China are described with respect to the emergence of the Judeo-Christian-Islamic, Hindu-Jainist-Buddhist, and Confucianist-Taoist-Buddhist theological spectrums. Differentiations are made between cultural factors and transcultural themes.

Chapter 6, "Matter, Fields of Information, and Incompleteness," describes the major paradigm shifts that have occurred in physics and computational theory which may shed light on the many aspects of consciousness. The shift away from the Newtonian/Cartesian Paradigm is described to illustrate the nonmechanistic, nondeterministic and nondualistic aspects of existence. The curious and dramatic finding of "nonlocality" is described. Finally, the changes in computational theory and the work of Kurt Gödel are noted. Gödel's Incompleteness Theorem illustrates the limitation of the use of logical systems to replicate and describe consciousness.

Chapter 7, "Self-Convergence," presents many of the provocative "para" phenomena such as psi experiences and near-death experiences. These paraphenomena illustrate that consciousness is sensitive to interconnective relationships that transcend the self system. On one hand, most of the scientific community reject these paraphenomena; on the other hand, many of those who do not reject these phenomena fail to discriminate among the various types. A sober analysis of these phenomena is presented. Parapsychological research is discussed and arguments for the validity of some and the lack of validity for other paraphenomena are presented. I then discuss and critique efforts that have been made to construct a transpersonal psychology. An alternative model is proposed which corresponds to a nondualistic and multidisciplinary perspective.

Finally, in Chapter 8, "An Evolving Unity," a unified theory of the evolution of consciousness is proposed. The phenomenon of nonlocality is related to many aspects of consciousness including transpersonal experience. The relationship between the arrow of time and the postulate of precognition is critically examined. In conclusion, an evolutionary theology that includes elements of the perennial philosophy with new developments in science and the study of consciousness is proposed.

Acknowledgments

No book is written in a vacuum. This book is no exception. I have been fortunate to have gained from the feedback of many individuals. The support and helpful suggestions have come in both the technical and editorial areas.

Selected chapters of this book have been read for technical accuracy by Dr. Bruce Boghosian of Boston University, Dr. Brian Goodwin of Open University in London, Dr. Basil Hiley of Birbeck College, the University of London, Dr. Stanley Krippner of the Saybrook Institute, Dr. Karl Pribram of Radford University, Dr. Roger Spence of Kaiser Permanente Medical Center, and Dr. Jerome Ward of Auburn University.

Editorial feedback has come from Vicki Arden, John Arden (senior), Kevin Brackett, Richard Cohen, Risa Aratyr, Barbara Monnette, Michael Skolinik, Dr. Pam Stevenson, Dr. Carrie Stoltzfus, and Diane Wiley. Finally, my thanks to Dr. Jim Sabin and Dr. George Zimmar of the Greenwood Publishing Group for their help and support. I am indebted to all of the above and especially to my wife Vicki for the illustrations and our sons Paul and Gabriel for their patience for the time it has taken to complete this project.

1

Then and Now

But no one puts a patch of unshrunk cloth on an old garment; for the patch
pulls away from the garment, and a worse tear results.
Nor do men put new wine into old wineskins, otherwise the wineskins burst,
and the wine pours out, and the wineskins are ruined; but they put new wine
into new wineskins, and both are preserved.

Matthew, 9:16–17

Throughout history we as a species have mapped out meaning for our existence.
Each effort can be described as an attempt to make sense out of the diversity of
experience. During the last few hundred years in the Western world this search
for unity has taken many turns. On one end of the spectrum various theorists
have proposed a completely materialistic approach, while on the other extreme
theorists have proposed theological explanations. Where does the truth lie?

In recent years many authors have touted a "new paradigm" from which we
can view the world and ourselves within it. Unfortunately, several of these
authors have used the term "paradigm shift" to mask old ideas that are merely
counter to the prevailing view. It would be misleading to say that these efforts
can be described as pouring new wine into old wineskins because the wine is not
new. Some authors have advocated an acknowledgment of "spiritual experience." Yet when promoting this emphasis any spiritual concepts, however far-
fetched, are uncritically embraced. These efforts are in juxtaposition to the materialists—those requiring a rigid five-sensory validation for any experience.

Dualism has offered fool's gold to its adherents. It comes in many forms.
Some authors have offered a "layer cake model" of existence, whereby each of
the layers has "metaphysical truths" that account for every reported experience.
However, simply because people have reported a particular experience which
seemed beyond natural explanation does not mean there is broad-based "truth" to
the experience that applies to other people. This type of approach promotes dual-

ism—the concept that splits off the material world from subjective experience.

There have also been efforts to gain new insights into consciousness using the new perspectives of chaos, complexity, and evolutionary theory, all of which will be explained in the following chapters. The emergence of these new perspectives is a very positive development. Unfortunately, the authors who have introduced these perspectives have essentially inquired into consciousness almost as an addendum.

Another recent trend has been to incorporate certain elements of modern physics into the study of consciousness. New developments in physics are compelling. Again, we find that the attempts to associate these new developments in physics to consciousness have been made by authors who know little about psychology and therefore include broad, obsolete, yet popular generalizations about consciousness. Thus, these efforts are comparable to sewing a new patch on an old garment. Consequently, what is offered as paradigm shift falls short.

I do not believe that these efforts constitute an actual paradigm. So then, what is meant by the term "paradigm shift"? A paradigm shift is a complete change in perspective. It is new wine in new wineskins. The concept of a paradigm shift is just over thirty years old. Thomas Kuhn proposed, in a now classic text, that the evolution of scientific thought has been characterized by major conceptual reorganizations—paradigm shifts.[1] His notion was that productive theoretical change occurs in spurts of innovation, followed by phases of routine research, the innovative spurts leading to a higher levels of theoretical organization. The accumulation of vast amounts of data creates a need for a more simplified, but more highly organized theorem or paradigm shift, and the process repeats.

Should there be a paradigm shift related to theories of consciousness? Pondered throughout history, the issue of consciousness remains one of the most misunderstood of human phenomena. To complicate this problem, the field of psychology, the field that should investigate consciousness, has fragmented and become compartmentalized into a plethora of schools and subschools. There are so many viewpoints and contrasting opinions about what constitutes consciousness that even the most rigorous investigator is often baffled by the lack of a coherent explanation. This problem is best capsulated by the popular analogy of several blind men all attempting to describe an elephant. The one touching the trunk will have a different explanation than the one touching the ears. In psychology most theorists have focused on either the biophysiological, sociocultural, or intrapsychic aspects of consciousness, emphasizing one particular theme and ignoring others. Consequently, these theorists believe that consciousness can be explained completely by biophysiological, sociocultural, or intrapsychic descriptions. Further, there has been an avoidance of theoretical approaches that have dealt with transpersonal experience—experiences that transcend the self. Conversely, when transpersonal phenomena have been addressed, the biophysiological, sociocultural, and intrapsychic aspects of such experience have been glossed over. A new model of consciousness is needed to integrate all of these aspects of consciousness, along with similar paradigm shifts in the natural sciences. Because consciousness is a natural and evolutionary process, the inclusion of the latest developments in the sciences is vital.

The time is ripe for a real paradigm shift in the study of consciousness. We cannot just affix new ideas to old concepts, just as we cannot add new wine to old wine skins. A real paradigm shift will require a conceptual synthesis of multiple processes. A multidisciplinary approach to the study of consciousness provides the perspective we need to facilitate such a shift. Consciousness is the result of multiple factors, including evolutionary processes. The integration of multidisciplinary influences places consciousness on center stage.

We must cover a considerable amount of theoretical territory: evolutionary theory and the application of this approach to an overview of the evolution of our species, of societies, and of what I have referred to elsewhere as self systems—individuals with their own subjective experiences.[2] A perspective that appreciates the diversity of experience, including individual reports of spiritual experiences, gives us the best vantage point from which to view consciousness. This perspective includes a discussion of how people have conceptualized such experiences. Also, this discussion needs a sober understanding of the physical world. But before immersing ourselves in these areas we must first discuss the philosophical foundations that led to the difficulty developing a coherent and unified understanding of consciousness.

THE SCHISM

Throughout history we have asked questions that have revolved around the central question: What is our place within the world and the universe? Before the development of agricultural settlements, much early speculation concerned our subsistence practices. During the Paleolithic Era, for example, mythologies were developed to explain the migration of game animals and our relationships with them. However, these relationships were embedded within an ecosystem that often seemed confusing or mysterious. The mythological system played the role that science now plays in interpreting or predicting natural phenomena. Essentially, myth, history, and science were probably part of one unified belief system in prehistoric societies. As tribes and social systems became more complex, so did mythological systems.

A pantheon of gods was assumed responsible for natural phenomena, such as the rain and wind. When someone became ill or injured, rituals were performed to seek favor from the gods. This contributed to a dualistic understanding of one's position in the world, in that individuals were not seen as responsible for or capable of managing their own lives. Instead, there was a reliance on external gods for health and good fortune.

With the development of the major theological systems, humans organized their lives according to the constructs prescribed by their theology. When individuals experienced "transpersonal"-type phenomena, they interpreted the experience within the parameters dictated by those theological systems.[3] In fact, they interpreted *any* experience through the dictates of their theological system. For example, if a fifth-century Christian were to have a dream with one dream character talking to the other about the humanity of Jesus, the dreamer might upon awakening have interpreted the dream as a warning against deviating from his or her church's doctrine of the trinity. This is because during the fifth century there was a great deal of controversy centered on the question of the true nature of Jesus. Those who embraced His humanity were regarded as blasphemous.

Although many people still adhere to only one conceptual framework, a variety of changes occurred during the European Renaissance and the Enlightenment that challenged the tendency of most people to adhere to a common dogma. These major shifts were precipitated by tremendous turbulence in Europe in the fourteenth and fifteenth centuries. During the mid fourteenth century the Black Plague occurred and one-third of the population of Europe died. The Islamic Turks conquered Constantinople and crushed the last elements of the Byzantine Empire, thereby opening Europe's Eastern door. Then late in that same century a theological schism occurred, throwing what conceptual unity the church had maintained into disarray. No longer were there simple conceptual frameworks from which people interpreted the world around them. Suddenly the world became increasingly complex.

The emergence of scientific inquiry was an attempt to make sense of this complex world. Yet many of the scientific observations conflicted with theology. This divergence of theology and science was fueled by the increasing sophistication of scientific methodology and instrumentation (e.g., the telescope). One of the most fundamental techniques employed by scientists was observation. It became clear that some observations were incongruent with church teachings, which had rigidified. For example, in Europe the Copernican view that the earth revolved around the sun threatened medieval church dogma. When Galileo began to teach the sun centered model he was told to renounce it. Even though he complied, he was placed under house arrest for the remainder of his life.[4] Over three hundred years later the Church admitted its minor oversight, a confession I find rather belated and bizarre! Did the leaders of the Catholic Church actually think that people still believed in their initial position?[5]

Other obsolete concepts still permeate Western culture. Many of these concepts are not as easy to discard as the earth-centered universe. They are far more subtle. For example, concepts such as determinism (i.e., the premise that everything that happens is predetermined) and dualism (the premise that there are two planes of reality—one for the natural world and one for the spirit world) are still adhered to by many authors who write about consciousness. Throughout this book I will show how the concepts of determinism and dualism in their modern forms are being challenged by the new paradigm shift now occurring in the sciences.

The adherence to the concepts of determinism and duality actually stems from the failure to understand the process of change. This failure dates back to the Greeks. The opposing perspectives of flux (change) and stasis (no change) in the West are best illustrated by two major pre-Socratic philosophers, Heraclitus and Parmenides. The historical legacy and importance of these residual themes proposed by both philosophers cannot be overstated.

Following the intellectual revolution initiated by the Ionian Greeks, the respective philosophies of Heraclitus and Parmenides allowed for a shift away from the sole domination of mythological world views. In this new tradition Heraclitus and Parmenides expounded opposing philosophies: Heraclitus proposed the perspective of eternal flux while Parmenides was an advocate of changelessness and stillness.[6]

The most celebrated quote attributed to Heraclitus illustrates his emphasis on the constancy of change: "You can't step twice in the same river, for other waters and others go flowing on."[7] For Heraclitus, the soul is in a continual process of change, which is critical for its constant growth. In this way the soul transcends itself and is "more than what it is." Heraclitus argued that all images of permanence are an illusion.

In contrast, Parmenides argued that all signs of change are an illusion, as no change actually occurs. Parmenides advanced a philosophy of permanence. Parmenides, regarded by Plato as a philosophical father, had argued that life is timeless and static.[8] A proponent of an unchanging sense of being, Parmenides had proposed before Plato that there was an unchanging permanence to the objects of knowledge. Thus, Parmenides has unfortunately had a more profound effect on Western society than has Heraclitus.

Plato, for his part, also proposed that ideas (i.e., love and beauty) and "ideal forms" (i.e., trees and humans) are permanent.[9] [10] Such concepts leave us no room for the reality that these "forms" and "ideas" are the result of evolution. They did not always exist.

Plato and his student Aristotle have had a pervasive effect upon Western thought. In fact, British philosopher Alfred North Whitehead once remarked that Western philosophy is "nothing more than a series of footnotes to Plato."[11] Several different philosophical views can be traced back to Plato, including dualism.[12] [13]

While Plato tried to develop a conceptual framework to deal with the overall unity of all aspects of the universe, Aristotle emphasized the observable aspects of the world that could be measured and understood by reason.[14] Not only were Greek philosophers the first to write extensive and comprehensive philosophies, but Hellenistic philosophy combined with Judeo-Christian theology formed the basis of Western civilization, science, and thereby our view of consciousness.

During the past 2500 years the philosophical and conceptual efforts to unify the diversity of experience has followed the same debate initiated by the Greeks. With an adherence to a dualistic framework and the concept of permanence taking hold, and an appreciation of flux not quite understood, there was a shift toward a debate about what we can know about human experience.

The difficulty making sense of both phenomenological experience (one's subjective experience of thoughts and emotions, or "internal truth") and empirical reality (what is assumed to be an objective external "reality") has resulted in opposing philosophical camps. One tendency has been to emphasize phenomenological experience and to de-emphasize the physical world. The other tendency has been to overemphasize the physical world and to de-emphasize phenomenological experience.

After the Renaissance and the Enlightenment there emerged two distinct schools of thought that characterize this dichotomy. One group, often referred to as the Rationalists, included such people as René Descartes and Baruch Spinoza. They argued that the mind is the only reality one can depend on to understand the world. The best example of this viewpoint is summed up in Descartes' now famous phrase "cogito, ergo sum"—I think, therefore I am. In other words, through "radical doubt" Descartes came to believe that the only thing he could be sure of was his own mind, as he felt he could doubt everything but himself.

In contrast, the Empiricists, personified by John Locke, argued that all one can depend on are sensory based experiences that are empirically derived. Locke stated, "The knowledge of existence of any other thing we can have only by sensation." In other words, if you cannot see, hear, feel, smell, or touch something, it does not exist. It follows that others must see, hear, smell, or touch something to make it an objective and mutually agreed upon reality.

By the twentieth century this dichotomy continued through the two broad schools, Logical Positivism and Phenomenology/Existentialism. The Logical Positivists are the philosophical heirs of the Empiricists. Here we see such figures as Gilbert Ryle and Alfred Ayers. The Phenomenological and Existential camp are the philosophical heirs of the Rationalists. They are personified by such figures as Edmund Husserl (Phenomenology) and Martin Heidegger (Existentialism).

According to the Logical Positivists, the task of any scientific endeavor must be to reduce to observable variables. Their obsession with reducing every question to little questions often misses the big picture. For example, concepts such as "consciousness" are viewed as troublesome at best. Consciousness does not exist for them. Ryle and more recently Daniel Dennett uses Descartes as a reference point. Ryle used the phrase "the ghost in the machine" to criticize the tradition of the Rationalists personified by Descartes.[15] He argued that humans produce thoughts and feelings, but it does not necessarily follow that a "self" or a "thinker" exists as a coherent whole.

The new wave of Logical Positivists conceives of consciousness as reduced to numerous parts with no real central organizing operator. Dennett refers to an "army of idiots" as the elements of consciousness.[16] This is in reference to the fact that the brain has numerous "modules" with semi specific functions. In other words, the cohesive experience of consciousness is just an illusion. There are just parts that only appear to be consciousness.

Those in the Phenomenological and Existentialist camp have taken an opposite view, maintaining that each individual's experience is unique to that individual, and that therefore, no objective reality is possible. All individuals have a unique contextual reality which no other individual can completely understand. Your experience is different from my experience because the specific context for our respective lives is different.

From Husserl's perspective, individuals "put the world into brackets," as we are always conscious of events, situations, and objects.[17] In other words, having lived in different contexts contributes to our unique perspectives. You may interpret the same events differently than I based on our different experiences in life.

Heidegger was a student of Husserl and went on to echo many of the positions of previous Existentialist theorists. He argued for the existence of free will over determinism and the responsibility for authentic living.[18] [19] Though you and I have inherited different lots in life, we have the freedom and responsibility to make the best of what we have.

In recent years many authors have written of "Post-Modern" and "Deconstructionist" approaches. The term "Post-Modern" has an ambiguous meaning. Nevertheless, when authors use this term the intent is to highlight contemporary relativist approaches to the study of meaning. The Post-Modern approach of French theorist Ferdinand de Saussure emphasizes a context dependent theme. Similarly, the Deconstructionist approach of Jacques Derrida highlights the contextual aspects of meaning.[20] The meaning that we can infer from each situation depends upon the unique context to which it applies.

Emerging from these philosophical antecedents are a diverse set of theoretical and research approaches to the study of consciousness. On the one extreme we have the "eliminative materialists," who maintain that there is no reason for any psychological descriptions of consciousness—just a description of brain firing patterns will suffice. This approach can be described by the phrase, "reductio ad absurdum."

On the other extreme we have the dualists, who regard the brain as relatively unimportant. People such as Rupert Sheldrake refer to the brain as something akin to a television set which only receives signals from some other source. Dualism is fool's gold. It allows its adherents to tack on popular ideas (i.e., transpersonal experience) but does not explain or validate anything.

Until recently, this fragmented and compartmentalized philosophical atmosphere has made it difficult to arrive at a comprehensive understanding of consciousness. Research has reflected a variety of limited and compartmentalized perspectives. If we were to adhere to any of these conceptual systems alone and exclude the rest, our attempt to understand the diversity of experience would be severely limited.

The sensible approaches lie between the two extremes of dualism and materialism. There are approaches that emphasize various neurophysiological, cognitive (thinking), affective (feeling/emotional), sociocultural, or transpersonal aspects to consciousness. However, these and the plethora of other approaches have not included a satisfactory synthesis of all approaches. I will address that task from a nondualist perspective. The resulting synthesis will constitute an actual paradigm shift.

We have the opportunity to develop a multidisciplinary and unified theory of consciousness—one in which both the biopsychosocial and the transpersonal are addressed. Our perspective will be greatly enhanced if we take advantage of the contributions of each conceptual system. Additionally, we must also factor in significant new insights from the natural sciences and relevant insights from theology. Without doing so, our effort to understand the unity of consciousness despite the diversity of conscious experience would falter. If we take keep considerations in mind, a true paradigm shift is possible.

THE NONDUALISTIC PARADIGM SHIFT

Alfred North Whitehead started his career as a mathematics tutor at Cambridge University early in this century. Now, at the end of the century, the themes he proposed are being embraced. Initially, he and his one-time student Bertrand Russell embarked on a project to reduce mathematics to logic. Whitehead came to realize that this project was unproductive. By the time he had become a philosophy professor at Harvard he had developed his "Process Philosophy"—a philosophy of flux. This was a shift away from reductionism and toward a philosophy of change. One could say Whitehead's perspective was a twentieth century version of the philosophy of flux introduced by Heraclitus 2400 years earlier.

What Whitehead had suggested was that science and philosophy had become out of synch, noting that there had been numerous changes in scientific thought since the seventeenth century but few changes in philosophical paradigms. Rather than leave religion as an illegitimate area for philosophical or religious exploration, Whitehead proposed the development of a "new cosmology" that fuses science, philosophy, and religion.

Whitehead was highly influenced by the paradigm shifts taking place in both relativity physics and quantum physics. He regarded the interrelationship between space and time (relativity theory—discussed in Chapter 6) and the complementarity between particles and waves (wave particle duality in quantum theory—also discussed in Chapter 6) as support for his Synthetic Process Philosophy.[21]

Whitehead tried to reconcile two troubling issues left over from Heraclitus and Parmenides—permanence and change. To do so he emphasized process—how things evolve. For Whitehead the battle between the dualists and the materialists is not necessary.[22] Whitehead's new paradigm is a philosophy of relations where nothing is permanent and everything is in the process of changing and becoming.

In Whitehead's critique of Western thought we see an attack on the antiquated concept of permanence illustrated by his phrase "The fallacy of misplaced concreteness." We have the tendency to think in terms of discrete and unchanging forms. This problem can be thought of as a hangover from Parmenides, echoed by Plato. This is a cognitive error that Whitehead thought plagued Western consciousness. Unfortunately, in the West we tend to disregard systemic interdependent relationships in favor of simple statements about where something exists and where it does not. In accord with the philosophical critics of language, Whitehead noted that Indo-European languages "bewitched" one to be pinned down in rigid and restrictive forms of thought.[23]

Envisioning phenomena as part of an ongoing process, Whitehead avoids dualism by noting that what would be seen by dualistic theorists as separate phenomena can be interpreted instead as different aspects of an unfolding process. This perspective supports a nonlinear view of consciousness advocated in this book, in which different psychological phenomena aren't bound, broken up, or compartmentalized by mechanistic explanation. Rather, consciousness can be seen as an inclusive, complete, and ongoing process.[24]

Whitehead was not the only one to advocate for a process philosophy. In many ways, the nineteenth-century American psychologist William James anticipated Whitehead's Process Philosophy in his widely quoted term "stream of consciousness" which addresses both unity and fluidity. So from my perspective, consciousness can be seen as a fluid process of potentialities. From this perspective consciousness and all "actual entities" are evolving processes in motion rather than static entities.

Just as Whitehead and James had both attempted to devise an overall unifying philosophy synthesizing science, philosophy, and religion, so do I in a modern context. Their efforts were ground breaking steps, yet they were premature because science had not reached a point to permit this synthesis. We now have an opportunity to develop such a synthesis. Recent developments in science have forced a reexamination of some of our fundamental beliefs. Collectively, these developments amount to a major paradigm shift in how we view ourselves and the universe we inhabit. The theme emerging is one in which all elements in the universe are coevolving. That is, we are part of a complex, fluid, and interconnected macrosystem.

The concept of "self-organization" emphasized throughout this book can aid us in developing a coherent theory of the unity of consciousness. This concept has emerged from advances in evolutionary theory and complexity theory. Though I will describe this concept in more detail in the next chapter, self-organization refers to the process through which complex systems (such as ourselves) are organized and de-emphasizes the component parts. To arrive at an appreciation for the concept of self-organization necessitates a multidisciplinary approach.

The reason we have had such difficulty understanding self-organizing processes and the phenomenon of consciousness is that we have employed those concepts and methodologies which now have limited utility, such as those noted above—"determinism," "reductionism," "linearity," "duality" and the belief in complete "objectivity." For example, most theoretical perspectives describe consciousness as pre-determined and as related to specific and one-dimensional causal antecedents. A causes B and B causes C.

Consciousness cannot be explained adequately by a linear chain of discrete events. The familiar billiard ball analogy, whereby one event, is the sole cause of another event is far too simplistic to explain the complexity of human experience or indeed of physical matter itself. When examining consciousness, reductionistic and mechanistic approaches are inappropriate. In other words, consciousness cannot be reduced to the sum total of discrete seemingly causal antecedents. Consciousness cannot be reduced to the sum of factors A, B, and/or C. Consciousness is far too contextual. Further, when one adheres to the assumption of complete objectivity, the rich contextual field of interrelationships that influence the phenomenological experience of both the observed and the observer is missed.

The antiquated belief that there is an objective reality out there about which all observers can agree conflicts with the contextual nature of all phenomena. Post-Modern theorists are right. Each person's point of view is contextually different. Individuals have different experiences and consequently have different perspectives, just as the Phenomenologists had proposed. Yet we agree on generalities, such as that killing others must be condemned. We share a consensual reality—a sociocultural system.

According to the concept of determinism, there is no room for free will. However, the future is not closed; it is open, allowing for the phenomenon of free will. Deterministic approaches envision the future as completely predictable. As we shall see in later chapters, this Newtonian/mechanistic perspective is not adequate to describe conscious human beings. You and I are not predestined to behave in any particular way. On the other hand, we can say we have the "potentialities" or "tendencies" to think and behave in particular ways based on the wide parameters of genetics and other factors including social learning and environmental factors.

Phenomenological experiences are significant to each individual, because people believe and behave in accordance with their particular experience. However, these beliefs do not necessarily verify broad and "transpersonal" objective truth that can apply to everyone. Consider the variety of folklore including the belief in possession by tree spirits in Borneo, and reports of "channeling" (i.e., the supposed transmission of spirits through a medium) in the United States. If one were to accept these reports as verification of actual phenomena existent in the biosphere, then it would appear that tree spirits only live in Borneo, and channeling only occurs in the United States since the 1980s. Currently there are numerous reports of contacts with angels, while reports of channeling experiences have subsided. Not so coincidentally, there is large scale commercial value in the shift from channeling to angels. Similarly, when religious cults report that catastrophes (i.e., wars or the end of the world) were foreseen "prophetically" but do not occur, it is proclaimed a "miracle." All this sensationalism is comically appetizing but smacks of pop dualism.

There are many forms of dualism that conflict with an adequate understanding of consciousness. For example, in the extreme are those perspectives which maintain that only spiritual dynamics are relevant to consciousness while the biophysiological, sociocultural, and intrapsychic are regarded as nuisance variables at best. In most theological systems dualism emphasizes the "immortal soul" and the "mortal body." More subtle forms of dualism assume there to be a stratified and hierarchical process that explains consciousness. With dualism in general there is no coherent explanation of how the so-called "levels" interact, change, or evolve.

Instead of being limited by such concepts, we now have the opportunity to understand consciousness from the perspective of the new paradigm of unity. In the next few chapters I will, therefore, explain and utilize the concepts of "nonlinearity," "bidirectional causality," "chaos," and "interconnectiveness," to illustrate this unity. Because consciousness is the result of evolutionary processes, I will also incorporate an evolutionary perspective.

Consciousness is not a static structure. It is a fluid process. Humans experience states of consciousness that are fluid and multidimensional. In other words, change occurs with nonlinearity. There have been discontinuities and bursts of development in the evolution of our species. Similar discontinuous bursts of development occur in the growth of an infant to an adult. Also, on a daily basis there are discontinuous shifts in states of consciousness. For example, during the sleep cycle we dream every ninety minutes and during waking consciousness we experience a daily cycle now referred to as ultradian rhythms. This is because multiple variables interrelate and coevolve in a nonlinear manner. In other words, changes in states of consciousness do not occur as the result of a neat, discrete, and isolated series of events (i.e., billiard balls on a table). In complex systems, sometimes change occurs abruptly and as a result of the reorganization of multiple factors. Our emotions would reflect all, not just one of these factors, as well as thousands of other mitigating circumstances too numerous to conclusively describe. Because consciousness is affected by so many factors, the collective contributions of these factors have exponential results. For example, if I am highly stressed at work, late for a meeting, had a poor night sleep, and get stuck in traffic, I may become irritable and say something to someone that would change our relationship irreversibly.

Because so many factors interrelate to create consciousness, interconnectiveness is a property fundamental to consciousness. This interconnectiveness can be experienced on many levels and in many dimensions. For example, one may experience acute anxiety and fear if attacked by a mugger. This fear is reflected on multiple dimensions. One's hands may tremble—a physiological response. Simultaneously, one may experience the self as threatened—an intrapsychic response.

On the most basic level the interconnectiveness between one's biophysiological, interpersonal, and intrapersonal experience contributes to the experience of selfhood. When the self is not threatened, one can have transpersonal experiences, such as a profound sense of unity with others and the universe. Although for most individuals these latter experiences are rare, when they do occur the connectiveness can be experienced subtly or as bliss.

A comprehensive analysis of consciousness requires an integration of the paradigm shifts in the natural sciences and what has often been referred to as the "Perennial Philosophy." This integration necessitates a discrimination between elements of each that are not complementary. Prior attempts at such an integration have assumed that there is broad and general agreement between the two. As will be illustrated throughout this book, the matter is far more complicated. There are areas where there is blatant conflict between elements of the "New Paradigm" and various theologies. For example, the new sciences of chaos theory and complexity theory envision the future as basically open and subject to change during far-from-equilibrium conditions. While this perspective may be consistent with some aspects of Taoism and Buddhism, the Judeo-Christian and to some extent the Hindu paradigms provide a perspective of dualism and linear determinism. Many theologies also propose that there is a reality that is independent from "earthly existence." This is dualism in its most primitive form. More subtle forms of dualism envision "levels of spiritual experience." I do not quarrel with the concept of levels of consciousness, but there are interactions between levels that have been overlooked, which I will discuss in later chapters.

Human consciousness has not always existed, as some theologies have maintained, but evolved as humans did. Consciousness is the experience of interdependent relationships and at each stage in the evolution of our species those interdependent relationships were different. In this sense consciousness is a coevolutionary process. As human consciousness evolved, so did the complexity of our coevolutionary relationships.

The complexity of these coevolutionary relationships depends on how our species was organized at each stage in our evolution. Therefore, central to the theme of this book is the concept of "organization." The emphasis on organization differs from approaches that have relied on reductionism. Consider the popular phrase: The whole is greater than the sum of its parts. While this phrase has become a cliché in recent years, it nevertheless illustrates the concept that the "organization" of the whole system has more significance than the analysis of the parts themselves. As we shall see in Chapter 2, the emergence of complexity theory has made this clear.

Explaining how systems such as organisms, species, and ecosystems are organized tells us much more about how life has evolved than solely detailing their microelements such as genes and cells. Similarly, consciousness can be explained by organizational contextualities. In other words, what one is conscious of depends on the context. While I write this sentence, I am not planning what to bring on my backpacking trip to the Grand Canyon. That would be out of context. Staying focused to the relevant context requires concentration. That is, of course, dependent upon the organization and flexibility of what I refer to as my self system. I will expand upon this issue in Chapter 3.

Since consciousness is contextual in nature, we coevolve with multiple systems. In other words, consciousness is relational and involves the awareness of our participation in the evolving biosphere and the universe. We are able to coevolve with multiple systems simultaneously. Individuals organize their lives on multiple levels, which all coevolve, and attend to levels of organization relevant to their needs and desires. For example, the degree of moisture in the air and our awareness of the dryness of our skin represent one of a multitude of dimensions one can, but need not, attend to. Other levels include but are not limited to the awareness of the feeling states and complexities of interpersonal relationships, sociocultural organization, and the intuitive awareness of the independence with others and the biosphere.

In this book, I will illustrate that within four broad subsystems—

biophysiology, sociocultural dynamics, intrapsychic, and transpersonal aspects—there exist further subsystems. Also, between these broad subsystems there exists a great degree of interconnectivity. In other words, you cannot conceptualize biophysiological processes without considering individual psychological, sociocultural, and transpersonal factors.

Consider the emerging field of psychoneuroimmunology—a field that studies the relationship between the immune system, the brain, thoughts, and emotions. We know through research in this field that one's beliefs and emotional states directly influence the viability of the immune system. To the surprise of many, recent research has found that in a double blind study those ill patients who were prayed for improved quicker than those who were not. Thus, there is an amazing transpersonal connection to the psychoneuroimmunological process.

Another excellent illustration of the interconnectivity of consciousness is the dream process. The dream has many dimensions. A discontinuous burst of change occurs when fluctuations in one dimension are reflected in another dimension. Changes in the dreamer's sociocultural system or changes in one's feelings about oneself may emerge as an influence for the storyline of the dream. For example, I may have a dream with a theme depicting a popularity contest between the dream characters, during a period in which one's society in working consciousness is proposing for a national election. Simultaneously, the dream may represent me as one of the characters losing the popularity contest, during waking consciousness in which I may be experiencing low self-esteem. A dream can also contain transpersonal content. For example, in the same dream an old close friend may appear in the dream as a consoling figure, while a phone call from that friend may wake me from sleep. So then, dreaming, like other aspects of consciousness, represents the complex multidimensionality of human experience.

Therefore, to explain consciousness in general we must utilize and synthesize many perspectives. The changes occurring in evolutionary theory, philosophy, mathematics and logic, and physics are integrated to describe consciousness. For example, consistent with evolutionary theory, consider that both the evolution of consciousness and shifts in states of consciousness occur in a discontinuous manner. After periods of far-from-equilibrium conditions, there often occur novel changes in the organization of consciousness. There has been a dramatic shift away from the Newtonian clockwork metaphor of natural phenomena where by everything was assumed to move in a mechanistic lockstep. The fluid and interconnective reality illustrated by recent developments in complexity physics serves better to reflect consciousness.

Overall, consciousness can be seen as an evolutionary process that can make nonlinear leaps to higher levels of organization. Consciousness can resonate with the central reality—that is, with the fundamental interdependence of all elements in the biosphere. Since consciousness is the result of the evolution of the biosphere, and the biosphere is the result of the evolution of the universe, we are now in the amazing position of being part of the universe looking back on itself. We now examine the universe of which we are a part. From this perspective one may envision an evolutionary theology in which the natural sciences, psychology, and the perennial philosophy achieve a coherent synthesis.

The above discussion is but a brief sketch of some of the central issues related to the evolution of consciousness. Now that we have gained some understanding of the philosophical evolution, it is time to explore the evolutionary process itself.

2

Evolution and Chaos

While Darwinian man, though well-behaved,
At best is only a monkey shaved.

W. S. Gilbert

Until the mid nineteenth century most of Western society had assumed that life was the result of instantaneous divine creation. When the concept of evolution was introduced, it was met with horror, because it threatened the concept that God had, without intermediaries of any sort, created human beings in His likeness. To assume that we were descended from apes was thus considered blasphemous, if not ridiculous, by Darwin's contemporaries. Many of these people ridiculed his concepts with such phrases as "I'll be a monkey's uncle."

Even Benjamin Disraeli, the British Prime Minister, waded into the debate. He proudly pronounced, "The question is this—Is man an ape or an angel? My lord, I am on the side of the angels. I repudiate with indignation and abhorrence the new fangled theories."[1]

Yet, with the accumulation of fossil evidence to the contrary, it become increasingly difficult to ignore the fact that there were earlier life forms on earth and that some species no longer existed. In fact, it has been calculated that 99 percent of all the species to ever inhabit our planet are now extinct.

To reconcile church dogma and the conflicting evidence that life on earth has changed, the Creationists (who believed that human beings were made in the image of God) referred to the concept of catastrophes. From this perspective the changes that have occurred in the biosphere and in surviving species are the result of catastrophes initiated by God, such as the great flood described in the book of Genesis.

By the end of the nineteenth century these efforts to support Creationism were wearing thin. Not only were new fossils found suggesting that humans may have previously existed in different forms, but many theoretical developments emerged that explained why catastrophism was an unlikely explanation of the physical findings. People such as Jean-Baptiste Lamarck, Charles Lyell, Russell Wallace, and Charles Darwin introduced ground-breaking efforts that led to a major paradigm shift. The concept of evolution has been referred to as the second major shock to civilization since the Copernican Revolution debunked the assumption that the earth was the center of the universe.

The concept of evolution has had a profound effect on the consciousness of Western society. Consider how evolutionary concepts have been modified to achieve social gain. Herbert Spencer, a contemporary of Charles Darwin, coined the phrase "survival of the fittest." This phrase came to be associated with strife between social groups. "Social Darwinism" implies subjugation of a "weaker" group by a "stronger" group. The graphic example of this model has been the exploitation of the working poor by the rich in many countries.

These sociocultural variants of early evolutionary theory were obviously quite crude. They express only part of the story. One of the themes of this book emphasizes coevolution, morphogenic fields, and self-organization. These concepts will be described in this chapter and will form the perspective from which we can begin to understand the evolution of consciousness.

How does evolution occur? Since we are the result of evolutionary processes, we must understand consciousness within an evolutionary context. I will, therefore, discuss evolutionary theory and related theories of change, and highlight how the initial theory of evolution has itself evolved.

EVOLUTIONARY PROCESSES

By the time Charles Darwin published his now classic *Origin of Species* in the mid nineteenth century, several supporting and competing views of evolution had already been put forth. Not only had Darwin's own grandfather speculated about evolution, but at the beginning of the nineteenth century the French scientist Jean-Baptiste Lamarck had developed a model of evolution, which the younger Darwin rejected by mid century.

Lamarck had proposed a model that is sometimes referred to as emphasizing "acquired characteristics," and the principles of use and disuse. He suggested that if a species were to develop a particular adaptive behavior, their offspring would be born with structural changes that support that adaptive behavior. For example, because giraffes stretch their necks to eat leaves in trees, later offspring would be born with longer necks. The Lamarckian model is inadequate for a number of reasons, the most obvious of which is that species cannot make dramatic structural changes in one generation. Another problem is that the mechanisms of evolutionary process are not explained.

Another significant development occurred in the field of geology. During the early part of the nineteenth century, Charles Lyell had published his classic *Principles of Geology,* in which he demonstrated that the earth was considerably older than most people had previously assumed.

Both Charles Darwin and Alfred Wallace were profoundly influenced by

Lyell's book. By the mid nineteenth century, these two young British naturalists gathered specimens in different parts of the world and arrived at similar conclusions. While Charles Darwin was in the Galapagos Islands and Alfred Wallace in Malaya, they were struck by how various species developed a wide range of adaptive strategies in the same ecosystem. Simultaneously, they concluded that species evolve through a random process of "selection" to their particular ecological niche. That is, those mutant characteristics advantageous to the species survive, and those disadvantageous to the species die off. This process became known as natural selection.

According to the concept of natural selection, a species produces variations in offspring. Some are adaptive to their environment and others are not. For example, in the Arctic, bears living in the snow and the ice survived and thrived more readily if their coats were white. In other words, the environment "selected" a breed of bears having this characteristic. Brown bears were at an evolutionary disadvantage and therefore not adaptive. The emergence of white "polar bears" was selected.

Since Darwin was not knowledgeable of genetics, he could not adequately explain the mechanisms involved in mutation. Although the study of genetics actually began with Gregor Mendel during Darwin's life, genetics was not combined with natural selection until the emergence of the "New Synthesis" in the mid twentieth century.

What has become known as the New Synthesis has wedded natural selection and genetics. From this perspective there is an emphasis on what genes are "selected" and a de-emphasis on Lamarckism.

The Synthetic Theory of evolution is more complex than Darwin's original ideas.[2] It involves mutation, genetic recombination, and selection. Genetic recombination results from both mutations and genetic recombinations, while natural section acts upon the variants and influences the direction of evolution. Essentially, the Synthetic Theory offers one mechanism by which natural selection operates.

The evolutionary picture becomes even more complex when the fossil record is examined thoroughly. There is evidence of distinct periods of explosive development and extinction, alternating with more static periods. For example, there were dramatic explosions of new life forms during the Cambrian Era 600 million years ago, then again during the Permian Period 250 million years ago. Occurring during these periods were massive extinctions, with 96 percent of the species dying out. It is clear that when examining the pace of evolution from the Cambrian Era on, there have been abrupt and explosive phases of evolution and extinction. Thus, the gradualism championed by Darwin, and later by proponents of the New Synthesis, fails to describe the pace of evolution.

To meet this challenge, two paleontologists, Niles Eldredge and Stephen Jay Gould, developed their theory of "Punctuated Equilibria" in 1972. This theory is considered a modification of the natural selection model, not an alternative to it. It reevaluated the problem with gradualism and the conflicting fossil record.

From this perspective there is a dynamic balance and equilibrium between a species and its environment. Species generally remain stable for long periods of time until they are abruptly destabilized. The abrupt changes or "punctuations" in a state of equilibrium allow for profound changes in the species. The destabilization of the environment can produce profound changes in the entire ecosystem. Species once dominant may abruptly die out and leave a vacuum into which species previously on the periphery may rush to fill the ecological vacuum.

Consider the abrupt demise of the dinosaurs 65 million years ago and the subsequent explosion in mammalian evolution. A consensus opinion is that a meteorite struck the earth and threw massive amounts of dust into the atmosphere, resulting in a dramatic climate change including a drop in global temperature. Those species that could not maintain constant body temperature were wiped out. Since most dinosaurs could not survive in severely cold weather, they became extinct. Existing in small populations and in marginal areas at the time were small species of mammals. They had been nocturnal scavengers and were warm-blooded. Once the dominant large reptiles were gone the mammals underwent rapid migrations into new ecological niches. The result was a variety of new mammalian species.

The punctuated equilibrium model serves to explain these rapid extinctions and explosions in new species. However, the model does not explain the persistence of recurring forms. It overemphasizes the premise of randomness. But random mutations, struggle, and competition alone cannot account for the tendencies of natural phenomena to repeat. For example, the similar or nearly identical positioning of bones in unrelated organisms that is not phylogenetically linked, or the positioning of the heart or the structure of the eye, are curiously recurrent. Nature somehow seems to "prefer" organisms with eyes and hearts structured in similar ways.

The biologist Brian Goodwin points out that Darwinian natural selection is adequate to explain the small-scale aspects of evolution such as "fine tuning varieties" of species to different habitats and their respective adaptations. However, it is inadequate to explain the forms of the species.

Goodwin has stressed that the natural selection model was organized around Calvinist metaphors of sin and redemption. These metaphors factor into the concepts of "fitness" and "struggle."[3] Organisms actually follow the path of least resistance—where there is potential for growth and development.[4]

One of the problems with the reliance on a theory that genes are the sole causal factor is that it neglects the organization of "morphogenetic forms" or species. Instead of focusing on how species are organized, evolutionary theory had become "genocentric." That is, genes were seen as the sole causal agent in evolution and development. Some theorists, such as Richard Dawkins, popularized this extreme reductionism by writing about "selfish genes."[5]

Genes act within an organized context, known as a morphogenic field, which describes the forces that generate the adult form of an organism from a fertilized egg. As genes change during evolution they can influence this field and so alter the morphology of organisms. Understanding evolution requires more than an understanding of genes. It requires also a knowledge of how morphogenic fields generate organisms as coherent wholes.[6]

The properties of morphogenic fields and how they generate the forms of organisms, a process called morphogenesis, show how emergent order and organization arises during evolution. How an organism is organized is as important as the parts of which it is composed.

Morphogenesis involves the process in which an organism develops into a complex adult form—from an egg or a bud. Goodwin points out that the process of morphogenesis has not been adequately explained by the reductionists. The emergent aspects to the order of organisms predominate over the quantities of such elements such as genes. DNA alone evolves to simplicity. Evolution requires movement toward complexity. Without a cellular context, DNA cannot evolve beyond simplicity. In other words, DNA does not exist in a vacuum. Within a cellular context, evolution tends toward complexity. Thus, inheritance depends not only on genes but also on *organization*. It is the relational order among the components that matters more than material composition. The emergent organizational qualities predominate over quantities. Goodwin clarifies this point well. He writes:

During morphogenesis, emergent order is generated by distinctive types of dynamic processes in which genes play a significant but limited role. Morphogenesis is the source of emergent evolutionary properties, and it is the absence of a theory of organisms that includes this basic generative process that has resulted in both the disappearance of organisms from Darwinism and the failure to account for the origin of the emergent characteristics that identify species. Many people have recognized this limitation of Darwin's vision and my own arguments are utterly dependent on their demonstration of the path to a more balanced biology.[7]

Therefore, until recently the overall organization of a morphogenic field (a living system) has been overlooked. The way in which a living system maintains organization while it grows and evolves is now the subject of inquiry.[8][9] I will turn to the work of two Chilean biologists to emphasize how widely this new perspective is being discussed.

During the 1970s Humberto Maturana and Francisco Varela introduced the term "autopoiesis" to describe the organization of morphogenic forms. Autopoiesis is the capacity for self-generation and self-maintenance. Autopoietic systems, therefore, are holistic systems that self-organize. They have the capacity to reproduce, and continually renew themselves while maintaining the integrity of their structure. We can think of the organization of an autopoietic system as its morphogenic field. You and I share the same organization as members of the same species (the same morphogenic field). Yet we are semi-autonomous—we are autopoietic unities.

Maturana and Varela differentiate between organization and structure. They propose that autopoietic systems have similar organization but varied structures. Thus, autopoietic systems differ from one another in structure, while they share the same organization. Autopoietic systems are autonomous entities that are unified by broad organizational systems. Maturana and Varela write:

Organization denotes those relations that must exist among the components of a system for it to be a member of a specific class. Structure dominates the components and relations that actually constitute a particular unity and make its organization real. Thus, for instance, in a toilet the organization of the system of water-level regulation consists in the relations between an apparatus capable of selecting the water level and another apparatus capable of stopping the inflow of water. The toilet unit embodies a mixed system of plastic and metal comprising a flood and a bypass value. This specific structure, however, could be modified by replacing the plastic with wood, without changing the fact that there would still be a toilet organization.[10]

Two or more autopoietic systems undergo "structural coupling" when they share a history of recurrent interactions. When this occurs all systems structurally coupled undergo structural changes to coevolve with one another in a process known as coevolution. The concept of coevolution will become increasingly important throughout this book. However, before expanding on this concept I must describe in more detail how change occurs. The contributions of chaos theory, complexity theory, and nonlinear dynamics illustrate beautifully how there is a dynamic balance between change and organization or chaos and order.

CHAOS AND ORDER

Up to this point I have emphasized the importance in the paradigm shift of evolutionary theory. Evolutionary theory initially overemphasized random changes in the microelements. We have now arrived at a balanced perspective in which the organization of the morphogenic field or organism itself is the subject of inquiry. How such systems maintain continuity on the one hand, while being able to grow and evolve on the other, will now be addressed.

Following World War II there were several parallel developments which together contribute to a coherent understanding of the change process. For example, in 1948 Norbert Wiener introduced the field of cybernetics. He fashioned the term "cybernetics" from the Greek word Kybernetes, meaning "steersman" and its Latinized form of "gubenator" or governor.

Cybernetics was an attempt to explain how machines maintain equilibrium through "error correction" or "feedback loops." Specifically, Wiener theorized that negative feedback loops function to stabilize the system. Consider how a thermostat signals a furnace to shut down when the temperature in the room exceeds a specified setting. Positive feedback loops temporarily destabilize the system to allow the system to expand and change. Consider what happens when a microphone is placed too close to a speaker—the sound amplifies. Positive feedback loops are a "feedforward" process because they allow the mechanical process to move ahead. Thus, negative feedback loops regulate a system and positive feedback loops amplify a system.

A theory more amenable to biological processes was introduced by Ludwig von Bertalanffy in 1968. According to him, cybernetics was too mechanistic and lacked an appreciation for how organisms function. From von Bertalanffy's point of view, Wiener's feedback loops or "circular causal loops" retain a linear perspective which misses the simultaneous and multivariable interactions. Dynamic interaction, which emphasizes holistic processing, seems more accurate when describing living systems.[11]

As von Bertalanffy pointed out, all living systems are "open systems." That is, they maintain an interdependent relationship with the environment in which they thrive. In contrast, "closed systems" cannot live because they cannot exist in a vacuum exclusive of interaction. Rocks can exist in a vacuum because they are closed systems and not living systems. They can exist on the moon because they need not interact with an atmosphere to exist.

Because open systems feed on the environment while they maintain organizational continuity, they are referred to as "self-organizing" systems. Autopoietic systems are open self-organizing systems. They grow, evolve, and self-organize, as they maintain organizational continuity.

Von Bertalanffy's model is referred to as General Systems Theory. It emphasizes a holistic interaction with the environment. Since organisms are considered open systems they maintain a multivariable interaction with the environment. That is, because they are complex systems, they are composed of multiple subsystems and interact with the ecosystem on multiple levels simultaneously.

The open systems model is particularly important when discussing human beings and consciousness. We coevolve on many levels with the environment and the social system we create and interact with. This multilevel interaction necessitates an open systems model.

Another significant theoretical development involves the field of thermodynamics and the phenomena of entropy. The term "entropy" was coined by Rudolf Clausis in the mid nineteenth century. He combined the Greek word tropos, meaning transformation, with en, representing energy. In the Second Law of Thermodynamics entropy came to represent disorder and "heat death."[12] Entropy means that fires die out and steam engines run out of steam unless refueled.

Since the late 1940s the Russian-born Belgian chemist Ilya Prigogine has reworked the Second Law of Thermodynamics and the issue of entropy. In 1977 he was awarded the Nobel Prize for his work. He emphasized the importance of nonlinear change or change that occurs abruptly and reorganizations that result from increases in disorder (entropy).[13] To illustrate how nonlinear change occurs, let's examine the popular phrase "the straw that broke the camel's back." When that last straw is placed on the camel's back the camel buckles to the ground. A linear illustration of this may depict the camel as slowly sagging until it lies on the ground. Nonlinearity occurs when the camel buckles to the ground.

This is an important conceptual shift because there are no completely linear living systems. Linear systems are closed and, as noted above, to be alive necessitates openness. Because open systems involve multiple variables, the interactions occur with nonlinearity. Prigogine points out that open systems use the "free energy" available in the environment to generate positive feedback loops critical for nonlinear growth. We need oxygen, food, and numerous other elements to thrive and grow. If we are closed off from an interaction with the environment we die. But through a coevolution with the environment we are more than what we were.

Prigogine proposed that entropy does not necessarily result in disorder all of the time. In some situations, such as during "far-from-equilibrium conditions," there is an opportunity for new order to emerge. The concept of far-from-equilibrium conditions refers to turbulence and fluctuations that can destabilize a system. In other words, under such situations a system is shaken up, and as a result of this destabilization, change is possible.

During far-from-equilibrium conditions, a "bifurcation point" can occur. Bifurcation points involve a shift and a "break in symmetry" or stability in the organization of a system. In general, bifurcations are novel changes that occur to a system after a period of instability. Bifurcations occur at the transition from a state of high symmetry and low complexity to one of low symmetry and high complexity. Therefore, the process of evolution involves symmetry breaking and an increase of complexity. Creative reorganizations can produce "dissipative structures." These are novel reorganizations that result in an increase in complexity.

Let us return to an example used before. After far-from-equilibrium conditions produced by major climatic changes, the stability of the dinosaurs was shaken. A bifurcation point occurred through which mammals proliferated into new dissipative structures—new species of mammals.

Prigogine's nonequilibrium thermodynamics conceives of time as a creative asymmetry that permits self-organization. Complex change is irreversible. In other words, the chances of dinosaurs reappearing on the planet are close to nil.

Benoit Mandelbrot has offered an example of the multitude of variables and irreducible complexity in existence. He illustrated this complexity visually by what has become known as the "Mandelbrot Set" or "fractal geometry." These fractals illustrate the seemingly endless complexity by intricate detail (see Figure 2.1). There is some degree of similarity evident in each detail but no symmetry. Because of this complexity, small fluctuations can potentially have dramatic effect on the entire system.

To summarize, all living systems are open and evolve through nonlinear change. This is because each living system is richly complex, as illustrated by fractal dimensions. During periods of far-from-equilibrium conditions there is an opportunity to change. This is because systems become destabilized during a major shakeup. These changes can occur initially as the result of sensitive fluctuations and then emerge as subsequent bifurcations—novel reorganizations and

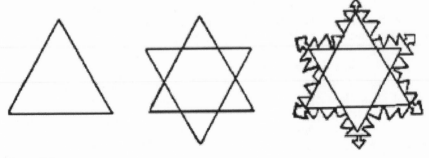

Figure 2.1
An Example of Fractal Geometry

branching in system (i.e., new species). Such change amounts to an abrupt reorganization and a leap to greater complexity. This new order is irreversible.

But how can disorder result in order and increase in complexity? In some ways this process is counterintuitive. To illustrate how this process occurs the concept of an "attractor" is useful. An attractor is a reorganizing theorem that constrains the behavior of a system. From a mathematical point of view attractors are always located in a "basin" because they pull and attract.[14] Generally, attractors can be thought of as organizational patterns that govern the long-term behavior of a system. Chaos theory has provided a detailed explanation and mathematical description of how organization emerges from chaos.

By the 1980s, the multidisciplinary field of chaos theory began to emerge. This development was aided by new developments in meteorology, mathematics, and physics. The work in meteorology actually began in the mid-1960s. In 1963 meteorologist Edward Lorenz stumbled onto a curious discovery. In an attempt to model weather systems on his computer he had made a slight error in a number he entered. He then left his M.I.T. office to get a cup of coffee. He had not anticipated what he would find when he returned. The entire pattern had reorganized. The popular illustration of his finding is now referred to as the "butterfly effect." If a butterfly flaps its wings today off the coast of Venezuela, there may be a hurricane in the Gulf of Mexico in a few days. Therefore, chaotic change results from "sensitive dependence on initial conditions."[15] Obviously, it is not as though butterflies cause hurricanes. The point here is that during periods of instability (far-from-equilibrium conditions) major changes can occur that result from subtle fluctuations.

Chaotic change is governed by a "chaotic attractor." These chaotic attractors, sometimes called "strange attractors," come into play after "far-from-equilibrium" conditions—chaos. In the "butterfly effect" illustration described above, the initial subtle air current precipitated by the flapping of a butterfly's wings set the conditions for the emergence of an attractor. The attractor in this case created the organizing theorem for the subsequent air currents in the Caribbean.

The central meaning of chaos theory is that there exists extreme sensitivity to a multitude of variables in all complex systems. This is especially the case when such systems are in flux. Changes occur nonlinearly because the multitude of elements that make up the system are interdependent.

In summary, nonlinear change involves abrupt transformations resulting from subtle fluctuations. Complex systems are open to interdependent nonlinear evolution. They are so sensitive that subtle changes can eventually lead to major changes in the organization of the entire system. Put another way, organizational change can be pulled by an attractor that initially occurs as a subtle fluctuation. The resulting bifurcation leads to a higher level of organization and increased complexity. From my point of view this is an important discovery. It means that all complex systems are exceedingly interconnected. Even the most subtle change can have a dramatic effect on entire systems.

In recent years there has emerged a broad, multidisciplinary approach to the study of complex systems. Many of the contributions of chaos theory and non-equilibrium thermodynamics have been incorporated into the new field of complexity theory. In fact, a few of the researchers who had contributed to chaos theory are now affiliated with the Santa Fe Institute—a multidisciplinary research institute devoted to the study of complex systems.[16]

Murray Gell-Mann, Nobel Laureate and one of the founders of the Santa Fe Institute, described complexity theory as dealing with "surface complexity arising out of deep simplicity."[17] He adds that complex systems are "pattern seekers." In other words, complex adaptive systems seek out organization.

Complex adaptive systems move toward a minimum of loss or useless expectations. But with perpetations, "noise," or randomness, the process becomes alive because there is a tendency to search ways to avoid settling in ruts or a "shallow basin" of an attractor. Noise or "perpetations" (chaos) jar one out of ruts in search of deeper and more rewarding adaptations.[18]

Complex systems have inherent order because they are composed of vast numbers of elements. Nonlinear interactions occur between these elements and produce the conditions ripe for emergent order. This is a dramatic conceptual change from the initial natural selection paradigm. The shift is toward conceptualizing the organism itself as a self-organizing holistic system.

Chris Langton, also affiliated with the Santa Fe Institute, describes the emergent process in complex systems as a nonlinear interactive process. In such systems the interaction of components in the various microsystems contributes to an emergent global property. That alone would result in what the reductionist paradigm offers (bottom-up causation). However, what also occurs is that the global property or the macrosystem effects feed back to the microsystems. This alone would be the Vitalist view of causation (top-down causation). From the perspective of complexity theory, both top-down and bottom-up tendencies do exist.

Langton has argued that complex systems adapt with dynamical interactions on the "edge of chaos."[19] The concept of life at the edge of chaos suggests that evolution involves the perpetual process of systems to move from order to chaos, then back again. In other words, organizational changes require periods of flux (chaos, far-from-equilibrium conditions, etc.) alternating with periods of stability.

Another term used to describe nonlinear change is "self-organized criticality." Peter Bak, also affiliated with the Santa Fe Institute, illustrated nonlinear change by the droplets of sand granules on a sandpile.[20] For a "critical" period of time there is a slow buildup of sand granules on the pile. Then there is an abrupt shift in the organization and distribution of the sand as the sand redistributes to a new steady state.

So what is emerging from these complementary theoretical approaches? Through chaos, complexity theory, nonlinear dynamics, and the overall self-organization paradigms we can now appreciate a coherent description of how living systems maintain relative continuity over time while making nonlinear adaptive change. Whether they are called complex adaptive systems, autopoietic systems, morphogenic fields, or simply living systems, they maintain some continuity as they grow and evolve. They remake themselves by both bottom-up and top-down processes while they maintain dynamic stability.[21] Simultaneously, the growth process itself contributes to stabilization and continuity.

Though living systems self-organize, as they have the capacity for growth and change internally, they also coevolve with the environment and other living systems. In other words, at all levels in the biosphere there exist coevolutionary relationships. The more complex the species, the more complex are the coevolutionary relationships.

Ascending up the phylogenetic chain, the more complex the species, the more dynamic and multidimensional the existence. As systems theorist Eric Jantsch has noted, behavioral change for simple organisms relies solely upon genetic and metabolic processing and takes place over generations.[22] Organisms with larger central nervous systems make adaptive behavioral changes throughout their lives as they adapt to new environmental demands and change.

Because human beings coevolve with many dimensions in the environment we have constructed exceedingly complex coevolutionary relationships with one another. Human consciousness reflects the complexity of these coevolutionary relationships.

To understand the dynamic and complex nature of our position within the biosphere we need only examine the dramatic phylogenetic differences in nervous systems between various species. To illustrate these differences examine McLean's popular image of the *triune brain*. His concept of the triune brain was an attempt to describe the evolutionary history of central nervous systems specific to phylogenetic stages. These stages are represented by three brain systems, each corresponding to a higher phylogenetic evolutionary level—a fundamental leap to a high organizational level.

The most primitive system is referred to as the *reptilian brain*. It is composed of the spinal cord and brain stem structures, such as the medulla oblongata, pons, and midbrain. This system coordinates many autonomic and self-preservative functions, such as digestion and the cardiovascular system. The more complex elements, such as the midbrain, are responsible for a primitive level of perceiving and selecting environmental stimuli that are essential for self-preservation.

This system is called the reptilian brain because many species with no more than these structures are limited to the consciousness metaphorically similar to that of reptiles. The reptilian brain is rigidly stubborn and inflexible. The stereotyped behavior associated with it includes fixed behaviors and territoriality. As humans beings, we have a reptilian brain, called the brain stem, and without one we could not survive. Interestingly, however, the common definition of being "brain dead" occurs when all other parts of the brain are dead and only the brain stem remains active. Yet in these tragic cases, the patient is only capable of respiration and circulatory functions. Actually, over evolutionary time many of the sensory functions migrated into more advanced brain systems as more advanced species evolved.

Sitting on and around the reptilian "neural chassis" is the more advanced *paleomammalian brain*. This dramatic leap to a higher level of organization represents a system that developed approximately 165 million years ago. The paleo-mammalian brain has also been referred to as the limbic system and includes the amygdala, the hippocampus, and the septum. It enhances the flexibility of action and involves such functions as emotional responsiveness, memory consolidation, and narrowing down the flexibility of cognition by strong emotionally fused convictions.

This advance enabled species endowed with this system to maintain emotionally bonding relationships and complex memories. Consider "man's best friend," the dog. Dogs are capable of developing emotional bonding relationships not only with one another, but also with human beings. You would not find this to be the case with a pet lizard.

Finally, the *neomammalian brain* exploded in development roughly fifty million years ago. This system represents an exponential leap to a higher level of phylogenetic evolution and is consistent with early primate development. This latest neuronal system is composed primarily of the neocortex, which facilitates all higher cognitive functions, including conceptual and abstract reasoning. The neomammalian brain is a leap to a much higher level of organization, with increased complexity and flexibility.

I will describe the cortex and the brain in general in the next chapter. However, the point here is that with the neomammalian brain, consciousness became exceedingly complex. No longer are we limited to simple emotionally bonding relationships and self-preservation concerns. With the neomammalian brain, the dimensions humans are capable of appreciating have multiplied exponentially. To more completely appreciate the evolution of human consciousness it will be helpful to chart what we do know about the emergence of our species.

THE EMERGENCE OF HUMAN CONSCIOUSNESS

Though mammals have been in existence for roughly 150 million years, they occupied a relatively limited ecological niche for more than half of that time span. They were small nocturnal scavengers.[23] Large reptiles dominated the biosphere until chaos overtook the worldwide ecosystem sixty-five million years ago. Because mammals were able to regulate body temperature during the dramatic drop in global temperature, they not only survived but also proliferated. The nonlinear evolution of mammals transformed the ecosystem.

Major climatic chaos occurred again fifteen million years ago, causing the forests to shrink and large savannas to emerge. Among the many species to coevolve with one another were many species of mammals, including a few ape species.

Through our ape ancestry we have inherited a number of evolutionary advances. For example, we see a layering of sense perceptions as we ascend in levels of morphogenic organization from mammals to primates and then to apes. Superimposed on the enhanced mammalian sense of smell and the ability to maintain emotionally based relationships, primates have proportionally larger heads than other mammals for their body size. The larger head is associated with a larger brain. As we shall see, the expansion in brain size coevolved with multiple behavioral and sensory capacities. For example, apes have keen stereoscopic vision and an associated expansion of the occipital (visual) cortex. Various species of apes rely to a greater degree on vision than do other species, such as dogs.

Generally, the larger the species, the slower the gestation period, the longer the infancy and the greater the longevity. In primates the complexity of all these factors is extended, including extended childhood. This is associated with a complex socialization process. In apes and human beings this social complexity is matched by an increased size and complexity of the brain.

Enhanced self-awareness is evident in apes. Merlin Donald has noted that self-awareness had adaptive value as it allowed for a more flexible problem-solving approach and permitted planning and foresight.[24] As our species evolved from the ape lineage, these skills expanded with a great degree of nonlinearity.

The bifurcation of human beings from the ape line occurred more recently than was once believed.[25] Evidence of this recent bifurcation comes from fossil discoveries and genetic mappings. The divergence of chimpanzees and hominids from a common line took place between five and seven million years ago.[26] Allan Wilson and Vincent Savich first postulated in 1967 that molecular evidence suggests this late divergence. By 1980 researchers used DNA sequencing techniques to confirm it.[27]

Clearly the pace of evolution does not conform to Darwinian Gradualism. As we shall see, the nonlinear evolution of the hominids has been marked by leaps to higher levels of consciousness. Consider the dramatic differences between our species and our closest primate cousin, the chimpanzee.

Chimpanzees and *Homo sapien sapiens* share 98.4 percent of the same genes, yet consider the fact that the human brain grows twice as much, by weight, than does the brain of a chimpanzee. Whereas the brain of the infant chimpanzee is roughly 60 percent of its potential adult weight, the weight of a human infant brain is 24 percent of its potential adult weight. This means that for human beings there is a greater degree of coevolution between the growth and organization of the brain and developmental experience. In other words, what human infants experience coevolves with the maturation of the brain to a greater degree than with chimpanzees during their infancy. In fact, the impact of human childhood experience upon brain development is extended by years. Human parents care for their offspring twice as long as chimpanzees care for theirs. This means that humans have the longest childhood of any species.

These factors are critically important because an intense degree of socialization occurs with an extended childhood. Children are bathed in an extremely complex sociocultural system. Simultaneously, their brains have an opportunity to develop the neuronal circuitry to support these complex experiences. Later, in this and other chapters, I will describe how consciousness is profoundly affected by sociocultural systems and how the brain organization coevolves with social experience. The point here is that humans have profoundly enhanced developmental flexibility, which results in the nonlinear emergence of higher levels of organization in consciousness.[28] Let us now examine the different levels of organization (or morphogenic fields) of this evolution.

The first dramatic evolutionary change came with the introduction of bipedalism. The currently available fossil evidence suggests that upright walking (bipedalism) was established at least by 4.4 million years ago. Tim White and his colleagues found the fossil remains of a hominid species now referred to as *Australopithecus ramidus*. The "pithicus" refers to apes and "ramidus" refers to the region where it was found.[29] This species walked upright but did not have a brain significantly larger than that of the chimpanzees. Similarly, the next identifiable species dating from nearly a half a million years later is referred to as *Australopithecus afarenis*.[30] This species walked upright but still had not developed a brain much larger than that of the other ape. Both of these species were found in what is now Ethiopia. Yet, it appears that *afarenis* had been established over a wide area. For example, footprints originally made by individuals of this species were found in Olduvai Gorge in present day Kenya by Mary Leakey.

The next identifiable species was *Australopithecus africanus* occurring by 2.5 million years ago. Africanus was followed by *Australopithecus robustus* and *boisei*. These species coexisted in the same ecosystem. For example, *africanus* was smaller and was an omnivore. *Robustus* and *boisei* were vegetarians with massive jaws.[31]

All of the australopithecines differed from their primate cousins by their child-rearing practices. The australopithecines weaned their infants later and had more offspring than chimpanzees. Presumably, the socialization process was more complex. But they were not capable of speech because their vocal tracts remained apelike.

A clear shift to a higher level of organization and consciousness occurred with a new species, *Homo habilis* (meaning "handyman"). This species emerged following a period of climatic chaos. There was a general drop in temperature and change in precipitation amounts between 2.5 and 2 million years ago. Associated with this shift there was a reduction in forests and a corresponding explosion in savannas and grassland. In contrast to the australopithecines, *Homo habilis* survived and evolved on the "edge of chaos." They leaped to a higher level of organization by developing a flexible diet and the innovation of tool use.

Habilis coevolved with this dramatic climatic shift by becoming a scavenger, consuming the remains of animals killed initially by carnivores.[32] The rudimentary stone choppers and scrappers were helpful in making use of these carcasses. Given that carcasses were widely dispersed and more difficult to locate than vegetable foods, the cooperation of teams of scavengers was critical. The scarcity of protein required food sharing, division of labor, and more elaborate forms of communication. The increased complexity of consciousness for *habilis* was the result of the coevolution of cognitive, and social factors, and increased size of the brain. Though *habilis* could not speak, they probably communicated through body language, hand movements, facial grimacing, and grunts.

Another dramatic shift in the evolution of consciousness occurred with the emergence of *Homo erectus*, roughly two million years ago. *Erectus* was different from *habilis* in a number of respects. For the first time hominids exceeded five feet tall. Unlike preceding species the difference between the size of males and females was more comparable. This suggests that there was less competition among the males for access to females.[33] Also, it appears as though females did not maintain an estrus cycle, which permitted sexuality to be within conscious control. This conscious ability allowed them to be consistently responsive to males sexually. This promoted family cohesion because of the continual presence of males in the family unit. Simultaneously, there was a prolongation of childhood, thus extending the socialization process. All of these factors contributed to dramatic changes in the level of consciousness.

The tools employed by *erectus* also became more complex. Simple stone choppers were transformed into bifacial axes by removing flakes from both sides of the stone.[34] The manufacture and use of these tools demanded and contributed to positive feedback on cognitive abilities and social complexity. In other words, it took planning and foresight to construct tools. It also required more complex social skills to teach others to make the tools. The combination of these factors contributed to more complex tools, and still greater social complexity and cognitive skills.

Eventually fire was discovered as a tool. This dramatic innovation transformed social systems with a great degree of nonlinearity. The use of fire made possible dietary, health-related, and migratory changes. For example, previously inedible plants became edible foods. Various foods tasted better and diet became safer because parasites and bacteria were destroyed by the heat. Previously uninhabitable ecosystems became habitable.

Approximately 900,000 years ago there was a major cooling trend. Also it appears that the African continent was broken up into separate regions. Coevolving with these changes, *Homo erectus* migrated to various distinct ecosystems and then *erectus* burst out of Africa.[35] Fossilized remains of erectus have been found in China (Peking Man) and Indonesia (Java Man).[36]

Merlin Donald has suggested that with *erectus* there emerged a complex new method of communication—miming. The ability to mime created the "Mimetic Culture."[37] Mimetic skills include the ability to reenact events through pantomime, facial grimacing, and nonverbal vocal communication. Repeated mimetic communication contributed to the formation of rituals. These rituals became organized means of communication. As rituals became standardized they formed the rich fabric of an increasingly complex society. As the enculturation process became more complex so did consciousness.

The consciousness of *erectus* was exceedingly more complex than that of preceding species. It included multiple dimensions of adaptation. For example, there was a greater degree of coevolution among members of this species. As the social system became more complex, so did cognitive abilities and neuronal organization. As a dramatic illustration of these factors the brain of *erectus* was significantly larger than that of *habilis*.

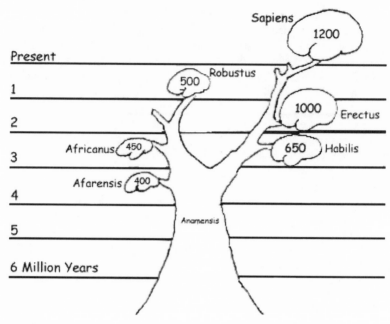

Figure 2.2
The Hominid Family Tree with the Relative Brain Size of Each Subspecies

No one is really sure how and when *erectus* phased out and the next subspecies emerged. But it is clear that brain size increased and sociocultural organization became more complex with the emergence of *Homo neanderthalis* (see Figure 2.2). The first anatomological characteristics of the Neanderthals appeared between 300,000 and 200,000 years ago, as evidenced by archeological finds on the Thames River and at the Swanscombe Gravel Pit and in Steinheim, Germany. Fossil evidence of Neanderthals has been found from Spain to Western Asia. Prior to this period there appears to have been general stability in structure for *Homo erectus* since the mass diaspora one million years ago.

Neanderthals appear to have hunted vulnerable prey and animals not in their prime. This is in contrast to *Homo sapien sapiens*, who hunted animals in their prime with sophisticated weaponry. Nevertheless, the *Neanderthals* had a complex social life. For example, there is evidence that they buried their dead with flowers, suggesting that social relationships had deep personal significance.

The latest known Neanderthal fossil finds date to 32,000 years ago. Interestingly, the brain of the Neanderthal was comparable in size to that of *Homo Sapien Sapiens*. Yet their speech was probably nasal and slowly delivered because their vocal tract was still rather primitive. Some theorists have suggested that because of their stocky build and specialization for cold climates, they were an evolutionary dead end.[38] On the other hand, they could have been assimilated by the invading *Homo sapien sapiens*.

Researchers have proposed that the emergence of *Homo sapien sapiens* took place relatively recently in evolutionary terms. Rebecca Cann, who worked initially under Allan Wilson, examined mitochondria DNA derived from placentas from individuals throughout the world. From this analysis she concluded that modern *Homo sapien sapiens* had emerged from one genetic stock originating from Africa. This genesis occurred in two bifurcations, one approximately 200,000 years ago (give or take 70,000 years) and the other occurring 100,000 years ago. This latest bifurcation was also associated with a major migration out of Africa. From then on, *Homo sapien sapiens* made their respective continental adaptations resulting in the races we see today.[39]

Homo sapien means "knowing man." Indeed, the emergence of this species represented a major transformation in consciousness. Culture became more sophisticated, tools more elaborate, and the brain more highly organized than in preceding species. Though they had a body type (i.e., slighter build) more adaptive to warmer weather than the Neanderthals, *Homo sapien sapiens* were behaviorally more complex. The major innovation of fluid speech had a tremendous nonlinear effect on all three factors. This complex coevolution resulted in a still more complex culture, intricately made tools, and a highly sophisticated brain.

As sensory input demands became more complex *Homo sapien sapiens* thrived in more complex social and environmental conditions. There was a simultaneous increase in the size and complexity of the brain. These changes occurred within the cerebral cortex—the neomammalian cortex. Specifically, the parietal and temporal lobes expanded to deal with new demands for more sophisticated sensory input, comparisons, and integration. The frontal lobes expanded exponentially to coevolve with the need for a powerful "executive function." In other words, the expanded frontal lobes allowed for the ability for focused initiative, planning, and selective inhibition.

As the sociocultural system evolved, so did the complexity of the brain and the complexity of individual selves. As our species became more complex the interdependence of these factors exceeded the pace of the evolution of consciousness. Humans are more than ever in coevolution with themselves.

As clans and tribes formed, distinct languages, rituals, and cultures emerged. The variation in sociocultural systems contributed to cultures with their own rituals and cultural histories. Donald has suggested that a "Mythic Culture" emerged out of the archaic mimetic base. In other words, myths developed as descriptions of tribal histories and origin.[40]

The collective observance of myth through rituals and the maintenance of sociocultural mores provided the clan and/or tribe with cohesion through a mutually agreed upon group identity. Myths can be seen as metaphorical, thematic, or mutually agreed upon cognitive sets.

In short, the mythic culture contributed to an increased complexity of individual self systems. Sociocultural dynamics organized and simplified human relationships. Individuals could rely on others for security on psychological, social, and safety dimensions. The point is that function (behavior) and structure (biophysiology) are intertwined and coevolve. Function does not precede structure in a Larmarckian sense, nor does structure precede function in a Darwinian sense. In other words, as biophysiology evolved, so did cultural systems, and so did the complexity of self systems.

In summary, human consciousness is the result of just a few million years of nonlinear evolutionary development from the ape phylogenetic line. It involves the dynamic interplay and coevolution of biophysiological, sociocultural, and intrapsychic processes. These factors will be addressed in the next chapter. The interdependence of these processes results in what I have referred to as the self system.[41]

The self system, as we shall see, is greater than the sum of its subsystems. It is an autopoietic form that "self"-organizes as it maintains a dynamic coevolution with multiple dimensions of the sociocultural and physical environment. It also maintains a curious interaction with itself.

Human consciousness, therefore, is exceedingly complex because of these dramatic evolutionary advances. The self-organizing aspects of morphogenic fields has reached such an extreme that we now engage in the most dramatic self-referencing process—the examination of consciousness itself.

3

The Self System

Trying to define yourself is like trying to bite your own teeth.

Alan Watts[1]

What are the factors that contribute to an identifiable self? Are they the result of biophysiological, sociocultural, or intrapsychic factors? These are questions that have troubled psychologists for over one hundred years. Unfortunately, the field of psychology has been splintered, fragmented, and compartmentalized into schools and subschools. For example, the Psychodynamic School has within it the Psychoanalytic School and within the Psychoanalytic School there are the subschools of Drive Theory, Ego Psychology, Object Relations, and Self Psychology. Each of these perspectives maintain different explanations regarding how the self develops. This would be fine if these perspectives were thought to be complementary. Yet adherents to these perspectives argue that *their* view is the most coherent and the only acceptable model to embrace.

Some schools, such as the Behaviorists, argue that consciousness does not exist. A well-known joke illustrates their view; what do two Behaviorists say to one another after making love? "Well, that was enjoyable for you, how was it for me?" In their quest for an "objective" viewpoint they have denied the reality that each of us has subjective experiences. It is no wonder that by the early 1970s many were fleeing behaviorism for cognitive psychology—a perspective that acknowledges that people actually think.

The cognitive psychologists view consciousness as primarily an information process. At the extreme of the cognitive perspective is the Artificial Intelligence proponents. For them the computer are the grand metaphor. They believe that the computer metaphor not only describes consciousness, but someday computers will replicate it.

As a psychologist, I have always been frustrated by these "clubhouses." I have regarded these schools as offering useful descriptions of certain aspects of self-development and consciousness. However, it would be a mistake to consider any of these perspectives as coherent and comprehensive descriptions of the development of the self and what consciousness is.

All the processes such as thoughts, emotions, biophysiology, and culture are interdependent. They all constitute dynamic systems, not independent "levels" or "worlds" unto themselves.[2] Collectively, they constitute a complex sea of influences on consciousness.

To correspond to the evolutionary aspects of the development of the self system and consciousness I will describe the biophysiological, sociocultural, and intrapsychic subsystems. Absent in this chapter are references to transpersonal dynamics, which will be left to later chapters. We need to understand the evolution of the self system to be able to understand human consciousness and it is not necessary to include transpersonal dynamics. This may disturb some readers, but the emergence of the self system can be explained without making reference to transpersonal dynamics. They are important, as I will stress later, but not critical for evolution to occur.

Because this is an evolutionary approach, I need to say a few words about the terms "consciousness" and the "self system" First consciousness is awareness. Different species are aware of different aspects of their ecosystem. It sounds simplistic to say, but it is useful to point out that the degree of complexity of a species relates to its respective level of consciousness. This is not meant to be a pejorative distinction. Common houseflies do not need to think in complex and abstract ways to be able to thrive. They don't write or read books on consciousness. Nor do they try to consider why human beings keep trying to swat them away from food. That simply is not their reality. They have less than 200 neurons, we have approximately 100 billion neurons. We have complex sociocultural systems and as many individual subjective realities as there are people. Flies and organisms similar to them have no variation between individuals or groups of organisms that genes do not determine. Human consciousness cannot be explained in such simple terms. There is a great deal of variation between us.

Theorists have identified several conceptual problems with respect to a successful theory of consciousness. For example, philosopher David Chalmers has coined the phrase "the hard problem," to emphasize the fact that researchers have been more successful at identifying how specific brain firing patterns are associated with specific sensory functions—which he has referred to as the "easy problem." However, researchers have not been able to explain the "hard problem" of how each of us has a unique subjective experience. In other words, there has yet to be an adequate theory to explain how you and I have completely different subjective realities.

Another problem that has been identified is referred to as the "binding problem." Again researchers have been able to successfully describe how these various perceptual functions correlate with specific brain firing patterns (i.e., the firing patterns of the occipital lobes are associated with the experience of sight). However, researchers have yet to describe how the collective firing pattern across the entire brain occurs to bring a unitary sense of being.

I believe that both problems are resolved by incorporating the concept of organization. As I noted earlier, there are levels of organization in any system. I refer to the organizational system that defines our individuality as our self system. Humans have extremely complex self systems. That is, the subsystems that contribute to the overall organization of the self system are complex and multidimensional. These subsystems coevolve with nonlinearity.

One subsystem involves not only nonlinear changes in its microsystems but coevolution with other subsystems. For example, dramatic changes in one's sociocultural system affect the subjective experience of individuals within that society. Individuals coevolve with major sociocultural changes (e.g., during an economic depression or a war) based on their position within the society and the way in which their self system is organized. Some may be very resilient individuals, some may exploit their neighbors, and still others may be so overwhelmed that they choke on their own entropy and psychologically decompensate.

Some self systems are relatively open. That is, they thrive on reciprocal interactions with others and their environment. Other self systems are relatively closed. That is, they are organized around the propensity to overprotect themselves. Yet these are superficial dimensions because each individual's situation is uniquely diverse and complex.

The model of the self system that I advocate is one which corresponds to many of the paradigm shifts in the natural sciences. We must understand the emergence of the self system from an evolutionary perspective. Self systems are the necessary result of this stage in the evolution of our species. The ability to have cohesive subjective experiences was and continues to be essential.

The self system is the result of systemic nonlinear relationships among the subsystems of which it is composed. Broadly speaking, biophysiological, sociocultural, and intrapsychic (subjective) systems are interwoven to contribute to the emergence of self systems. Yet the self system cannot be reduced to any of these dimensions.

The self system can be referred to as a morphogenetic form or an autopoietic system that supersedes its elemental parts—it is greater than the sum of its parts. It is the actual organization of the self system that makes it so dynamic. It "self"-organizes as it maintains an interdependent relationship with the environment and with others.

Consciousness is what the self system does. In other words, self systems are differentially aware and sensitive not only to their own subjective experiences but to the environment and to others. Consciousness is not a static structure. It fluctuates daily and is a fluid process. Later in this chapter, I will describe how biophysiological, sociocultural, and intrapsychic factors coevolve to contribute to the fluidity of consciousness. Let us, however, begin with an appreciation for the complexity and nonlinearity of biophysiological processes.

THE BIODYNAMICS OF THE SELF SYSTEM

To arrive at a coherent understanding of consciousness necessitates an appreciation for biophysiological processes. Therefore, we must dismiss dualistic perspectives in which there is the Cartesian split between the brain and the mind.

As illustrated in the last chapter, the evolution of the brain was interdependent with the evolution of higher levels of consciousness for each of the hominid subspecies. Further, the hominids retained the evolutionary legacy of mammalian development, so well exemplified by the McLean triune brain.

Based on our paleomammalian ancestry and its associated neuroanatomical structures (the paleomammalian brain, generally called the limbic system) we have great affinity for emotionalism. Obvious examples of this aspect of consciousness include how hearing a piece of music resonates with limbic structures. When this occurs we often remember poignant emotions we had experienced in various relationships. Similarly, a smell can evoke powerful memories instantaneously. This is because the olfactory bulbs lie just on top of the hippocampus, one of the limbic system structures closely associated with memories.[3]

The paleomammalian cortex allowed for more flexible behaviors, as it factored in emotional and thereby motivational aspects of consciousness. With the increase in emotional processing there was also an increased demand for the nurturance of offspring. Therefore, the bonding process is profoundly important to consciousness. Although I will describe the psychological aspects of the bonding process later in this chapter, the critical point I am trying to make here is that we have inherited a brain that has coevolved with the bonding process.

The "neomammalian cortex" has coevolved with dramatic innovations in cognitive capabilities and behaviors.[4] The cortex is composed of two hemispheres, each with its own capabilities. For example, the right hemisphere is generally more involved with spatial awareness, and because it has more connections with the limbic system (paleomammalian brain), it has been associated with emotional expressiveness.[5] The left hemisphere, in contrast, is associated with the perception of detail, language functions, and is less associated with the emotional content of words.[6] The left hemisphere is generally considered to correspond to logical-deductive capabilities and has sometimes been referred to as the "interpreter." In contrast, the right hemisphere has been shown to have very poor problem solving capacity.

The split-brain research, pioneered by Roger Sperry and others, has demonstrated how profoundly different are the left and right hemispheres. For example, when the bundle of fibers that connect the two hemispheres (referred to as the corpus callosum) is cut, the left and right hemispheres operate like different brains. In fact Michael Gazzaniga's research has shown that each hemisphere is unaware of the thoughts of the other hemisphere. This fact argues strongly for the position that the brain is composed of "modules" or semiautonomous subsystems that, when they operate together, provide the rich complexity of consciousness.

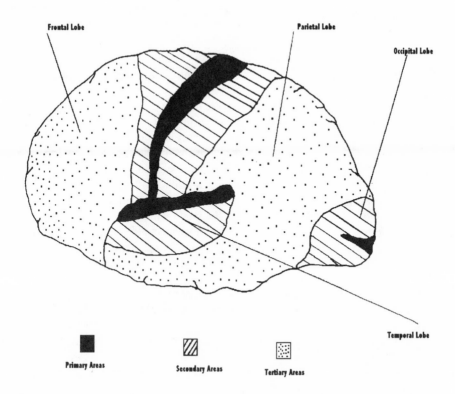

Figure 3.1
The Brain's Four Hemispheres and Three Zones of Organization

Each hemisphere is further divided by four "lobes": the frontal, temporal, parietal, and occipital (Figure 3.1). The lobes have a primary, secondary, and tertiary area. The primary areas correlate with a specific sensory or motor (movement) function. For example, the primary area of the occipital lobes is associated with vision, the temporal with hearing, the frontal with movement, and the parietal with body sensation. Each of the lobes has association areas that correlate with the mixing of modalities within that sensory function. Finally, the tertiary areas correlate with the blending of multiple functions. For example, the posterior tertiary area involves the mixing of sight, sound, and space perception.[7] Damage to this area on the left side would impair one's ability to understand what another person is saying in communication.

The expansion of the frontal lobes was a significant part of the evolution of our species. No other species has as large and complex frontal lobes. The far-frontal cortex can be seen as an executive processor. It is involved in the direction and allocation of resources for the rest of the brain. To illustrate how critical the frontal lobes are to consciousness we need only to witness the behavior of those individuals with frontal lobe damage. Generally, they are unable to inhibit autonomic response when not practical. Imagine how impractical it would be to let anyone you encounter know exactly what you think of him or her.

Damage to the frontal lobes also results in indifference and loss of anticipation of the future. A sense of one's possible future is critical to human consciousness and distinguished our species form others. We are the only species that is able to develop complicated plans to achieve long-range goals and adjust those plans in changing situations.

Another illustration of how important are the frontal lobes to our level of consciousness can be seen in the developmental process. The far frontal lobes are the last to fully mature—some estimate that they are not completely developed until the late teens.[8] Think of the developmental challenges of adolescence. Adolescents deal with self identity, inhibition of behavior, goal planning, understanding what is dangerous and what is not, as well as anticipating the future.

The gender specializations in neuronal processing occurred over millions of years. Men have generally functioned as the hunters in hunter-gatherer societies. Coevolving with the skills necessary to be a good hunter were neuronal areas that facilitated keen spatial perception and gross motor abilities.[9] Though most present day humans no longer live in hunter-gatherer societies, the residual effects of the evolutionary legacy are reflected in the developmental process. For example, boys mature more quickly in gross motor movements.

Women, in contrast, probably spent more time verbally communicating and enculturating children in hunter-gatherer societies. Fine motor skills were probably more important than for men because of the gathering tasks, assembling items, and care of the children. Again, we can see the residual evolutionary effects of this legacy in the developmental process. Girls mature more quickly in fine motor and language skills.

There are also distinct structural differences between the brains of males and females. For example, there is a smaller degree of cerebral asymmetry in brains of females than males. In other words, the relative shape of each hemisphere is more similar for women than for men. Differences are also found in the relative sizes of the corpus callosum, the bundle of fibers connecting the two hemispheres.

The posterior part of the corpus callosum, referred to as the splenium, is larger in the brains of women than of men. This suggests that the brains of women support more efficient connections between the posterior parts of each hemisphere. In support of this finding are studies that indicate that women suffer less deficits following neurological insult to the right hemisphere. Thus, women use the hemispheres more equally than do men. Perhaps this is one reason why women have been described as having more associations to the emotional content of words than do men.[10]

Regardless of gender, the brain consumes 25 percent of the oxygen supply used by the body and 10 percent of the calories consumed, despite the fact that the brain amounts to only 2 percent of an adult's body weight. It is by no means irrelevant to consciousness, as the dualists would have us believe.

At birth an individual has as many neurons as he or she will ever have, even though the brain is roughly one fourth of its potential adult size. The growth generally takes place in the connections between the neurons (axons and dendrites) and support cells.[11]

The human brain has roughly 100 billion neurons and maybe a trillion support cells. These neurons are organized by how they are connected to one another. It has been estimated that each neuron has synaptic connections with several thousand other neurons. These connections are facilitated by experience, and obviously everyone's experience is different. The greater the differences in our experiences, the greater the differences are in how or brains differ in organization. Even for identical twins, brains differ with experience. These differences are not in the gross structure of the brain but, rather in the connections between the neurons themselves.

To appreciate how the brain modifies itself with experience over time we must understand that the brain is an electrochemical organ system. Neurons communicate between themselves through chemicals called neurotransmitters, which travel through a gap called a synapse. These synaptic connections change and modify based on our experiences. Neurons themselves fire electrically in an all-or-nothing manner referred to as an action potential.[12] But they do not fire if a specific neurotransmitter has not unlocked the key on the other side of the synapse to trigger the firing.

Thus, experience is critical to brain organization. It would take an astronomical number of genes to dictate the propensity for every behavior, every thought, and every feeling.[13] We are not "hard-wired" to behave in stereotypical ways, as do species with vastly less neurons, such as bees and house flies. The human brain, culture, and subjective experience all coevolve. As Gerald Edelman has pointed out, an individual's genes alone are insufficient for the synaptic structure of the brain. In other words, it is silly to build an analogy that the brain is hardwired along the lines that advocates of artificial intelligence have proposed. An individual coevolves with his or her environment and the "structure" of the brain's synaptic connections is malleable.[14] The brain is much too complex to reduce to a "hard-wired" reductionistic perspective. Yes, brains are critical to experience, but they coevolve with experience. They are part of the same process.

To illustrate the coevolution of brain organization and experience I will use the concepts of "structure" and "function." Whereas structure refers to the actual physiology, function refers to behavior, thoughts, and feelings. There is a bidirectional causal relationship between function and structure. As changes occur in structure, so are there changes corresponding in function. As there are changes in function, so are there changes in structure.

Let me start with structure, the easiest to understand, and then proceed to function. As a psychologist with neuropsychology training, I have evaluated people who have major problems with brain structure. For example, I have given neuropsychological tests to people who have bullets still lodged in their brain. The parts of the brain damaged by these bullets had profound effects on these patients' abilities to think and function in particular ways. The brain damage profoundly disrupted their ability to perform certain functions. For example, one patient had prepared taxes as a vocation prior to being shot. This requires an ability to calculate and perform many mathematical manipulations. My neuropsychological evaluation of this patient revealed a profound disability in calculation abilities and visual spatial capabilities.

With respect to function first and structure following, let me turn to two developmental phenomena, dendritic arborization and the myelination process. With dendritic arborization we can appreciate how novel thinking produces structural change in the brain. The dendrites are the part of the neuron that reaches out to other neurons to receive information. Dendritic arborization occurs as dendrites branch out and coevolve with new experience. The opposite of dendritic arborization is dendritic pruning. This results from little use. It is a kind of atrophy process. We can surmise that Einstein's brain was rich in connections between neurons. This is an empirical fact. Slices of his brain are in neuroscience labs in different parts of the country! In contrast, we may speculate that a person who watches television all day and/or belongs to a right-wing militia or white supremacist group is vigorously pruning dendrites. This is because he explores few of the complexities of life and centers rather on a few single constructs, however bizarre.

The myelination process occurs during development to aid the brain in facilitating particular types of functions. Myelination involves the coating of axons with a fatty substance called oliodendral glial cells. Axons are the part of the neuron that sends messages to other neurons. The myelination of axons facilitates more efficient neuronal firing. Those areas myelinated are those areas that correspond to specific functions. For example, axons from the motor (movement) and sensory areas are myelinated early in life, which parallels the acquisition of these movement and sensory abilities. Myelination facilitates more efficient firing of motor and sensory neurons. The more the use, the better the myelination of axons facilitating that function, the more efficient that function. Thus, function and structure coevolve. Stated more generally, the brain and behavior modify each other.

The interconnection between brain and experience is illustrated by how parts of our brain work together. Because humans are endowed with the paleomammalian limbic system and an expanded cortex, memories are referred to as "state-based" memories. There is tremendous interaction between cortical firing patterns and subcortical limbic system firing patterns. An example of how this occurs is illustrated in how one can retrieve various memories when experiencing the same emotional state during which the memory was encoded. Also, as noted earlier, a simple fragrance or smell may bring into consciousness a whole series of memories. This is because these memories were coded when smelling that particular fragrance.

No one neuron contains a thought, feeling, or memory. When clusters of neurons fire together they form the basis for thoughts, feelings, and memories. This is why thoughts, feelings, and memories are so complex. They are not "fixed" but rather they are multidimensional and always subject to modification.

The point I am trying to make is that thoughts, feelings, and perceptions are correlated with the collective firing of groups of neurons. The organization of these clusters of neurons changes with every thought, feeling, or perception. This fact has led many theorists to adopt models that metaphorically describe clustered firing patterns. Terms such as "connectionism" and phrases such as "neural nets" have been used by neurophysiologists, psychologists, and researchers in the field of artificial intelligence.[15] Reductionism does not work when analyzing the brain. Instead, we must appreciate the dynamic organization changes of clustered firing patterns of neurons to understand how the brain operates.

The actual firing patterns of neurons in the brain illustrate the great degree of versatility, self-organization, and nonlinearity in the brain.[16] Chaos is one of the chief properties of the brain. It is chaos that provides the brain with versatility and the potential for self-organization.[17] An example of a completely nonchaotic firing pattern is an epileptic seizure. With a seizure the electroencephalographic (EEG) pattern appears intense but relatively even. In contrast, an alert and active state of mind produces an EEG pattern with great variation in "dimensionality" of firing patterns. This is hopefully what is occurring while you read this sentence.

The chaotic nature of neuronal firing patterns involves the discontinuous firing of neuronal groups. The nonlinear reconfigurations that result from these fluctuations revolve around various attractors that may emerge.[18] For example, the clustered firing of a small groups of neurons may have a "butterfly effect." In other words, during periods of extreme flux other firing patterns subsequently revolve around a brief clustered firing of neurons. That pattern is represented as a thought or a feeling such as how one feels about one's son. When stressed (i.e., put in danger in some way) the thought about one's son can trigger the feeling of concern or worry about one's son.

Yet the brain does not behave completely with chaos. Clusters of neurons fire together and the more they do so the more they will in the future. The more you review a memory, the easier it will be to retrieve or be reminded of that memory sequence.[19] However, those clusters of neurons are always subject to modification. These modifications and restructuring of neural nets take place through new experiences. Memories are reworked and modified over time. This is facilitated by the inclusion of other connections with other neurons not initially part of the neural net/memory. Psychotherapy is based on this fact, even though the neurophysiological aspect is not understood by most therapists. Nevertheless, the retelling and reworking of memories reframes them and allows the client to move forward with a new perspective.

Because neural nets are always subject to modification and because one of the properties of neural firing patterns is chaotic, thought processes are fluid. This fluidity provides the brain/mind with a ready state and flexibility. In other words, in changing circumstances the individual is capable of making adaptive behavioral changes. An extreme example of not being able to do so is the person who continues to try to exit a building the same way he had initially learned, despite the remodeling of the building. Though the location of the door was changed, he continues to run into the wall where the door had been, expecting to get out of the building. So we are not preprogrammed computers. We learn, adapt, and change. The dynamic quality of the brain permits us to do so. It is the most complex organ system on the planet today.

The brain is a holistic system. Its holistic qualities are exemplified by how memories are distributed throughout the brain. They are not contained in any particular part of the brain. Memories are composites that involve the input of various collective configurations.

One of contemporary neuroscience's prime proponents of the concept of a holistic brain is Karl Pribram. He has proposed that the brain functions holographically.[20] Just as with a hologram, each part has limited capability of reproducing the whole; it is through a holistic configuration of all of the parts that the actual image comes into focus. Memories occur in the same way. A small cluster of neurons contains only a fragment of the memory and only with the combined firing of the other relevant clusters does the memory have significance.

So then, mental events are correlated with holistic firing patterns of clusters of neurons. The thoughts and feelings themselves can have an effect on subsequent firing patterns of other firing neurons. In this sense a "top-down" process evolves.[21] For example, as I write this chapter I exercise "top-down" constraints by not including in this discussion comments about the weather.

There are also "bottom-up" processes that occur in the brain. Bottom-up processes occur when unanticipated insights or perceptions are freely associated. For example, while working on a sculpture, I begin with a particular form in mind, but as I continue to work, new dimensions or visual-spatial configurations may occur to me. Such creativity represents a bubbling-up type of phenomenon.

There is a bidirectional interaction between top-down and bottom-up processes.[22] The brain is organized in such a way to allow this to occur. This coevolution of top-down (macroprocesses) and bottom-up (microprocesses) does away with the need for the old models of materialism and dualism. Both extremes do not allow us to fully appreciate the complex coevolution of biophysiological processes and psychological processes.

The developments of the field of psychoneuroimmunology represent a major breakthrough in understanding the systemic nature of our mind/body. This field demonstrates the multidirectional interaction between culture, cognition, emotions, brain, and the immune system.

Consider the well-known placebo effect. The placebo effect occurs when an individual who is ill takes a pill that he or she is convinced is a medicinal compound. It has been often reported that in such cases the individual experiences a lessening of adverse symptoms, despite the fact the pill taken contains no medicine. It is the *belief* that it is curative, not the pill itself. However, as I noted elsewhere, this is not a simple case of "mind-over-matter."[23] Rather, there is a complex interconnected relationship between biophysiological, sociocultural, and psychological processes.

Researchers have demonstrated that there is a bidirectional interaction between the brain and the immune system.[24] For example, individuals who have experienced a great deal of stress have been found to have suppressed immune systems.[25] A common finding is that widowers have been shown to have suppressed immune systems as long as two months after their spouse dies.[26]

A dramatic example of the interaction of sociocultural belief systems is the so-called voodoo death reported in Haiti. In such situations the individual comes to believe that he or she has been manipulated by a voodoo priest and dies, often by a heart attack brought on by panic.

While detrimental effects of stress on the immune system have been widely reported, other studies have shown that various psychological techniques have been correlated with the amelioration of stress and the corresponding hardiness of some individuals' immune systems. For example, during the last thirty years it has been reported that psychotherapeutic interventions, such as hypnosis, biofeedback, and imagery, have helped with individuals who are seriously ill.[27]

Specific personality types have been identified that have been correlated with healthy immune systems. So-called "hardy" individuals have been identified as people who relish a challenge and feel in control of their own lives. While they encounter stress, they manage it more effectively than those who experience "uncontrollable stress." Consequently, "hardy" individuals incur little detrimental effect on their immune systems, despite the stress.[28]

These findings clearly illustrate that how one thinks, feels, and generally approaches life has a dramatic effect on the body. It is no wonder that many researchers now refer to the mind/brain/body as one integrated system. One element of the system does not supersede the others—rather they all coevolve.

CULTURE AND CONSCIOUSNESS

As I noted in the previous chapter, the evolution of our species coevolved with sociocultural systems. There was a profound degree of bidirectional causality between the increased complexity of sociocultural organization and the complexity of the brain.

Interestingly, the size of the brain stabilized approximately 100,000 years ago. Though the enfolding of the brain continued, culture became increasingly fluid and less dependent on changes in physiology. This is not to say that culture superseded the importance of physiology.[29] The point is that cultures change at a greater pace than does physiology. Both coevolve with one another but sociocultural systems are more fluid. For example, a dramatic change in sociocultural organization may occur in just a few days. In fact, changes of this kind take place over a shorter period of time than they had earlier this century, thanks to changes in technology, extensive traveling, and the mass media. People simply have greater access to information and it is this information that forms the basis for a fluid sociocultural system.

For centuries theorists offered a variety of models of how culture evolves and affects consciousness.[30] The new paradigm envisions cultures as organized holistic systems. That is, they cannot be reduced to the sum of their constituent members. They self-organize over time and are subject to great nonlinear evolution.[31]

Information coupled with interaction between people fuels sociocultural organization. Consider the massive exchange of information taking place on the Internet. At no point in history has such a large scale of information been shared. It is no wonder people characterize this period in history as the Information Age.

People organize their lives and conform to mutually agreed upon rituals and views of reality. Every college student is familiar with Stanley Milgram's research on conformity and obedience.[32] The study involved convincing each subject that he or she would be the "teacher" in an exercise while another subject (a confederate) would be the "learner." The teacher was asked to get the learner to recall a list of words. If the learner were to make a mistake, the teacher was ordered to give the learner an electric shock. Each shock progressively increased in intensity. The closeness in proximity of the learner to the teacher affected how likely the teacher was to obey the experimenter's order to shock the learner. The closer the learner and the teacher were together, the less likely such obedience were to occur and vice versa.

Several factors have been associated with conformity—for example, if a generally unanimous decision is made by a group on an individual, if he or she is in the extreme minority, and especially as the size of the group increases. If individuals feel they are of lower status than others, they will conform out of fear of being deviant. Finally, the greater a group's cohesiveness, the greater the conformity of its members.

Conformity, social history, and enculturation were factors throughout the evolution of our species. As I noted in the previous chapter, Donald has developed a useful model of sociocultural evolution.[33] He had proposed that the culture of *Homo erectus* was based on mimetic behavior, including ritualized gestures, grimaces, and modeling of events. With the emergence of *Homo sapien sapiens* and language, rituals became verbalized. The result was the emergence of myths.[34]

Culture based on myths instilled a rich fabric of symbols, metaphors, and archetypes into the consciousness of its constituents. These mutually agreed upon self-referential images reinforced a strong sense of group cohesion and provided a context from which individuals could interpret their lives.[35] Much of this process occurs unconsciously. Anthropologist Claude Levi-Strauss stressed this point well by saying, "I therefore claim to show how men think in myths, but how myths operate in men's minds without them knowing it."[36]

As sociocultural systems leaped to higher levels of organization, so did the complexity of myths. In other words, as sociocultural organization leaped from clans, to tribes, to kingdoms, and then to nation states, there was a corresponding increase in the length and complexity of myths. An illustration of how myths became more complex and interwoven with theological organization will be described in Chapter 5. My point here is that, as there was an increase in complexity of sociocultural organization and corresponding mythic systems, so was there an increase in the complexity of consciousness. There was and continues to be a coevolution of sociocultural organization and consciousness. They are one interdependent and complementary aspect of the same reality.

Consciousness, therefore, responds to the metaphoric, symbolic, and archetypal fabric of sociocultural systems. We view our interactions with others through the filters prescribed by the culture we are embedded within.[37] These symbols and archetypes function as attractors. In other words, they serve to organize the thoughts and feelings of individuals embedded within the culture.

The effect of language on consciousness has been studied for decades.[38] Language is a popular illustration of how cultural systems instill characteristic metaphors and symbolic imagery into the consciousness of individuals speaking that language. The initiators of the extreme version of this viewpoint were anthropologists Edward Sapir and Benjamin Whorf. Writing in the 1940s, both of these theorists emphasized the extreme degree to which the perceptions and beliefs of specific language speakers are determined by the constructs inherent to that language. An often used example is the categorical system employed by Eskimos to describe snow. Reportedly, they had numerous and elaborate descriptions of snow. However, more recent anthropological studies have demonstrated that the Sapir-Whorf Hypothesis was grossly exaggerated. Language systems do influence consciousness but do not determine it.

The model I am proposing in this book is the coevolution of all systems that influence consciousness. This means that one-factor determinism does not work. Individuals within various sociocultural systems are influenced, not determined by these systems. If this were not the case, all members of a sociocultural system would respond exactly the same to the same metaphors and symbols. You and I may be of the same general sociocultural system, but we are individuals whose experiences vary even within the same sociocultural system.

Even if our sociocultural position were relatively similar, we come from different family systems. Even if we come from the same family system, variations in personality occur between siblings. Though individual differences will be explored in the next section, what is important here is that we are self systems that interact within a social context. Our attempts to communicate are only approximations of what we truly feel and believe. We use common metaphors and symbols embedded within the language we employ and the imagery we convey. But our subjective experience is different.

"SELF"-ORGANIZATION

As there were dramatic increases in the evolution of sociocultural systems and a corresponding increase in the complexity of the brain, so was there a profound complexification of self representations. The combination of emotional bonding relationships, extended childhoods, and language development contributed to the increased complexity of subjective experiences.

The bonding process not only contributed dramatically to the further complexity of consciousness for members of our species, but also provides major differentiation between individuals. The degree of warmth, empathy, and consistency experienced during infancy and childhood has a profound influence on the self system.[39] One's self system evolves during infancy through feelings and perceptions of others. In psychodynamic language these psychological images are interjected as "self objects."[40] As an infant matures and tries to "individuate," he or she tries to "cast out" the self objects to build a greater sense of self as an independent entity. This is done by differentiating what one is and what one is not.[41]

Self systems can be organized in an infinite number of ways. Yet there are open self systems and closed self systems. What I mean by these distinctions is that some self systems are organized to deal with the world in reciprocal and dynamic ways. These are "open self systems." Of course, very few people achieve complete "openness"—Christ and the Buddha perhaps exemplify this extreme.

In contrast there are "closed self systems," people who are organized to over-protect themselves. These are people who tend to inappropriately cut themselves off from reciprocal interactions with others. The result is psychic entropy—disorganization. We all tend toward some degree of closure, but some people are more closed to outside input than others. Thus, they are emotionally malnour-ished. In the extreme, they may exploit others with maladaptive maneuvers or crude attempts to feed a disorganized and starved self system.

The degree to which we tend toward closure is based on many variants, in-cluding traumatic state-based memories, developmental experiences that pro-mote the concept that others cannot be trusted, or the degree of curiosity about the world. Those individuals who have been traumatized and/or emotionally malnourished tend toward closure and ironically, because of the tendency to overprotect themselves, are less able to grow without reciprocal interactions with others. For example, those people abused as children may themselves go onto abuse others in a crude attempt to feed a malnourished self system. They do not gain psychologically from this abuse. Rather, they experience further disorgani-zation as a result. The metaphor of cancer comes to mind.

From an evolutionary perspective, the development of an organizational sys-tem that could deal with an increase in the complexity of sociocultural systems resulted in the increase in complexity of the self system. The concept of a self system is more complex than the terms used in psychology, such as the self, ego, and the personality.[42] It is greater than the sum of its contributing subsystems.

To paraphrase Terence McKenna, "The function of the ego is to keep us from putting food in the wrong mouth in a restaurant." The ego is an aspect of the self system. It serves primarily a social function. It provided us with a dynamic and complex organizational system that allows one to coevolve in a complex social environment.

The importance of decentering the ego cannot be overstated. I have stressed elsewhere that the ego is best thought of as a socially constructed face, beyond Jung's concept of persona.[43] It comprises a functional personality.

I have always been struck by how, when ego inflation occurs, something can happen to force the contraction back to a more reasonable image. Perhaps con-sciousness sends out "guide waves" that refer to reality as a whole. An excellent example of how dangerous it is not to decenter the ego is the actor or sports celebrity. They confuse their entire self with their ego. When they find that they do not perform well or are not gratified by fans they experience a crisis of the self.

The self system is an organizational field of cohesive, but fluid, self-referential subsystems. The self system supersedes its elemental subsystems. It is not separate from, but includes, biological, sociocultural, and intrapsychic dimensions.

In recent years two general theoretical trends have emerged to describe psychological process—Connectionism and Constructivism.[44] Connectionism represents the effort by those who envision psychological processes as the result of multiple microprocesses. Contributors to this model include many neurophysiologists who emphasize the "module" concept, described earlier in this chapter.[45] They argue that what we call consciousness is the result of the synthesis of these microprocesses.

Constructivism, in contrast, has emphasized the "macroprocess"—or the self. Constructivist theorists have argued that the self as a whole undergoes a self-organizing process. I have argued that the Connectionist and Constructivist perspectives can be combined. Yes, there are subsystems that make up consciousness (Connectionism) but consciousness cannot be reduced to the sum of subsystems. The self is the higher organizational system that self-organizes (Constructivism).[46] The flow of ideas, associations, and emotions is orchestrated by the central organization of the self system (Constructivism) but is choppy and scattered because of the multiple subsystem from which it is composed (Connectionism). Thus, we are composites, but these composites have a central organization.

Some authors have described the self as always in a state of becoming, or striving for self-actualization.[47] From this perspective the self system always attempts to develop to its potential. This humanistic perspective envisions everyone as endowed with potentialities that strive to be actualized. The old model still retains the concept that the self need only to be allowed to reveal itself and develop according to its predetermined potential. The new paradigm envisions potentialities emerging as one evolves. In other words, as one develops there are organizational changes that contribute to new goals and potentialities that had not been previously identified.

More recently some authors have used the image of the "empty self" to describe the fact that there is no such thing as a static self.[48] The utility of this metaphor is that it draws attention to the fact that the self is not "filled up" with enduring patterns. It is not an object or a "thing" that can be quantified or reduced to its "parts." That is why I prefer to use the term "system" when using the term "self."

Over a century ago the great American psychologist William James introduced many concepts that are only today being fully appreciated.[49] According to James, there is a fundamental unity of each conscious thought. He regarded thoughts as complex wholes that are irreducible to their constituent parts. James emphasized the contextual nature of consciousness. His naturalistic approach cannot be isolated from one's unique position in the world. Therefore, the contextual unity is not a static structure, but rather a process.

When describing how the self is a system, it is important to emphasize that it fluctuates as it grows, and is capable of discontinuous reorganization. This is what I mean by the term "self"-organization. The self system is recursive in self-identity but not static. It refers back to itself and can have a relationship with itself. Self systems maintain some cohesiveness, while also having a changing contextual nature. That is, self systems maintain and thrive on relationships with others. We behave, think, and feel differently in each relationship.

Self systems are active processes. They do not exist as a noun alone. The term "self system" is better thought of as verb and a noun. We as individual self systems are "selfing" when we coevolve as selfing processes. We are contextual self systems within families and sociocultural systems and so on.

The emphasis on selfing, action, and coevolution cannot be overstated. We as self systems are always fluctuating, evolving, reorganizing. At this stage in the evolution of our species, our lives evolve on many levels simultaneously with nonlinearity. Change in one dimension changes other dimensions. These changes are irreversible.

For example, when I was twenty-two years old I spent one year traveling through Asia and the Middle East. By the time of my return, my view of myself and the world was irreversibly changed. There was no going back to perspectives and self states that had existed prior to my departure. I came back with a much expanded sensitivity to the diversity of human experience. Obviously, one does not only change through such experiences. We can also change each day in subtle ways. Changes occur discontinuously with nonlinearity—in spurts. Each change is so complex and nonlinear that identifying any of these changes in a comprehensive way is an impossible task.

This is why memories are reconstructions of past events from the vantage point of the present. We cannot move backward in time as if we are reviewing pictures or tape recordings. We are simply not the same people we were yesterday. However, I am more like myself today than I am like you and you are more like yourself than you are like me. There is obviously continuity to self systems. The point I am trying to make is that this continuity is fluid.

One aspect of consciousness is the subjective experience of being yourself over time. Even though you are always changing, your experience is in the present. Your memories of the past are actually continually evolving memories seen from the vantage point of the present.

It cannot be overstated how important the development of complex memory systems has been for the evolution of human consciousness. Memory serves to synthesize interrelationships that take place in space-time. Without this synthesis the self system would be fragmented and disorganized. Since memories evolve just as the overall self system evolves, these interrelationships take on different meanings.

Much of the cognitive and emotional processes that occur with the self system is unconscious. This belief has been around since Freud's era. However, there was no real evidence of this fact—it was only a theory. More recently, however, numerous studies have demonstrated that some unconscious processes do in fact occur.

The "blindsight" phenomenon also makes the direct or positivist position far too simplistic. Here individuals with damage to their occipital cortex (the area of the brain associated with vision) operate or navigate "as if" they can see, when in fact they themselves report blind spots associated with corresponding occipital location.

Blindsight represents an example of how an individual can perform a behavioral procedure necessitating visual input without awareness of that visual input. While individuals with this disorder suffer damage of the visual cortex their eyes track visual stimuli.

A particularly provocative series of studies was performed by Benjamin Libet, at the University of California at San Francisco. Libet's "Time-on" Theory suggests that most volitional movement is initiated unconsciously. According to Libet, the only uninhibited mental process occurs in dreaming.

During neurosurgery, Libet attached electrodes to an area of the brain associated with the sensation of a tingle to the hand. He also attached electrodes to the patient's hand to compare the experiential difference between actual stimulation to the skin and stimulation to the brain. He found that the experience of a tingle occurred as much as half a second after the electrical stimulation to either the skin or the brain, exceeding the time it took for the electric current to travel to either site.

Libet also stimulated the skin on the left hand at the same time as stimulating the left hemisphere (which controls the right hand). As expected, subjects reported tingles to both hands. Surprisingly, they also reported that the tingle to the left hand had occurred first. This is puzzling because the brain presumably is the site where the tingle is registered—the seat of consciousness. Libet argued that the tingle to the skin on the left hand is "referred back in time" to when the actual stimulation occurred.

Much has been written about what Libet's findings may mean regarding consciousness. I find most compelling the evidence of the multidimensional process occurring in consciousness. This multidimensional process evolves with nonlinearity. We perceive time as flowing, or rather specific moments in time are strung together and seen as continuous.

Consciousness is the result of the synthesis of multiple systems that unfold in many dimensions. These systems coevolve in space-time and are organized loosely in a higher organization—the self system. Biophysiological, sociocultural, cognitive/emotional processes all represent important contributing processes to the overall experience we call consciousness. Individual self systems occur within the "evolutionary field" of their unique experience of biophysiology, their position within a sociocultural system, and the fluid cognitive/emotional dynamics.

This open systems model envisions self systems as dynamic "self"-organizing systems. However conflicted they are from trauma, they still have the potential to reconfigure and continue to grow. The overall organization of the self system can grow through broadening oneself. This requires perceiving interdependent relationships with others. Reaching out beyond oneself allows for the perception of the reality of an interdependence.

4

Nocturnal Consciousness:
The Nature of Dreams

Everyone dreams on a regular basis. But what do dreams have to do with consciousness? In what way are the images envisioned in dreams relevant to the person who produces them or to that person's community? Such questions have concerned and intrigued people throughout history.

I have always been fascinated by the process of dreaming, and as a psychologist, I have invested considerable energy into reading the relevant research literature. Yet it was not enough for me to simply study theories of dreaming. I needed to be the direct subject of inquiry and for this reason I maintained a dream journal for nine years (from 1972 until 1981). So was I intrigued by the study of my own dreams that I kept a tape recorder next to my bed to ensure that if I awakened at 3 A.M., those dreams would not be wasted. What struck me about my own dreams was how they revealed an incredible diversity of perspectives of one life—my own.

To my dismay, I did not find a comprehensive description of the dream process in the psychological theories I reviewed. Instead, I found discreet descriptions of the dream process. This problem resembled, in many ways, the overall fragmentation, the compartmentalization, and the theoretical clubhouses of psychology.

In recent years, dream research has revolved around the biophysiological, sociocultural, intrapsychic, or transpersonal aspects. Although each of these dimensions represents a wealth of interrelated dynamics, none of these dimensions alone can represent a complete explanation of the dreaming process. However, biophysiological, sociocultural, intrapsychic, and transpersonal dynamics coevolve to produce the dream process. As I noted in the last chapter, these dimensions coevolve to produce the emergence of the self system. Correspondingly, the dreaming process is composed of, but cannot be reduced to, these dynamics.

The point I am trying to make regarding the fluidity of consciousness is best illustrated by the dream process itself. Dreams are erratic, chaotic, and multidimensional. Consider how the sequencing of dream images shifts abruptly. At one moment in a dream you may envision yourself talking to your mother, then abruptly the scene changes and you are at the beach flying a kite. At the beach you may find yourself talking to an old friend.

Not only is the dream process in this sense nonlinear and an interconnective synthesis of several subsystems, but there is evidence that dreams may reveal broader dimensions of consciousness than has been assumed by causal reductive paradigms. For example, if we assume that dreams are the result of neurons haphazardly firing we are lost in obsessive reductionism.

Many states of consciousness are possible within human experience. Dreaming itself can be seen as a unique state, or a unique series of states of consciousness. But the dream state is not hinged to the restraints dictated by presumptions of waking conscious about the nature of reality.

There is strong evidence that one can affect one's own dream imagery either by issuing directives from waking consciousness or by undergoing posthypnotic suggestion. This phenomenon is easily assimilated within our current conceptual system. It is when we move to lucid dreaming, when the dreamer knows that he is dreaming when in the dream, that new questions arise.

We then move further from theoretical "equilibrium," if you will, to discuss parapsychological research on the dream process. As we will observe in Chapter 7, the perplexing issue of psi phenomena presents problems for the paradigm of one-factor material causalities and limited dimensionality. Dreaming represents a highly sensitized level of consciousness that, at times, reflects nonlocal interconnectedness.

I am not suggesting that the transpersonal aspects of dreaming preclude or supersede the biophysical, sociocultural, or subjective aspects. Rather, all dimensions of dreaming are just that—dimensions that operate simultaneously. But these dimensions do not exist independently. There is considerable nonlinear coevolution among all aspects of the dream process. Changes in one dimension can have dramatic effects on other dimensions.

Over twenty-five years ago I had a dream about finishing a course I was taking. Within the dream I was experiencing a sense of accomplishment—I turned to a friend and remarked that I had learned much. The image of the friend became an old girlfriend who had left the country one year earlier, and whom I had not heard from since. I was awakened from the dream by a knock at the door. To my surprise she was the person at the door.

Dreams have many dimensions and contain layers of meaning. There are broad dimensions involved, such as the biophysiological, sociocultural, subjective, and transpersonal. I will discuss each of these dimensions in this chapter and emphasize how each coevolves with the others.

THE BIODYNAMICS OF THE DREAM PROCESS

Although theories of the dreaming process have been in existence since organized culture emerged, the biophysiological factors related to dreaming have only recently been researched. The reasons for this omission are twofold. First, the dualism that has stifled a comprehensive theory of consciousness for so long has also effected theories of dreaming. Second, the advances in research techniques and the maturation in the neurosciences during the last sixty years permitted a sophisticated analysis of how dreaming relates to the brain.

The first major advance in the biodynamics of dreaming occurred in the 1930s. This breakthrough was facilitated by the invention of the electroencephalograph (EEG). This instrument allowed researchers to track brain waves. By 1937 the EEG was applied to the sleep cycle. Five stages of sleep were identified. By 1953 one stage of sleep was correlated with frequent rapid eye movement (REM). When researchers woke their subjects during the REM period the subjects reported that they had been dreaming.

These REM periods occur every ninety minutes and are more densely concentrated toward the end of the sleep cycle (see Figure 4.1). The REM period also appears to be more intense in EEG activity than during other stages.[1] In contrast to slow wave sleep, where the immune system is revitalized and general physiological restoration is evident, the REM period is characterized by brain activity similar to that of waking consciousness. In fact, during REM sleep there is an increase in "dimensionally" (chaos or variation and randomness) in neuronal firing patterns.[2] The dream pattern emerges from this chaos. The initial neural fluctuation for the dream process begins deep within the brain stem. The giant cells in the pontine tegmentum (part of the brain stem) fire immediately prior to "PGO" spikes, which are sharp, "monophasic" waves emerging in the pons, oculomotor nuclei, lateral geniculate, and visual cortices.

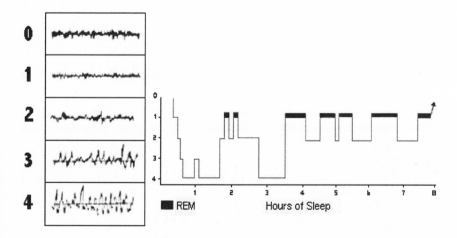

Figure 4.1
The EEG Patterns Associated with the Stages of Sleep

These events eventually result in the tonic activation of the frontal lobes. In other words, fluctuations in neuronal firing patterns occur first in the most primitive parts of the brain, then more complex parts of the brain are activated. At face value this appears to be a "bottom-up" process. Yet, as I will make clear, the dream process is far more complex.

Based on this series of brain events, J. Allan Hobson and Robert McCarley proposed their "Activation Synthesis" model of dreaming.[3] The basic premise of this model is that the cortex receives chaotic messages from deep within the most primitive parts of the brain and it does a poor job constructing a reality from them.[4] Hobson and McCarley proposed that dream imagery is meaningless and should be ignored. This extreme reductionistic approach has been partially abandoned in recent years, even by Hobson himself.[5]

Although the reductionistic perspective is unproductive when examining the dream process, the brain events themselves cannot be overlooked. I will describe how neuronal events coevolve with other aspects of the self system. They have their roots in the evolution of the species and the developmental process.

It appears as though the REM cycle is an evolutionary artifact of species that have a complex central nervous system (CNS). The REM cycle is unique to the mammalian species. The functions of REM sleep include self-protection and cortical self-stimulation for these species. For example, given that the REM cycle is more neuronally intense in EEG activity than slow-wave sleep, it allows for an easier arousal. In other words, REM sleep provides a safety arousal threshold during which one could awaken quickly if a predator were threatening.

It is the self-stimulating function of REM sleep that I find more interesting. Consider the fact that for all mammals REM sleep takes up more overall time early in the animal's life. In fact, for humans the REM cycle is apparent in utero and during infancy it takes up more than half of the sleep cycle. These facts have led to the premise that REM sleep provides the maturing brain with critical stimulation for adequate development. In other words, the brain needs stimulation to mature. REM sleep provides the critical stimulation during the night. The point here is that while maintaining cortical growth and tone, the stimulating images of the dreams are essential factors for the developing self system.

Another important aspect of the REM process is memory consolidation. The structures in the brain stem I noted earlier also activate the septum and the hippocampus. Both the hippocampus and the septum are involved in memory consolidation and emotional arousal and are part of the paleomammalian cortex—the limbic system. Emotions and memories are intertwined in what has been called state-based memories. Thus, stimulation of these parts of the brain also stimulates and rehashes state-based memories and emotions.

Jonathan Winson has found a relationship between state-based memory consolidation, emotional arousal, and mammalian evolution.[6][7] It appears that REM sleep provides a means to deal with the increasing complexity of psychosocial experience for complex species.

The cortical stimulation that occurs in utero and during infancy can be understood as an aspect of the self-organizing process that prepares the brain to deal with the rich complexity of psychosocial experience. Memories of experiences that have occurred during waking consciousness need to be reprocessed and worked over during sleep. REM sleep provides a means for this to occur.

But one remaining question still lingers. Why is there a drop-off in REM time as an individual ages? The answer may be that the sociocultural system in which the individual is embedded provides one of the channels through which an individual can work through his thoughts and feelings.

Therefore, biophysiological and psychosocial experience coevolve even in the dream cycle. They are not separate dimensions, but are interdependent evolutionary processes. This interdependence becomes more complex when we consider what happens to the dream process as we age.

HUMAN DEVELOPMENT, GENDER, AND DREAM CONTENT

As one ages so does the complexity of dream content, which illustrates the interdependency and coevolution of the self system and its dreams. In other words, as an individual's life becomes more complex through rich psychosocial experiences, dreams both reflect and work through the state-based memories derived from these experiences.

Over the past forty years a vast body of research has accumulated supporting the view that there is a coevolution of dream content and increasing complexity of the self system. For example, research in the United States indicates that as one ages so does the level of aggression evident in dream themes.[8]

During childhood dream themes become progressively cognitive—more oriented toward thoughts than exclusively emotional. Between ages three and four, for example, dreams are described as expansive and expressive. By ages five and six dreams double in length and the cognitive factors express concern with interpersonal relationships. This parallels developmental experiences of the early latency years in which interpersonal relationships outside one's family become increasingly important.

The dreams of boys are different than those of girls. Boys dream more of male strangers, untamed animals, and aggression. Girl's dreams, in contrast, express more friendly interactions and resolution of conflict.

By the turbulent years of adolescence, dream themes express more conflict and frustration. Paralleling the major physical changes that occur in growth and puberty, dream themes become more bizarre.[9] It is not uncommon for an adolescent to produce a dream in which he images himself as a physically distorted individual who has a great deal of difficulty fitting in socially.

By adulthood the gender differences in dreams become more pronounced. The dreams of men often have more men in them than women. In contrast, women dream equally of men and women. Often the dreams of men reflect more aggression between the men in their dreams. Dreams of women depict relationships that are friendlier than those in the dreams of men.[10]

Aggression continues to be a factor in the dreams of men and the degree of physical violence increases. Often the violence occurs with individuals whom the male dreamer does not know in daily life. For women, dream characters often include people the dreamer knows in waking life and the themes reflect more cooperation between those characters.[11]

To what degree are these factors reflective of the differences in enculturation? To explore this issue researchers have compared the findings from dream content studies in the 1950s and 1960s with those performed in the 1980s and 1990s. During the last thirty years sex roles have changed significantly in Western culture. Indeed, in one study it was found that there was less differentiation in social interaction, misfortune, and aggression between the sexes.[12] However, in another study it was found that there continued to be a preponderance of male characters in the dreams of men and that women continue to dream more of babies, family members, and indoor settings.[13] Interestingly, the level of aggression in dreams seems to reflect the region of the country that the dreamer lives in more than the gender of the dreamer. Specifically, dreams of subjects in the Eastern United States had higher levels of aggression than did the dreams of subjects in the West and Midwest.[14]

In general, as with sociocultural systems there appears to be a slight shift in the dream content of men and women in Western culture. The point here is that there appears to be a coevolution of sociocultural factors and the content of dreams. We will explore these factors in the next section.

THE SOCIOCULTURAL ASPECTS OF DREAMS

As noted in Chapter 3, sociocultural systems have a profound effect on consciousness. Culture, consciousness, and dream content are interdependent and coevolve. An individual within a sociocultural system not only responds to culturally based images and metaphors but the same imagery is reflected in the content of his or her dreams. Thus, there is a creative feedback process in dream imagery and sociocultural systems. Sociocultural systems provide a rich fabric of symbols and metaphors that act as attractors for the content of dream.

For over thirty years an extensive body of research has accumulated on the cross-cultural aspects of dreaming. Samples of dream reports have been taken from cultures all over the world, and have collectively shown that the differences between cultures are also evident in the content of dreams. In other words, people from different cultures have dreams that differentiate their cultures. My dreams are different from your dreams. But assuming that you live in a Western industrialized culture, our dream content has more similarity with one another's when compared to the content of dreams produced by a member of the Amazonian Kalapalo tribe.

One of the most extensive series of studies to explore how the content of dreams differ in individuals from culture to culture was performed by Calvin Hall and Robert Van de Castle in the 1960s.[15] They had on file at the Dream Research Institute some 30,000 dream reports from areas as diverse as Peru, Australia, Nigeria, and the United States. They found major differences based on socioeconomic group, gender, and the physical health of the dreamer.

The prevalence of animal figures in dreams is characteristic of the culture of the dreamer. For example, the incidence of animal references ranges from 51 percent of recorded dreams for the Australian Yir Younts, to 23 percent for the Hopi of the Southwestern United States.[16] Even within the same country dream content can vary based on tribal affiliation. For example, in Nigeria the three main tribes are the Ibo, the Hausa, and the Yoruba. These tribes have been described in the anthropological literature as having generally different degrees of achievement motivation. In a study that examined the content of dreams taken from subjects of these three cultures it was revealed that tribal affiliation was evident as expressed by characteristic differences in achievement motivation. The dreams of Ibo subjects reflected more achievement motivation than the dreams of subjects of the Hausa and the Yoruba tribes.[17] Thus, dream themes reflect those in the sociocultural system.

For cultures that regard dreams as important messages, the telling of one's dreams serves as both positive and negative feedback. For example, when individuals within a sociocultural system describe their dreams they do so within the context of their cultural system. Dream characters are often mutually agreed upon as representing either mythological figures revered by the culture or characters within the group itself. When an individual has a dream in which a mythological figure is thought to convey a particular message, the clan or tribe may modify some behavior dictated or metaphorically implied by the dream.

A good example of this process occurs with the Australian Aboriginal culture. According to their concept of dreamtime, all that exists in the universe is part of a great spirit's dream.[18] When individuals have dreams they gain insight into the great spirit's plan. The retelling of dreams in a social situation serves to enculturate members of the society. Both the dreamer and those hearing about the dream gain a sense of belonging to the same social system—occurring within dreamtime.

The telling of dreams in a social context serves not only to reinforce enculturation, but also has a sociotherapeutic function. In other words, the telling of dreams in a social context provides a psychotherapeutic outlet for individuals. For example, among the Mapuche tribe in Chile, discussing dreams is a regular practice. For example, in most sociocultural systems this is especially the case during periods in which the dreamer has experienced stress. The support and feedback elicited from others after the telling of one's dreams has been reported to contribute to more warmth in the family system and better general communication among tribe members.[19]

Another interesting example of the sociotherapeutic function of dream reporting occurs with the Cuna tribe in Panama. The Cuna share a high value for "moral" behavior. Dreams expressing interpersonal difficulties with peers are shared and discussed. Reported, the Cuna have a relatively low incidence of violence, aggression, and competition.[20]

Overall, there is a coevolution of the individual, his dreams, and his place in the sociocultural system. Since cultures are made up of individuals with con-

sciousness, the incorporation of dream reports into the rituals of the culture allows the involvement of individuals in a common experience. From this perspective one could say that the sociocultural system is having dreams. These
dreams provide a healthy self-regulatory and self-organizing function. In other
words, they support the culture from which they emerge and they contribute to
that culture's growth.

Dreaming also illustrates the degree to which consciousness is made up of
metaphorical images, culturally relevant symbols, and archetypes. All of these
support the "self"-organization of individuals. They do this because they are part
of the fabric of cultural experience of each individual.

It is reasonable to postulate that in the paleolithic mythic period dreams were
indistinguishable from daily consciousness. Given that myths formed part of the
fabric of a sociocultural system, they also serve as reference constructs for individuals within a society. Dream imagery has a more subtle meaning for individuals in contemporary industrial societies. In general, myths are condensed
through symbols and are expressed by the members of a society through various
forms of interpersonal interaction and intrapersonal dream content. For example,
one may suggest to another individual that his inclusion in a political party
serves as a "Trojan Horse." The inference is that the individual's political influence will "sneak in" and take over the party. On an intrapersonal level an individual may dream of a Trojan Horse entering his or her house. This covert take-
over may imply that outside influence may take over the perspective of the individual.

THE SUBJECTIVE EXPERIENCE OF DREAMS

During the last ninety years more has been written about the significance of
dreaming with respect to subjective experiences than about any other area. For
this reason I will not attempt to summarize the historical developments in psychological theory, but rather comment on what I view as the most important issues, drawing on some of the points made elsewhere.[21]

I have stressed that as with other aspects of psychology, there has been a tendency to fragment and compartmentalize psychological processes. With respect
to dreaming, researchers have gravitated toward a particular aspect of the subjective significance of a dream—one causal factor. Human consciousness is far
too complex to be explained by one causal factor and so are the subjective aspects of dreaming.

As I noted earlier in this chapter, dreaming had evolutionary functions. It
provided a critical arousal threshold (so the animal could arouse easily if it were
in danger) and important nocturnal stimulation for the developing brain (to ensure the continued maturation of the brain). Dreaming also aids in the process of
memory consolidation and reworking state-based memories derived from complex psychological experience.

The self-referential aspects of the self system and dreams cannot be overemphasized. Dreams by nature are self-referential—they are produced by a self

system always in the process of self-organization. The self system emerges in a complex sea of factors and self-organizes. As noted in the previous chapter, many subsystems coevolve and are organized into self-referential imagery. Metaphors derived from the sociocultural system and aspirations are reflected in one's experiences and dream imagery.[22] Just as there are fluctuations in waking imagery, so are there fluctuations in dream imagery. But the fluctuations in dream imagery are more extreme. This is primarily because during the dream process interaction with the world is based solely on memories and creative reconstructions of experience.

Therefore, dream imagery can serve as creative feedback to waking consciousness. For example, the initial expression of the commonly used chemical periodic table was reportedly envisioned in a dream. In 1869, Dmitri Mendeleev claimed to have had a dream in which he envisioned a table in which all the chemical elements were arranged according to their atomic weight. This makes the dream imagery reveal, work through, and project the creative reorganizations of thoughts and concerns of waking consciousness.

From this perspective we can say that dreams provide an important self-organizing function. They deal with many of the factors identified by theorists over the past one hundred years. Though Freud overstated the sexual aspects of dreaming, they do, nevertheless, play a part in dreams. Who can deny that sexual dreams do not occur more when one feels deprived of sensuality?

Dreams also express and project concerns about possible courses of action that one is considering in daily life. We are beings who strive, plan for, and are concerned with our struggles in a complex psychosocial world. Freud's early colleague Alfred Adler was right to draw attention to these factors. Most people recognize that their dreams reflect concerns they are dealing with in their conscious lives.

Dreams also appear to compensate for and express one's internal struggle to balance opposing thoughts and feelings one has regarding oneself. Carl Jung was right to point out the compensating and internal balancing function that dreams provide. It would be difficult for any astute investigator of one's own dreams to deny that compensating factors occur in dreams.

What is most interesting to me, however, is that the dream process itself revolves around the multidimensional self-organizing process. However seemingly fragmented, the dreaming process is reflective of rich self-referential imagery. This metaphorical imagery accesses, recombines, and fuses elements derived from state-based memory networks. In recent years cognitive theorists have overemphasized, but nevertheless pointed out, the importance of cognitive factors in the dreaming process. Yet cognitions are fused with and coevolve with emotions during dreams, just as in waking consciousness.[23]

Because there are so many subsystems coevolving to produce the dream process, they evolve with a great deal of nonlinearity. Again, this occurs more so than in waking consciousness because the environmental demands are not as critical. The abrupt changes in the story line of a dream reflect this high degree of nonlinearity. For example, when describing our dreams we often remark,

"And the next thing I knew I was . . . talking to my boss . . . or . . . at the beach and the President walked up and said . . ."

Even though these discontinuities and seemingly chaotic dream story lines do not appear at face value to be cohesive, they do revolve around the same organizing central system—the self system. Why do your dreams always portray you as the central character? This is because dreams are an aspect of consciousness that reflects, maintains, and self-organizes the self system.

Perhaps the most extreme example of the self-organizing function of dreaming occurs when an individual decides prior to sleep what she will dream about. Yet one of the assumptions that the general public and even some researchers make is that dreaming is a passive process. Dreams are thought to just happen. Remember, the discontinuous scene changes—"the next thing I knew was."

In some cultures and most shamanic practices there is a belief that one can decide what one will dream about. The purpose is to gain some answers to concerns and questions that need addressing in conscious life.[24] The individual may talk to a spirit god, or advisor or manipulate and change her perspective.

The shamans interviewed in anthropological studies report that they achieve novel perspectives of their lives, and the lives of others, through lucid dreams. They project themselves in the dream to prearranged tasks and bring back to waking consciousness information obtained during the dream.[25]

Is this really possible, or is it intriguing folklore? The more precise question we need to ask is: can one decide before sleeping what he will dream about that night? The answer to this question was resolved experimentally thirty years ago. In these cases, subjects were successfully exposed to post-hypnotic suggestions concerning what they should dream at night.[26][27][28]

Now what would happen if these directives were instilled by the dreamer himself while he was in the middle of a dream? The issue of the supposed passivity of dreams is addressed head on. This is what happens during lucid dreams. Lucid dreaming, as the name implies, refers to dreams in which the dreamer "knows" he is dreaming. Often during a lucid dream the dreamer "decides," (since he is "just dreaming") to make changes in the dream imagery. Instead of the usual sort of dream where one experiences abrupt changes in the story line of the dream (i.e., "the next thing I knew was. . . "), lucid dreams transform this experience to direct decisions regarding what will occur in the dream (i.e. "the next thing I decided to do was. . .").

Research directed toward control of lucid dreams prior to sleep onset has been explored during the past fifteen years. Subjects have been asked to perform certain tasks during the dreams. The success of these predirectives reveals the multidimensionality of the self system. Other researchers have found that experienced meditators have significantly more lucid dreams than nonmeditators.[29] This suggests that people who have cultivated an ability to focus attention and screen out extraneous stimulation also achieve control of their own dream content.

Interestingly, prelucid dreaming has been associated with bizarre imagery and with nightmares. As with nightmares it is relatively easy to awaken someone from lucid dreaming.[30] This suggests that lucid dreams, like nightmares, represent the self system in far-from-equilibrium conditions. Perhaps what emerges out of these conditions is that a higher level of organization is possible. Lucid dreams represent a higher state of consciousness possible within the dream cycle.

This leap to a higher level of organization represents how the self system is greater than the sum of its parts. Put another way, the emergence of a conscious self within the dream (a self-representation) illustrates the dynamic qualities of the self system. In other words, the self system is a dynamic self-organizing process that supersedes its elemental constituents. It can reach beyond self-maintenance and enhance itself even within the dream process. It can also reach beyond itself. It is in that provocative direction that we now turn.

SELF-TRANSCENDENCE AND DREAMS

Most ancient cultures attached great significance to dreams and regarded them as having practical as well as mystical value. The literature of the ancient Babylonians, Egyptians, Chinese, Greeks, Hebrews, and Romans contains countless references to prophetic dreams.[31] Joseph was said to have interpreted the prophetic dream of a pharaoh. Alexander the Great supposedly conquered the city of Tyre after his dream interpreters told him that his dream foretold the fall of that city.[32]

It is probable that dreams were regarded as an important spiritual medium by cultures during the Paleolithic period, as is now evident in many contemporary hunter-gatherer societies. Lucid dreaming provided the shaman with a sense of power and versatility. Shamans regarded dreams as expressions of archetypal visions, and insight into the spiritual undercurrent of the world. For example, among the Cushininahua in Eastern Peru, the Siberian Chuckahee, the Australian Urambal, and the Naskapi Algonquin in Labrador, dreams are regarded as an important tool for shamanic visions.[33][34] Among the Kagwahi of the Amazon, it is believed that "spiritual beings" in the form of deceased loved ones provide spiritual insight to life.

In all of the major sociotheological systems, dreams are regarded with reverence. For example, in Judaism, the Talmud contains 217 references to dreams. Gabriel, the most important angelic figure, has been referred to as the "Prince of Dreams." Since dreams were thought to have been avenues by which angelic entities could communicate to mortals, Gabriel and others were believed to have served as guides or special messengers in dreams. Much of the early developmental history of the life of Jesus was said to have been envisioned in dreams. For example, in Matthew it is written that Joseph was told the source of Mary's pregnancy through a dream. Mohammed envisioned his divine mission through a dream. In fact, much of the Koran was believed to have been revealed to Mohammed through dreams. Some of the imagery in the dreams weaves together figures from Judaism and Christianity into the emerging Islamic motif. For example, Gabriel was believed to guide Mohammed through the seven celestial spheres. During the journey, Mohammed meets Abraham, Joseph, and Jesus.

But by the late eighteenth century, educated people began to regard these be-liefs as occult nonsense. The possibility that dreams might produce phenomena with undefined spatial and temporal order was seen as being incompatible not only with the Aristotelian laws of logic but also with the Newtonian laws of space, time, and causality. Such beliefs in the spiritual power of dreams was in-consistent with the general positivist attitude that followed. Belief in this possi-bility—like the belief in telepathy and precognition—was attributed, until re-cently, to uneducated superstitious people.

During this past century, however, serious efforts have been made to investi-gate the dream process from a parapsychological perspective. For example, of 7,000 cases of extrasensory perception (ESP) studied in the United States and 1,000 cases studied in Germany, almost two-thirds were related to dreams. And a study of cases among schoolchildren in India gives a figure of almost 50 per-cent.[35] Therefore, dreams represent a sensitive state of consciousness through which the dreamer may have psi type experiences.

In the 1960s the REM phenomenon was first applied to the study of telepathy in dreams at the Maimonides Medical Center in Brooklyn, New York. The stud-ies on dream telepathy at Maimonides were conducted by Montague Ullman and Stanley Krippner between 1962 and 1971. The design of these studies usually involved a subject who was connected to an EEG, while an agent (in another room) would focus attention on a vivid painting depicting strong emotions. Throughout the ensuing night, the subject would be awakened during REM sleep for dream reports. The researchers found a strong congruence between the con-tent of the paintings and the dream content. They also surmised, based on anec-dotal information, that a strong emotional bond between agent-subject was very important in facilitating telepathy. Similar findings have been noted with twins; these findings suggested that strong emotional rapport between twins was more facilitative than genetic similarities alone.[36]

Inclusive emotions, such as love and compassion, because of their connective quality, appear to facilitate the telepathic connection between the dreamer and the sender. Emotions such as anxiety and depression, which are aspects of closed self system dynamics, do not seem to facilitate this connection. Thus, the issue of telepathy may be related to the process of emotional facilitation of interconnec-tivity and occur during significant life events.

The connection of an emotional bond between individuals and telepathic communication in dreams suggests that interconnectivity at one level (emotional) facilitates interconnectivity at another level (telepathic). In other words, inter-connective relationships promote sensitivity to other interconnective relation-ships. Further, there is a natural tendency toward the promotion of interconnec-tive relationships between elements in the biosphere that can be reflected in dreams as well as cultivated in human communication.

Transpersonal dreams also can include archetypal imagery. Like lucid dreams and telepathic dreams, dreams that are infused with archetypal imagery are rela-tively resistant to free association.[37] In other words, while most dreams can be linked to self system attractors through the aid of free association, lucid, telepathic, and archetypal dreams are transpersonal. Interestingly, Jung proposed that psi phenomena in dreams cluster around emotionally laden archetypal symbols.[38] Telepathic dreams often occur just before or after a personally significant event. Dream reports in the laboratory differ from dream reports derived from home. Specifically, home reports are more emotionally intense and elaborate than are laboratory reports.[39]

How can emotion, which is an aspect of the self system, be resistant to free association? The connective quality of love and compassion can be extended to others in such a way that what binds us transcends the immediate concerns of one's self system. In this sense dreams fused with emotion can be self transcendent.

The dream process, like all aspects of consciousness, is multidimensional, nonlinear, and interconnected. All the dimensions of the dream process operate simultaneously and they coevolve. It is difficult to influence one dimension without influencing all others. Further, not only is the dream process interconnected at all levels but it represents a very sensitive altered level of consciousness. The restraints that are operative in waking consciousness are less apparent during dreaming. One may say that conditions during the dream process are far-from-equilibrium, and that they are subject to multidimensional bifurcations in dream imagery. For example, Rhine had reported that spontaneously reported ESP type dreams had generally occurred around life-crisis-type experiences.[40]

It may be useful to consider the correlation between significant life events, archetypal imagery, and transpersonal experience as convergence points. The periodic convergence of these phenomena reveals the inherent flux and evolutionary aspects of consciousness. In other words, consciousness is not a static, one-dimensional process. It is an evolutionary phenomenon that occurs on many levels. As we evolve, the meaning we are capable of placing on phenomena evolves. We become more aware of interconnective relationships among the multiple dimensions of consciousness. Theologies have dealt with these aspects of self transcendence. We turn our attention to that area in the next chapter.

5

Perennial Philosophy and Sociotheological Systems

> Most men worship the gods because they want success
> in their worldly undertakings. This kind of material
> success can be gained very quickly [by such worship]
> here on earth.
>
> Bhagavad Gita

Over forty years ago Aldous Huxley popularized the term "Perennial Philosophy."[1] He and many others since have argued that there exists a consistent message conveyed by all theological systems. The two main tenets of the Perennial Philosophy are compassion/love and the concept of unity/inter-dependence. Is there a Perennial Philosophy? In other words, is there a common theme of unity and compassion inherent in all theological systems? If there is, does this theme emphasize a deep interconnective fabric to all existence? Or, are there great discrepancies among theologies? If there are discrepancies, can these variations be explained by the sociocultural systems in which they emerged? How can there be both wide cultural variations between theologies and themes that are cross-culturally similar?

In support of the Perennial Philosophy, many authors have argued that cultural variation is irrelevant; that all theologies simply reflect the Perennial Philosophy, expressing it in different styles. Others, however, argue that the variation between theologies reflects each culture's effort to compensate for uncertainty and deal with sociocultural tension. It is undeniable that cultural factors exert considerable influence on the emergence and evolution of theological systems. Each theology is a cultural expression. For this reason I shall refer to theological systems as "sociotheological systems." To assume that each sociotheological systems expresses *exclusively* a Perennial Philosophy would be terribly naïve and misleading. On the other hand, deeply embedded within the rich culturally relevant mythology of many sociotheological systems there exists a consistent theme of interconnectivity as well as unique cultural elements that characterize not only the particular culture, but perhaps the Perennial Philosophy as well. In this chapter I will differentiate between the cultural influence, which is often referred to as exoteric, and the Perennial Philosophy, which is often referred to as esoteric.

The emergence of sociotheological systems illustrates the nonlinear evolution of sociocultural systems. Sociotheological systems influence the way in which sociocultural dynamics influence the way in which members of these systems organize their lives. The central theme of most sociotheological systems is that there is a broad and unifying order in the universe. Interestingly, many theologies emerged during periods of social flux, often organizing around a charismatic reformer who reported having experienced a mystical insight of universal order. This report, and the social context in which it was reported, often contributed to the emergence of a new theological system or a revitalization of a preexisting theology.

New developments in sociotheological organization lead to varying degrees of influence or feedback on the "self"-organization of individuals. In other words, individuals within these cultures use the central constructs of theologies to reorganize their lives and interpret novel experiences. When individuals who adhere to these belief systems have experiences that are not easily understood, they may define the experiences within the constructs of the sociotheological system to which they subscribe. For example, the fundamentalist Christian may view his curiosity in evolutionary theory as a temptation to deviate from his faith. Or a Hindu might interpret the same evolutionary curiosity as an attempt to trace the complex workings of Maya, or worldly illusion.

In far-from-equilibrium conditions within sociocultural systems, new sociotheological systems acted as attractors for the sociocultural systems from which they arose. In other words, new theological systems emerged during and after social and cultural upheaval. Most major sociotheological systems began during such turbulent periods.

The attractor in each case was the innovative and reformist philosophy of an individual who, as noted above, communicated a theme of interconnectivity and/or ethical behavior. Many of these individuals did not themselves live to see the sociotheological systems that they had initiated. Rather, they served as archetypal attractors for a later nonlinear transformation of the sociocultural system. For example, Jesus of Nazareth became the Christ image for millions of people outside of the small community in which he lived. Moses never saw the Promised Land; and Mohammed died long before the full extent of his influence was realized.

It is important to note that the philosophies that derived from the original teachings did not necessarily retain the essence of those teachings, although they may have embodied the same general themes. For example, the plethora of Christian denominations depend on the same story, but do not necessarily agree on issues at the heart of Christian belief. The contemporary contrast between Mother Theresa and the Christian Right Wing in the United States illustrate this disparity. Thus, sociotheological systems were, and are, self-organized systems that bifurcate and evolved within sociocultural macrosystems.

But the mystics who initiated these sociotheological systems were not just re-acting to the sociocultural conditions of their respective eras. They were also responding to their own creative and intuitive visions of transcendental unity during periods of social chaos. The sociocultural significance of their mystical revelations further added to the mystics' own power as attractors. Even myths constructed around the lives of these mystics modeled the ideal transformation from mortal existence to reunification with the ultimate macrosystem. For ex-ample, Jesus is believed to have been resurrected after three days and risen to heaven forty days after crucifixion. This ascension was thought to represent a reunification with his father after a period of semimortal existence.

It is also fascinating to note that many sociotheological systems began during the "Axial Age," 800 to 200 B.C.E., Christianity and Islam being notable excep-tions. These, however, can be seen as modifications of the initial Judaic theol-ogy, which was forming during this time frame. During this Axial Age there were many parallel cultural developments such as the emergence of large king-doms and a market economy. The major sociotheological systems emerged dur-ing this period of collective and nonlocal connective flux in the evolution of the species.

Written script and the external memory capability that it provides contributed to major cognitive reorganization. Written script served as a structural bridge from the Mythic to the Theoretical Cultures.[2] During the Mythic Culture there was an oral tradition which we can know little about. In effect, written script intensified the emergence of sociotheological systems all of which have had a profound influence on the organization of sociocultural systems. For example, the central organizing themes in all the major sociotheological systems have eventually been put forth through sacred written texts (i.e., the Old and New Testaments, the Vedas, the Tao Te Ching, and the Koran).

Not only is the evolution of sociocultural systems consistent with the emer-gence of organized theological systems, but the influence of these sociotheologi-cal systems on the evolution of consciousness is pervasive. In short, the factors related to sociotheological dynamics are multivariate and interactive. An indi-vidual is embedded in a complex field of interconnected sociocultural variables, and his or her personal experience coevolves with these dynamics. Individual and sociocultural far-from-equilibrium conditions allow for creative bifurcations within a given sociocultural system. This is the process by which the individual and the system coevolve.

PRESACRED SCRIPT AND ORAL THEOLOGIES

What can we assume that people thought about before there was written script? All that is available for us to infer from are fossils and artifacts. Neverthe-less, many of these fossils and artifacts are very provocative. They leave us with much room for speculation.

During the past 500,000 years, individuals and societies probably devoted time and thought to speculation about, and the belief in a supernatural world. Consider two rather macabre fossil finds. In what is now China, skeletal remains of *Homo erectus* indicate the cutting off and preserving of heads 500,000 years ago. Compare that finding to another from the Paleolithic period. In the Placard cave in what is now Charente, France, skulls had been found that were separated from the bodies. Two of the skull tops have been fashioned into bowls. Other skulls had been used as drinking cups. The fossils found in China and those found in France are separated by roughly 450,000 years and different subspecies. As I pointed out in Chapter 2, the brain size difference between *Homo erectus* and *Homo sapiens* was immense. But why would individuals from both groups do this? Explanations concerning the meaning of these findings have ranged from trophy taking and ancestor worship to the ingestion of the contents to derive the vitality of the deceased.

I think that the confusing phenomenon of death must have been as provocative to them as it is for us today. It was probably thought that by using the skulls of people who died as drinking cups, the power of the "other world" could be harvested. This may be the core concept of ancestral worship.

Of the mythology of this period, we can only conjecture. The mythology undoubtedly was a model of reality carried in the minds and permeating the cultural system. Joseph Campbell has written eloquently of this period.

The animal forms of the mural art now masterfully rendered in a powerfully painterly style, with fluent lines and rich coloration, through eyes that had looked at animals in a way that has not been known since, and by hands perfectly trained. This art was magic. And herds are the herds of eternity, not of time—yet even more vividly real and alive than animals of time, because of their ever-living source. At Altamira the bulls—which are almost breathing, they are so alive—are on the ceiling, reminding us of nature; for they are the stars.[3]

The magic of life and death generated a sense of awe throughout our evolutionary experience. The belief in a meaningful or at least complex universe often included an "other dimension" after life. For example, archeological evidence of the worship of the dead is almost universal. In central Europe, Neanderthals buried their dead with flowers and food presumably for the journey to the afterlife. Red ocherous powder has been found in burial sites all over Europe, often with seemingly sacred items such as carvings and shells. A common practice in these cultures was to place the deceased in a fetal position in the tomb, suggesting preparation for rebirth.[4]

In Northern Iraq, there is a Neanderthal burial site from 60,000 years ago in which the corpse had been placed in pine boughs. Pollen was found in the grave indicating that a bouquet of flowers from eight plant species was intentionally placed there. These plants are used to this day in the region for medicinal purposes.

Trances and altered states of consciousness may have been a part of the Upper Paleolithic culture, as evidenced by the "Dead Man" in the cave paintings at Lascaux, in present day France.[5] During this period the practice of shamanism is illustrated by the now acclaimed "sorcerer" painting/engraving. This figure appears with a human face, large eyes, the beard and claws of a lion, and the tail of a horse. Near Leride in the Spanish Pyrenees, a cave painting depicts a ritual dance of nine women dancing around a small naked man. This painting is generally interpreted as a depiction of a fertility dance. All of these findings illustrate a profound degree of ceremonial ritual directed toward the unknown.

Death and rebirth are prominent themes in European cave art from about 40,000 years ago. For example, at Lascaux a carving of a nude pregnant woman holding a bison horn in her right hand had been covered with red ocher apparently to further sanctify or venerate the carving.

Early rituals also seemed to be directed toward efforts to influence the environment (e.g., good hunting and/or weather).[6] Paleolithic art found in cave paintings at Lascaux, southwestern France, and Altamira, northern Spain, have revealed a preoccupation with hunting game animals. The reverence for specific game animals gave way to totemism and clans that worshipped one or more animal images.

Apparently shamanism was the dominant means of ritualistic and spiritual inquiry in most societies until the advent of written theological systems. In fact, in most remaining hunter/gatherer societies shamanism is still widely practiced. It was only with the advent of sociocultural systems based on agriculture that shamanic traditions were superseded by traditions that centered on pastoral related deities.

About 30,000 years ago maternal figures, often referred to as "Venuses," appeared in what is now Spain in the West to Lake Baikal in Siberia. These figures symbolize life in what has been called the Mother Goddess Cult.[7] Let us turn to Campbell again.

We are clearly in a paleolithic province where the serpent, labyrinth, rebirth themes already constitute a symbolic constellation, joined to the imagery of the sunbird and the shaman fight, with the goddess in her classic role as protectress of the hearth, mother of man's second birth, and the lady of the wild things and the food supply. She is here a patroness of the hunt, just as among planters she is the patroness of the fields and the crops.[8]

In the eastern Mediterranean and western Asia, the Mother Goddess worship was prevalent throughout the early agricultural period. Most evidence indicates that the inhabitants of these early city/states were peace-loving egalitarians with little division between the sexes. In contrast, tribes that practiced herding and whose clans were ruled by priests and warriors brought with them male-dominated gods of war and paternalism. When these clans invaded the early city-states, many of the Mother Goddesses were demoted or eliminated from positions of central worship by male gods who were either promoted from minor status or adopted outright from invading cultures.[9]

Early Indo-European theology was organized around one central concept, a paternalistic "Father Sky." Many of the subsequent kings of the early Indo-European civilizations tapped into this motif and proclaimed that they themselves were divine.[10] Yet the residual influences of the Mother Goddess survived in many civilizations. For example, the Great Mother was referred to as Ishtar in Babylon, Isis in Egypt, Irana in Sumeria, Anat in Canaan, and Aphrodite in Greece.

The later major sociocultural systems evolved as open systems, subsuming and synthesizing the sociocultural dynamics of earlier theologies. This "syncretism" illustrates how fluid and dynamic such belief systems are.

Each of the three theological spectrums, the Judeo-Christian-Islamic, the Hindu-Jainist-Buddhist, and the Confucianism-Taoist-Buddhist, exemplifies the dynamic interplay between numerous nonlinear, sociocultural subsystems. Through each spectrum there has occurred an intriguing absorption process not only of previous and competing theological systems but also of macrosystemic symbols which Jung referred to as archetypes.

THE JUDEO-CHRISTIAN-ISLAMIC PARADIGM

The Judeo-Christian-Islamic God is a hybrid. It evolved over thousands of years as several cultures coevolved. It is an amalgamation of myths. The genesis of the Middle Eastern theological paradigm developed in the great agricultural civilizations of the early Neolithic period. For example, as we shall see the concepts of good and evil may have emerged in Persia. The concept of divine retribution may have emerged in Mesopotamia, and the concept of the repudiation of sins in Egypt. A nomadic and patriarchal Semitic tribe absorbed and synthesized these varied but related concepts into a new creation: the Middle Eastern Theological Paradigm.

We can look to Sumeria for the first contributions to Judeo-Christian-Islamic theology. Written language provides that trail. The first evidence of written language appeared about 3000 B.C. at Uruk in Sumeria. Over half a million documents in cuneiform script have been found on clay tablets.[11] Because of this, Sumerian cosmology and religion have been easily traced, including their later influence on Babylonian, Elamilitie, Assyrian, and later the Judaic cultures.

For example, one of the earliest works in literature is the myth of Gilgamesh which had a profound effect on the theologies of the Middle East. In the epic Utnapishtim told Gilgamesh that he had been approached by Gods who warned him of a great flood. The Gods told him to stop everything he was doing and build a great boat. He was then to gather pairs of every species and gather them onto the boat. After the horrendous flood that waged for six days and six nights the boat rested on the summit of Mount Nisir. After an additional seven days Utnapishtim sent a dove free, then a swallow, and finally a raven. When the raven did not return he knew it was safe to leave the great boat. There are few differences between this myth and that of the story of Noah in the book of Genesis. Indeed, there are many parallels between this myth and others in the eastern Mediterranean.[12]

Fundamental to Sumerian religion are the premises that there is universal order to the cosmos and that whatever mankind can perceive reflects the activity of the divine mind. The subsequent Babylonian concept of divine retribution, in the guise of sickness, problems, and even death, was seen as the result of human "sin." This concept is easily recognized as a fundamental tenet of the later Judeo-Christian tradition. Of course, the Hindu concept of Karma, discussed later, is a similar parallel. In the early Mesopotamian culture, the fatalism of the sufferer could be mitigated by painstakingly noting the will of God through various forms of divination, including astrology.

The widely regarded father of Judaism, Abraham, initially lived in the Sumerian city-state of Ur. It was he who was credited with taking a large number of fellow Semites from his tribe and fleeing the city. They left Ur in approximately 1850 B.C. and eventually settled in Canaan.[13]

The Canaanite culture, specifically its creation myth, and the subsequent Judaic myth were influenced by the much earlier Babylonian epic poem *Enuma Elish*. According to the *Enuma Elish*, Gods emerged two by two from a watery substance. The sun god, Marduk, emerged victorious in a battle with the water goddess, Tiamat. Marduk decided to create a new world and humanity. This creation took six days after which he rested on the seventh day. Again, the many parallels in the book of Genesis are compelling.

Once settled in Canaan, the Hebrews blended Mesopotamian beliefs with Canaanite theology. Religious historian Karen Armstrong has noted that there was a considerable variety in theological beliefs among the early Hebrews. She writes,

Indeed, it is probably more accurate to call these early Hebrews pagans who shared many of the religious beliefs of their neighbors in Canaan. They would certainly have believed in the existence of such deities as Marduk, Baal, and Anat. They may not all have worshipped the same deity: it is possible the God of Abraham, the "Fear," of the "Kinsman" of Isaac, and the "Mighty One" of Jacob were three separate Gods.[14]

Further, it is quite possible that Abraham's God was El, the high God of Canaan. Armstrong points out that this deity introduces himself to Abraham as "El Shaddai" or "El" of the Mountain, which according to Genesis is one of El's traditional titles.[15] The name of El may have been absorbed by such Hebrew names as Isra-El and Ishma-El.

Early Judaism involved ritualistic sacrifice, both animal and sometimes human. Although these practices gradually faded, its most famous example is the sacrifice involving Abraham and his son, Isaac. The central message of the fable was that one should hold no one above God.[16] But what a powerfully disturbing way to demonstrate faith!

Inherent to the Judeo-Christian system is the belief that time is linear in that historical events do not repeat themselves. The scrupulous honoring of oral and written history and the linear notion of time bind the religion and culture of the early Hebrews. The concept of linear time emphasized the historical integrity of the society and the religion. This was a break from the earlier Babylonian concept, based on astrology, that time is cyclical by nature, therefore repetitive by nature.

A significant number of Hebrews were later enslaved in Egypt, thereby absorbing aspects of Egyptian theology. As described in the *Egyptian Book of the Dead*, if the correct ritualistic practices are performed by the living, the deceased's soul can make a transition from the earth to the great judgment hall of Osiris.[17] This is a precursor of the Judeo-Christian-Islamic great judgment day at the gates of heaven and hell.

Monotheism preceded the Judeo-Christian-Islamic continuum. One example of monotheism was introduced by Amenhotep IV in Egypt. He renamed himself Ikhnaton after Aton, who was regarded as the one supreme God. Freud had speculated, albeit erroneously, that Ikhnaton and Moses were the same person. Nevertheless, Moses may have been influenced by the monotheism in Egypt.

By about 1200 B.C.E., Moses was said to have led his people "into the promised land." They took with them many aspects of Egyptian theology. In fact, Moses picked up where the Egyptian "Repudiation of Sins" left off. His "Ten Commandments" is similar to its Egyptian forerunner, the myth of Osiris. Both are moral codes.

Moses claimed that a God he referred to as Yahweh aided the Hebrews in their flight out of Egypt. He was able to convince the Hebrews that Yahweh was one and the same as El. Yet the transition to naming the "one god" as Yahweh at times demanded coercion. Joshua was said to proclaim . . . "Cast away alien Gods from among you![18] Finally, in the prophet referred to as the second Issiah we hear Yahweh state "I am Yahweh . . . there is no other God but me."[19] Thus, the book of Genesis was combined with the collection of writings we now refer to as the Torah. This God of early Judaism was a harsh God. Consider the following passage.

"'Come no nearer,' [God] said, 'Take off your shoes for the place on which you stand is holy ground. I am your father,' he said, 'the God of Abraham, the God of Isaac and the God of Jacob.' At this Moses covered his face, afraid to look at God."[20] This is a vision of God as "other"—out there. The mystical bliss of connectiveness seen in the mystical traditions is really not seen until much later in the history of Judaism. In this sense the Perennial Philosophy, in the form of social ethics, was to emerge in Judaism during this period.

The Kingdom of Israel had been established in Palestine by approximately 1000 B.C. Once settled, it consolidated all the preceding myths during the reign of three kings: David, Saul, and Solomon. With Solomon's reign, Israel went through a period of societal chaos. The Kingdom bifurcated into two kingdoms: Israel, with its capital in Samaria, and Judea, with its capital in Jerusalem. Israel was the wealthier of the two states and was somewhat influenced by the Canaanites and their God Baal, Goddess Asherah, and the fertility cult associated with her.[21] Judea, a more pastoral and poorer society, in effect, was in religious competition with Israel. Elijah, a Judean prophet, proclaimed a holy war between Yahweh, the god of Judea, and Baal. Following the collapse of the Kingdom of Israel, the evils of wealth, greed, and polytheism were devalued and supplanted by monotheism and concern for the poor. Both the serpent image associated with the Mesopotamian image of the Tree of Life and the Goddess were incorporated as negative images into the Book of Genesis. Eve was depicted as too weak to resist the temptation introduced by the serpent and as a result mankind was brought down from an idyllic innocence.

It is ironic that the Goddess was converted into a negative motif because what emerged from the destruction of Canaanite mythology was a renewed emphasis on morality and social ethics. The theme of social justice was one of early Judaism's main contributions to the Perennial Philosophy.

After wars with the Assyrians, Israel was invaded in 722 B.C.E. and the legendary ten lost tribes of Israel disappeared. Several Jewish rituals and cultural holidays such as the Spring Renewal Festival, the legend of Unleavened Bread, and the liberation from Egypt were synthesized into the Passover motif—when the Jewish kingdom was consolidating in Judea after the disintegration of Israel. In this transformation, the Jewish state was in far-from-equilibrium conditions, and the emergence of the Passover holiday served as a unifying attractor for the sociocultural system. Passover had become one of the most important holidays for Judaism. It symbolized not only deliverance and revitalization but also the belief in the coming of a Messiah, who would deliver them from persecution.

In 586 B.C.E. a large number of Jews were brought into captivity by the Babylonian king Nebuchadnezzar. It was during this period that the concept of Yahweh, the ultimate creator of the universe, solidified. Also, the Babylonian concept of "an eye for an eye, a tooth for a tooth" (lex talionis) was absorbed.

Another abrupt change to the theology occurred when the Persians overran Mesopotamia and allowed the Jews, who had been held captive there, to return to Palestine. Upon their return, all of the books of what would later become the Old Testament were edited together as one sociohistorical religious text. This history of nomadic movement and of persecution heavily influenced the evolution of Judaism. Because of the persecution and near extinction experienced by the Jewish people, the two central premises of Judaism became morality and group membership.

It is important at this point to highlight the significant influence of Persian religion. In Persia a prophet named Zoroaster preached a theology that was to later influence the Judeo-Christian-Islamic spectrum. He advocated a view of reality that revolved around the battle between good and evil. It is interesting to note that the popular folklore associated with Zoroaster was that he was born from immaculate conception and was a "wonder child."[22] This is a motif repeated throughout the mythologies of the world. Consider the Virgin Mother of the Christ Child. Zoroastrianism had a profound influence on the Judeo-Christian-Islamic spectrum of theologies, especially illustrated by the battle between good and evil, the concept of heaven and hell, the resurrection of the dead, and the final judgment.

In many ways the God of early Judaism was anthropomorphic. He was a male figure who imposed punishment on those who did not revere him and sacrifice to him. For those who developed a personal devotion to him through ritualistic practice, he was regarded as a compassionate father. God had periodic dialogues with humans. It was believed that he created humans in his likeness. Despite this, he was often punishing to both individuals and to nations. During this period, however, Judaism was a religion of racial and national experience. As we shall see, it is not until the mystical reform movements that there is a shift to a religion of personal experience for those who were not prophets.

Early Judaism was a religion of faith, obedience, and morality. It emphasized social justice and compassion for those less fortunate. These elements were consistent with the Perennial Philosophy. Indeed, the theme of compassion for others is inherent to theologies.

Prophets such as Hosea, Isaiah, and Amos modified to some extent the concepts of God. Instead of a primarily tribal God of redemption, God became a more nurturing universal force. These prophets served to organize Judaic theology onto a higher plane as they denounced corruption and materialism and expounded a social philosophy of altruism. In many ways they paved the way for the teachings of Jesus and his efforts to promote brotherly love, even among one's enemies.

The author of the Book of Proverbs suggested that wisdom was part of the plan of God. This new theme in Judaism reflects the increasing contact between the Jews and the Greeks. In fact, during this period Alexander the Great defeated Darius III of Persia and there began a tremendous Greek colonization of the area.

During the period between 200 and 200 B.C.E. the dominant theme of Jewish writings was apocalyptic.[23] In this sense it was widely believed that the Messiah was to deliver the Jewish people from foreign oppression. Another theme evident in the Psalms of Solomon, and in other writings, was the reference to the Kingdom of God. Later Jesus, in effect, brought this concept down to earth.

During this period of social flux the Pharisees became a politically powerful sect. They compiled oral law and modified Mosaic law. Subsequently, a group of scholars known as the Amoraim produced a series of treatises known as the Talmud. The Talmud described the Holy Spirit as presiding *over* people as a rushing wind or as a blazing fire. The idea of God had not yet reached the level where people thought they could experience God internally. In this sense Judaism had not reached a monotheism of unity.

From my point of view this "split off" concept of God perpetuated a dualism we have yet to recover from. In other words, there is the world and there is God—two separate entities. Perhaps this is what Jesus tried to reconcile by his phrase "The Kingdom of God is within you."

Christianity emerged during the period of flux and instability ultimately resulting in the Roman destruction of the last temple of Jerusalem. During this period there was tension between the Greek speaking (Septujut) and the Aramaic-Hebrew-speaking Jews. Considerable hostility also existed between the Rabbinical faction and the Temple faction of Judaism, with Rabbinical Judaism dominant since the destruction of the last temple. Judaism in its various forms has served as the binding force for the Jewish sociocultural system for the past 2000 years.

It was prior to the destruction of the last temple and during this era of instability that Jesus lived. The Jewish sociocultural system was in a turmoil, and in far-from-equilibrium conditions. Roman domination had stirred up enormous resentment. Those Jews who collaborated with the Romans were regarded by several subgroups as impious. To counter the threat of destabilization to the power structure, religious figures who criticized the Judaic religious institution were suppressed.

One of the religious sects dissatisfied with the closed religious system made its semimonastic settlement at Qumran, near the Dead Sea.[24] Jesus perhaps was indirectly influenced by the Qumran group through John the Baptist, who may have associated with the group.

The mystical insights of mutuality, love, and compassion that Jesus conveyed in his teachings were brilliantly clothed in the language and scripture of the Jewish sociocultural system—"I came not to overthrow the Law and the Prophets but to fulfill them."[25] During this era the coming of a messiah who would revitalize Israel was eagerly anticipated, and the books of the prophets were interpreted literally as prophesy. The metaphors and parables of Jesus expressed themes of love and compassion. He announced a new era by using the metaphor of the arrival of the Kingdom of God. These concepts exerted a bifurcating influence on Middle Eastern religion resulting in the emergence of Christianity.

Jesus understood that in order to express high organizing principles that would outlive him, he needed to use language which was highly symbolic and organized in symbolic stories or parables. Perhaps he knew that the prevailing sociocultural system was ripe for a leap to a higher level and understood how to position himself within significant sociocultural rituals. When Jesus was asked if he was the long-awaited messiah prophesied in the scriptures, he responded with no denial: "Thou sayest."[26] Knowing that going to Jerusalem would be inviting his martyrdom, he arranged to enter the city just as the prophet Zechariah had prophesied. Knowing that going into the temple and accusing the religious power structure, the Sanhedrin (Jewish Council), of blasphemy would ensure his execution, he did so anyway. All this occurred during the holy period of Passover, which garnered great symbolic significance.

The most profound message conveyed by Jesus was that of love. He advocated that one should "love thy neighbor" and "turn the other cheek." To illustrate the grace of forgiveness, he openly accepted tax collectors, prostitutes, and individuals rejected by the general populace, saying he came not for the righteous but for the sinners. He also was, in effect, a feminist who saw the sexes as equals. As the prophet Ezekiel in 397 B.C.E. had been called "Son of Man" by Yahweh, so too did Jesus refer to himself frequently as the "Son of Man." The phrase Son of Man in its original Aramaic (*bar nasha*) stresses the mortality of the human condition. It was only after his death that his followers began to refer to Jesus as the Son of God. This is unfortunate because it stifled his message and contributed to a dualism—the separation of the holy and the mortal. In other words, by not appreciating the concept that he was the "Son of Man," Mankind again split off God as an external.

It was not until the mid sixties or early seventies B.C.E. that the Gospels were written. This was thirty to seventy years after the crucifixion of Jesus.[27] Further, it is not clear who actually wrote these documents. As a consequence we are left with crude approximations and distortions of the message. Historical accuracy was sacrificed through sociocultural filtration. Let us examine the cultural filters and competing philosophical perspectives.

The development of the early Christian movement included the nonlinear evolution of Judaism, the religion of classical Rome, and a form of Zoroastrianism based on the worship of Mitras, the Persian god of light. Another influence included the Cybele cult, active in Rome. This cult was practiced on Vatican Hill and involved self-mutilation and dancing. Of particular importance was Cybele's lover, Attis, who was thought to have been born from a virgin. He was resurrected annually. The usual festival began on "Black Friday" and ended after three days of rejoicing about the resurrection. This ritual predates the Christian Easter by roughly 200 years. In fact, the other Roman and regional myths coevolved with early Christianity.[28]

The question is—was the story of the crucifixion and death of Jesus adjusted to compete with myth or was the story consistent with this myth because it represents an archetypal transformation process? My guess is that both were factors coevolved and synthesized with other myths.

There was also an interesting coevolution of Judaism and Christianity. In the second and third-centuries mysticism in Judaism developed around what has been referred to as "Throne Mysticism." Here there was an emphasis on imagination, language, and mythology. Visions were described that incorporated Jewish mythology and an emphasis on the indescribable aspects of God. The purpose was to bypass the intellect. Similarly, within some forms of early Christianity, such as with the tradition of the Desert Fathers, there was a strong emphasis on working around the ego and the false self.

In the early forms of Christianity there were several sects and interpretations of the meaning of the life of Jesus. One very diverse group, referred to as the Gnostics, proposed there were two deities, God (the Supreme Being) and a lesser deity characterized by evil. Some Gnostics believed that God did not create or have anything to do with the world. This was the work of a being referred to as "Demigourgos." Consequently they viewed the world as an unholy place, taking an extreme position and rejecting any form of humanity of Jesus. Here Christ was regarded as a divine spirit whose mission was to bring mankind back to God. Again we see an unfortunate dualism where matter was viewed as inherently evil.

It is not quite clear what impact the Gnostics had on the theology in the East. Until just recently our knowledge of the Gnostics came largely from the orthodox church, sources who, as we will see, moved to suppress their influence. Through the deciphering of Gnostic texts recently discovered in Egypt (the Naj Hamadi Gospels), it has become evident that the Gnostics were a mystical sect without central paternal organization.[29] Women held at least equal status as men and, in fact, some people have suggested that there is reason to believe that the figure Mary Magdalene was one of its leaders.

The Gnostics were a catalyst for the orthodox central church in an ironic way.

The central church found its theology threatening to the Roman domination of social, economic, and political control. To meet the challenge presented by the Gnostic metaphysical doctrine, the central church relied heavily on the Gospels. The church then proposed what was referred to as the "Apostles Creed." In fact, the effort by the church to suppress the Gnostics culminated with the gathering together of the books of the Gospels, which became known as the New Testament. They proposed that the church alone could interpret the word of God through the "learned" reading of these Scriptures. Gnosticism, however, did not die out. Forms of its dualistic (good versus evil and worldly versus "above the world") doctrine were absorbed by the church itself.

In the first three centuries C.E. several competing Christian theologies had developed. One school advocated by Athanasius, of Alexandria, is often referred to as the "logos doctrine." From this perspective, Jesus Christ was regarded as a God-man, equated with the divine.

Another school arose around the doctrine of monotheism. Led by Arius, also of Alexandria, it viewed Jesus as mortal. Arius believed that Jesus was created by God and, therefore, subordinate to the Father. Concerned about a split in the church and loss of central control, Emperor Constantine summoned the Council of Nicaea (325 C.E.). It was in Nicaea that the Arian doctrine was put down in favor of the belief that the Father and the Son are one (the Logos Doctrine). The council of Nicaea had a profound effect on the later development of the dogma of the church. It was here that one can say Christianity became "Churchianity."

Interestingly, many historians date this period as the beginning of the "monastic revolt." This alternative model counterbalanced the rigid adherence to the dogmatic Nicaen Creed. Once again we see a coevolution of the exoteric and the esoteric movements with the church carrying the exoteric movement and the monasteries attempting to preserve the esoteric movement.

More sociocultural turbulence arose in 428 C.E. when Nestorius, the patriarch of Constantinople, and Cyril, the patriarch of Alexandria, continued the debate about the nature of Jesus. The latter maintained a position closer to the Nicene creed solidifying the Father and the Son. In response to this dispute, the Church intervened again and imposed judgment at the council at Ephesus in 431 C.E.. Again, the effort to view the humanity of Jesus' was institutionally rejected.

Yet the surge in monasticism, mysticism, and aesthetic theologies occurs at this same period, perhaps as a protest against their counterparts' "selling out." Tension brewed throughout the Middle Ages. Some of the most influential Christian theologies bubbled up from this stream.

Theologians from Cappadocia, in modern-day Turkey, proposed an addendum to the Athanasian position of the God nature of Jesus. They proposed that it would be useful to think of God as represented by a trinity: Father, Son, and Holy Spirit. They argued that contemplation of the Trinity was inspiring to religious experience and that the Trinity implies that God is beyond human intellect. In this way, there was a refusal to engage in an analysis of Jesus Christ.

The Greeks and the Armenians believed that it was the destiny of men and women to be reunited with God. By following the example of Jesus the God-

Man this Eastern view held that reunification could be a joyful and peaceful process. In contrast, the Western concept of "original sin" made a peaceful reunion difficult.[30] This conflicted reunion necessitated a denial of earthly pleasures, regarding spiritual discipline as a painful process requiring a great degree of sacrifice. Central to much of Western Christianity is the notion of suffering.

The contrast between Eastern Christianity and Western Christianity is best illustrated by the imagery employed by both. While in the East God was experienced as light, in the West God was experienced through strain in the darkness.[31] Though there was more emphasis on the "sanctification" in the East and "sacrifice" in the West, following Greek/Armenian and Roman cultures, respectively, both East and West saw a significant rise in monasticism. Asceticism "training" was the basis for both paths.

Further to the south and east another Semitic theology emerged during a major cultural transformation. Prior to the emergence of Islam there were several tribes competing violently for water, trade, and domination of the Arabian Peninsula. In the seventh century C.E. Mohammed introduced his uniquely Arabic form of Judeo-Christian theology. Like so many venerated figures before him, Mohammed was given his name after achieving prophetic status. Originally called Vbulkassim, he was renamed Mohammed, or "The Praised One." He was of the Hashim clan of the Meccan tribe, the Quraysh. Two generations before Mohammed, the Quraysh had gone through a major transition. Though they once were a nomadic society, they settled into a capitalist life-style in Mecca. During the nomadic period the tribe came first and the individual second. With the shift to an urban life-style, individuals came first and group cooperation was destabilized. Mohammed was troubled by this state of cultural change.

Mohammed professed to have been visited in the desert by the angel Gabriel while praying to the high God of the Arab pantheon, al-Lah. He regarded al-Lah as the same God as worshipped by the Jews and Christians. Mohammed stated that he received a series of revelations experienced in a trance state and at times would lose consciousness altogether. During these episodes he received messages from God. The result was the Koran.

The Koran is beautifully written when read in its original Arabic. It echoes the monotheism of the Judeo-Christian tradition in prose:

There is the One God;
He is God, the Eternal, the Uncaused Cause of all being.
Neither does He beget, and neither is he begotten
and there is nothing that He can be compared to. [32]

Note that he begets not and neither is he begotten. He is all and precedes all. This monotheism was not only built on the Judeo-Christian concept of God but it incorporated all preceding Arab deities into an enhanced al-Lah. Mohammed stressed that he was not introducing a new religion, but was "reminding" people of a God worshipped by the Jews and the Christians. This God was the same as the God of the Arabs, referred to as al-Lah.

Mohammed's new religion was to be referred to as Islam, meaning surrender to God. His followers were called Muslims (traders) by people of his own tribe. The term Muslim came to mean "those who submit to Islam." The holy book, written entirely by Mohammed, was referred to as the Koran, or "thing to read." This book was basically an extension of Judeo-Christian morals and theology. Its morality is consistent with Judeo-Christian charity, humility, and justice. With Islam we also find strong reference to Judgment Day, heaven, and hell and contempt for nonbelievers.

Mohammed understood that by incorporating important religious sites he would draw popular appeal. He, therefore, moved on the Kaaba. The Kaaba in Mecca was a pre-Islamic holy site. This large black stone of meteoric origin was absorbed into Islamic religion. Prior to Islam Arabs would make a "hajj" or pilgrimage to the Kaaba. Since pre-Islamic Arabia was rife with conflict between tribes, this stone provided the only unifying force.

Mohammed's persistent effort to win converts to his cause served to galvanized the previously warring tribes into the common cause—the spread of Islam. Though Islam made many of its converts by the sword, their eventual conversion ushered in a leap to a higher level of sociocultural organization. Indeed, during the Middle Ages Arabic culture far surpassed European culture in science, philosophy, and architecture.

The essential early message of Islam was that al-Lah was the one and only God. Mohammed was just one of a series of prophets, including Abraham, Moses, and Jesus. Muslims were encouraged to look for signs or messages from God and use their minds and imagination. It was a religion with a social conscience. Care of the poor and the disadvantaged was encouraged, while the accumulation of wealth and power was discouraged. Like early Christianity, Islam was initially a religion of equality between the sexes. Only later was it corrupted to favor men over women.

Although each of the major religions in the Judeo-Christian-Islamic spectrum shares a common mythology, there were clear efforts to differentiate them. For example, the holy day celebrated by each is different with Islam identified with Friday, Judaism with Saturday, and Christianity with Sunday.

Like Judaism and Christianity, Islam went through periods during which it became more institutionalized. Following periods of institutional and societal rigidity the resulting closed system promoted sociocultural instability. Out of these far-from-equilibrium conditions, bifurcating revitalization movements appeared.

Islam broke up into multiple sects, such as the Shah and the Sunni. Like Christianity, there were those who emphasized philosophy, such a the Faylasuf, and those who emphasized mysticism, such as the Sufis.[33] The Faylasufs were highly influenced by Greek philosophy introduced to them by Nestorian Christians. It was partly through this Hellenic influence that the Arab world flourished in astronomy, mathematics, and medicine. For example, our number system was imported into Europe from the Arab world.

By the eighth century Sufism developed around the central construct of "love of God." This love was expressed experientially through chanting, music, dancing, meditation, and night vigils. The Sacred Tradition (Halith Qudsi) involves the mystical experience of loving God so completely that the practitioner feels part of Him. This was a highly personalized devotional practice, the goal of which was to dissolve the boundaries of the self and experience the ecstatic absorption in God. This is referred to as "fana," or annihilation.

The Sufi axiom "He who knows himself, knows his Lord" represents the contemplative and intuitive approach of Sufism. But unlike the Socratic axiom "Know thyself," Sufism emphasizes the non-rational.

One Sufi order, the Mawlawiyyah, was founded by Jalala ad-Din Rumi in the 13th century. This order is known in the West as the "Whirling Dervishes." Here the practitioner would spin around and around until the boundaries of the self dissolved and he experienced fana.

Rumi wrote a poem, the Masnawi, that is often referred to as the Sufi bible. The Masnawi challenges people to work to minimize the ego and see God's presence deep within everything. Consistent with Sufism in general, God is here only understood subjectively.

Paralleling this mystical reform in Islam there were similar developments in Judaism and Christianity. For example, within Judaism there arose another mystical revitalization movement known as Kabbalah. The Kabbalists called God En Sof, meaning "without end" and emphasizing the unknowable aspect of God. They preferred to interpret the Bible symbolically rather than literally.

The Kabbalists envisioned there to be stages of God's manifestations in human consciousness. En Sof was conceived of as having ten different "sefiroths," or numerations. These numerations were illustrated visually as an upside-down tree (Tree of the Sefiroth) with the top descending into the unknowable depths of En Sof. The emanations were considered the ten stages of God's unfolding revelation of himself.

Various Kabbalists developed methodologies, such as meditation with a mantra, breathing, physical postures, and using imaging of the sefiroths to achieve union with En Sof. They developed a method of concentration, called Devekuth, which they believed helped the practitioner be aware of God everywhere. The practitioner of Devekuth they believed may become aware of an energy field, referred to "refish," that surrounds each individual. In some ways, this is similar to the concept of the Holy Spirit, and as we shall see, "prana" in Hinduism and "Qi" in Taoism.

The concept of "kenosis" was embraced by mystics of the Kabbalah and Sufism. Here the goal is to experience a self-emptying ecstasy of God. Overall, unity with God was the primary purpose of these mystical sects. This esoteric concept of God can be considered part of the Perennial Philosophy. In this sense Judaism and Islam came to esoteric fruition again through the Kabbalah and Sufism.

The widespread practice of esoteric Christian mysticism continued to flourish into the late Middle Ages, especially in the monasteries. Individuals such as Saint Francis of Assisi in Italy, Meister Eckhart in France, and Richard Rolle in England argued that we must abandon the anthropomorphic imagery associated with God. Eckhart, for example, proposed the mystic must reject finite ideas about God. Without this emphasis on the mystical, esoteric Christianity (like all theologies) became rigidified and drifted away from the Perennial Philosophy.[34]

THE HINDU-JAINIST-BUDDHIST SPECTRUM

In the Indian subcontinent, the development of the Hindu-Jainist-Buddhist spectrum followed a similar nonlinear sociocultural evolution with tension between the esoteric and exoteric aspects of the theologies. The first identifiable seeds of Hinduism emerged in the Indus River valley after an invasion of a tribe of Indo-European speaking Aryans, perhaps by the Mitanni. During the era of the Hittites in Anatolia, the Mitanni were a strong force in the upper Mesopotamian region. The gods they worshipped would later appear in Hinduism. For example, Mi-it-ra became Mitra, Aru-nu became Varnu, and In-da-ra became Indra.[35]

The destabilization that followed the Aryan invasion in the seventieth century B.C.E. led to the creation of the Vedas (knowledge), a series of texts that outlined theological and ritualistic traditions. The Vedas served as the central organizing doctrine of Hinduism. The most prominent of these is referred to as the Rig Veda.

The Rig Veda is less philosophical in terms of speculations concerning the nature of reality than are later theological works such as the Upanishads. Much of the Rig Veda is legalistic and concerns simple pastoral worship. However, within the Rig Veda there was a significant step toward a unifying paradigm. Consider the following passage: "The truth is one, but the wise see it in many ways."

Gradually, a priestly caste (known as the Brahmins) gained control of the developing religion. Religious experience became more ritualistic, sacrificial, and formalized. Commentaries referred to as Brahmins were written and attached to each of the Vedas.

By the eighth century the closed system imposed by the Vedic priests created conditions of stagnation, which in turn were broken by another creative surge. The so-called forest treatises (Aranykas) were composed by sages outside the priestly community. Eventually these mystical commentaries were combined with elements of the Vedas to form the Upanishads. By the fifth century 200 such commentaries were written. The period of the Upanishads represents a shift toward the esoteric from the exoteric.

The fundamental premise of the Upanishads is that each individual's spirit (Atman) is ultimately interconnected to the Infinite Spirit (Brahman). The concept of Atman is in contrast to the orthodox Judeo-Christian-Islamic concept of soul, because in Hinduism, as well as Buddhism and Jainism to follow, there is a de-emphasis on individuality and a denunciation of desire and attachment. However, as noted earlier, there is a similar emphasis in the contemplative or esoteric traditions in the West.[36]

In the Hindu Upanishads, 3,306 gods are reduced to one, Brahman. People were encouraged to envision Brahman as the source of all existence. This mystical monotheism predates its counterpart in the Middle Eastern paradigm. As I stressed earlier in this chapter, early Judaism was monotheistic but God was seen as external and to be feared. While on the one hand early Judaism offered the Perennial Philosophy of ethics, compassion, and social justice, early Hinduism offered a class system.

Buddhism and Jainism emerged as alternatives to Hinduism and threatened its mass appeal. The concept of Brahman was too abstract and lacked popular appeal. As Hinduism coevolved with the popularity of Buddhism and Jainism, the Vedic became popularized. The more personalized aspects of Brahman (Shiva and Vishnu) had emerged as part of the Hindu Trinity (Brahman, Shiva, and Vishnu), and two cults or sects developed around these newer deities.

Vishnu is conceived to represent benevolence toward humanity. This concern and love for all people, especially those disadvantaged, is similar to Christianity. The two most popular "avatars," or incarnations, of Vishnu are Rama and Krishna. Shiva, in contrast to Vishnu, personifies fear. The "dance of Shiva" is a powerful, many-armed image of change, movement, terror, death, and the whole phantasm of the material world. He is conceived to be both the creator and destroyer, characterized by Rudra, the author of sickness and death; he can also be helpful to those suffering and, therefore, he is worshipped by those experiencing difficult psychosocial stressors such as poverty, famine, and illness.

Conditions within Indian society became unstable. Out of far-from-equilibrium conditions, a broader and more simplified form of Hinduism emerged. The dual influences of the Sutras (scriptures) and the popular epics resonated with the Indian masses. Most of the Sutras are essentially formalized rituals that provide structure for ceremonies, language, and even science (e.g., astrology).

Among the most popular of the epics is the Bhagavad Gita, or song of God. This epic is a portion of the large "Mahabharata." The main principle in the epic is how one can achieve union with God and live in the world. To illustrate this theme Krishna, the avatar or incarnation of Vishnu, aids Arjuna, a prince with good intentions, in practicing religious ethics while trying to save his community from oppressive forces in a great battle. Consider the following passage from the Bhagavad Gita:

Arjuna: What power is it, Krishna, that drives man to act sinfully, even unwillingly, as if powerfully?

Krishna: It is greedy desire and wrath, born of passion, the great evil, the sum of destruction: this is the enemy of the soul. All is clouded by desire: as fire by smoke, as a mirror by dust, as an unborn babe by its covering.[37]

Here we see Krishna advocate for moral behavior and an Indian emphasis on detachment. He tells Arjuna that he must fight for the common good and ignore his immediate personal concerns. The emphasis on moral behaviors is consistent with the Perennial Philosophy.

Inherent to Hinduism is the belief that experience in one's current life should not be confused with the ultimate reality. Rather, one's experience in superficial life, referred to as the dance of "maya," is an illusion. Maya can be thought of as a different level of organization than the ultimate unity. From this perspective, maya is not an illusion but a potential diversion for the unity. Maya is the world of the ego.

How one behaves has an influence over one's future existence. If, for example, one behaves according to a moral path, or "dharma," then his/her residue of immoral acts referred to as Karma can be, in effect, worked off. However, if this does not occur, one has to repeat a life and try again. In this way the concept of reincarnation contributed sociocultural stability, much in the same way the concepts of heaven, hell, and divine retribution were introduced into the Judeo-Christian-Islamic spectrum of theologies.

The concept of Karma represents an important milestone in the theology of India. It symbolizes the development of personal responsibility. In other words, it is harder to blame gods for one's misfortunes when the concept of Karma is taken into consideration. One reaps what one has sown across the span of several lifetimes.

The concept of yoga (meaning "yoking" one's consciousness) also represents a conceptual shift toward the view that one can achieve spiritual elevation individually by various methods. A combination of meditation and physical posturing is employed to cultivate the experience of oneness with Brahman. Through these practices the practitioner may experience a sense of harmony with the spiritual/energetic life force referred to as "prana" or life—breath. Jainism and Buddhism did not promote the same concept.

Jainism and Buddhism are bifurcations that developed during one of the many fluctuating phases of Hinduism. As the priests became a more dominant force in Hindu religion, rituals became rigid and impersonal. At the same time, sociocultural conditions became turbulent: tribal federations were disappearing and the monarchies had not yet formed. In these far-from-equilibrium conditions, individuals sought mystical revelation outside of Hindu dogma.

One such individual was Vardhamana Mahavira (599–527 B.C.E.).[38] He was a wealthy man who became dissatisfied with a materialistic life and set off to become a religious sage (Shrmanas). After he achieved Kevala, (the state of "supreme knowledge"), and intuition, he spent the next thirty years preaching his basic message of nonviolence, renunciation of all bonds, and fundamental interconnectivity.

He believed that the leap to oneness with the infinite macrosystem freed him from the karmic cycle of transmigration, or successive reincarnations. His later followers were referred to as Jainists after the Sanskrit word "jina," meaning victorious. The central goal of Jainism is to be victorious in breaking the karmic cycle.

Like other religions, Jainism underwent many sociocultural fluctuations. A major bifurcation occurred when a large group of Jains migrated to southern India during a major famine. After twelve years, this group returned to northern India. Though both groups still professed to renounce all bonds including emotion, the returned migrants diverged into a separate sect—the Digambaras—while the remaining Jains became known as the Shvetambaras.

Prior to the divergence, the Jainists had forsaken clothes. When the two groups reunited, the group that had remained in the north (the Shvetambaras—white clad) had taken to wearing white robes. They also wore cloth masks to demonstrate that they would not even harm insects by breathing them into their lungs. In contrast, monks from the other sect (Digambaras—the sky clad, meaning naked) demonstrated their non-attachment by a vow of nudity.

Jainism diverges from Hinduism in that the latter regards the nature of reality as both momentary and eternal while the former regards reality as far more complex. Within the theology of Jainism, one finds a type of process philosophy. All is regarded as in a constant state of flux—the process of origination, destruction, and permanence. From this perspective the soul is thought to be continuously changing, yet eternal.

According to Jainist theology the world is composed of an infinite number of units of consciousness, referred to as "jivas," or eternal souls. Similar to Hinduism, Jainism conceives of these jivas as trapped at different evolutionary levels in every life form (i.e., frogs and people). Consistent in both Hinduism and Buddhism, there is a belief that one may work one's way to unity with the ultimate oneness through nonattachment, thereby transcending the separation of one's own particular diva.

In the fifth century B.C.E., Buddhism broke from Hinduism during the same turbulent period that led to the emergence of Jainism. Its founder, Siddhartha Gautama, was a prince who left his comfortable existence in Kapilavashtu (north of present-day Benares, India) for the ascetic life of a religious sage. Eventually he renounced the ascetic life and is said to have achieved enlightenment following a great mystical experience. In many ways, he was a social reformer as well as a mystic. He renounced the caste system and many other social conventions separating people.

Interestingly, the legend surrounding his life and the life of Vardhamana Mahavira have striking similarities. Siddhartha was also said to have left his comfortable existence during the sixth century B.C.E. for an ascetic life of a religious sage. In fact, during that period, the life of a wanderer on a spiritual quest was quite common. These individuals were referred to as "Shrmanas." Their teaching served as alternatives to Brahmanism. Siddhartha eventually left the Shrmanas and, like Vardhamanna Mahavira, sat under a tree, in the Buddha's case a botree, and had a great mystical experience. When asked if he was enlightened, he responded by saying, "No, I am just awake." He, thereafter, was referred to as the Buddha, or "the awakened." He, too, gathered a large following.[39] During the period of Buddha's life, sociocultural conditions were in a far-from-equilibrium state as the tribal federations were disappearing and the aggressive monarchies had not yet formed.

For a time after the death of the Buddha, his teachings were communicated through an oral tradition of parables and similes. Several hundred years later, perhaps during the first century C.E., these traditions were written down. This initial body of works was referred to as the Pali texts. These documents describe the sociocultural traditions of the early Buddhist community. One tradition was that the Buddha had argued for a "middle path" between the life of luxury and sensuality, on the one hand, and the life of asceticism or intense denial of earthly indulgence.

The Buddha offered hope through "right living" (or "the truth about right living"). Through right living one could achieve liberation from suffering. Essentially, suffering is experienced as a result of attachment. Since nothing is permanent, living a life of compassionate nonattachment is one of the primary goals.

Consistent with Hinduism, there is a fundamental belief in the cycle of rebirth into "painful lives" (reincarnation). Like both Hinduism and Jainism the goal of Buddhism is to end this cycle by working off one's Karma. This is achieved through right living.

Buddhist doctrine is founded on "four noble truths." The first of these is referred to as dukkha, which suggested that mortal truth (samodaya) argues that uneasiness arises out of desire and craving. The second truth identified craving as the cause of suffering. In response to this craving, the third truth (nirodha) proposes a "cure" that leads to nirvana. To achieve this cure and experience the state of nirvana one must "cool" (mibbuta) the passions, desire, and greed. The usage of the term "cooled" was prevalent during Buddha's period as it meant to cool after a fever and was analogous to health.[40] Nirvana literally means "cooling off." The fourth truth suggests that there is a way to achieve the cessation of desire. That "path" (magga) was demonstrated by the Buddha. The path was initially described as threefold: morality, meditation, and wisdom. This path was later expanded into an eightfold path. Briefly, it involves right understanding, right thought, right speech, right bodily action, right livelihood, right moral effort, right mindfulness, and right concentration. Thus, it is apparent that in Buddhism, action and behavior are critical.

In Hinduism the "Atman" is thought to represent the soul of the individual that is part of the greater Brahman. Buddhism proclaims no such permanent structure exists. According to Buddhism, like Jainism, everything is in a constant state of flux and it is a mistake to believe in an unchanging individual soul. To broaden one's scope beyond individual aspirations, one should "see things as they are" (vipassana). Consider the following passage:

Thus when he perceives a form with an eye, a sound with the ear, an odor with a nose, a taste with the tongue, a contact with the body, or an object with the mind, he neither adheres to the whole, nor to its parts. And he strives to ward off that, through which evil an demeritorious things, greed and sorrow would arise, if he remained with unguarded senses, and he watches over his senses, restrains his senses. Possessed of this noble control over the senses, he experiences inwardly a feeling of joy, into which no evil thing can enter.[41]

The study of Buddhism is in many ways the study of the self. Yet the Buddhist study of the self is to forget the self. The selfless self implies an egoless self. Paradoxically, one can say that the "empty self" is full. In this sense empty does not mean "nothing."

Eventually Buddhism bifurcated into two distinct schools of theology, Hinayana (or Theravada) and Mahayana. The Hinayana branch is a more conservative theology. Within this school was a sharp division between monks and lay people, as the monks were viewed as more capable of achieving nirvana. From this perspective, the early Abhidhamma teachings were interpreted more literally.

Mahayana Buddhism is more populist and has appeal to the wider sociocultural system. In many ways Mahayana Buddhism was a reaction to the religious elitism of the Hinayana school. From this perspective the existence of the dhammas is a contradiction within Buddhism. Since all is in a state of flux, there is no need to think of dividing up the world into forms or dhammas.[42]

A populist form of Buddhism arose around the concept of the bodhisattva. Here the emphasis was on the proposed existence of "friendly spirits"— enlightened beings who choose to remain available to mortals who called upon them for help. The bodhisatva concept provided a way for the Mahayana school to absorb indigenous local Indian deities.[43] In this way Buddhism both competed and coevolved with Hinduism.

The emergence of the concept of bodhisattva represents the difficulty the populace had with the emphasis on nonattachment in the Hindu-Jainist-Buddhist spectrum. There needed to be a method through which the spiritual world becomes tangible for the world of everyday life. The bodhisattva provided that link and ironically conflicts with the wisdom of the subtle concept of nonattachment.

Around 500 C.E., a new form of Buddhism emerged in India just as Buddhism in general was disappearing, having been absorbed by Hinduism. Vajrayana (Tantric) Buddhism in some ways resembled Yogic Hinduism and contributed to the former's emergence. Buddhism was also absorbed by adherents to the deity Vishnu, with its liberal view of the caste system and vegetarianism. Yet, in both Hinduism and Buddhism there arose a tendency toward devotion (bhakti) to deified figures such as Shiva and Vishnu.

In contrast to Jainism, Buddhism did not survive within India itself.[44] Rather, it became a dominant spiritual tradition in Sri Lanka, Burma, Thailand, Laos, Tibet, and Cambodia and a significant influence in China, Korea, and Japan.

THE CONFUCUCIANIST-TAOIST-BUDDHIST SPECTRUM

Because of its geographic position, the sociocultural system in China developed in relative isolation compared to the other great Neolithic civilizations. After the tribes on the middle and lower Yellow River regions unified their respective totem symbols, the dragon and the phoenix became interwoven into the emerging Chinese culture. With the first dynasty, the Xia (2200 to 1700 B.C.E.) the tradition of family sovereignty and ancestral worship became incorporated into the belief in heaven and earth with the emperor absorbing divine and absolute rule.[45]

It was actually not until the introduction of Buddhism in the second century that a nonindigenous religion was introduced to the Chinese people. Even the Chinese written language reflects their relative isolation. The Chinese written script is ideographic rather than phonetic, like most other languages. Despite these differentiating factors, the evolution of Chinese religion reflects the same nonlinear dynamics of other sociocultural systems. There was a tension between the esoteric and exoteric functions as we have seen in the sociotheological systems further to the west.

Beginning as early as the sixteenth century B.C.E., there is written evidence that during the Chang dynasty divination formed the heart of institutional rituals. These highly organized rituals were based on ancestral worship, which would be a theme throughout Chinese history. From the inception of the Chou dynasty (1000 B.C.E.) we see evidence of "priest-kings." These monarchs functioned in the dual roles of head of the religion and head of the state. Because of the tendency toward ancestral worship, the deceased kings were revered and asked special favors.

Shamanism flourished in the countryside and away from the city-states. The only evidence of these practices are a series of hymns referred to as "wine songs." Apparently, shamans served as the practitioners of divination, healing, and magic.

During the period now known as the Age of Philosophy (700 to 400 B.C.E.) Chinese society was in a state of flux. A technological change occurred with the advent of iron. An economic change occurred with the major restructuring of the economy. These sociocultural transformations prompted a great deal of philosophical and theological speculation among the so-called "Hundred Schools." During this turbulent period the attractors for two of the major Chinese religions—Taoism and Confucianism—first appeared.

During the Age of Philosophy, one of the Hundred Schools centered around K'ung Fu-Tzu, better known in the west by his Latinized name, Confucius. His teachings were not mystical; they centered largely on reverence for the Chou dynasty, but they placed great emphasis on ethics. This emphasis constituted a leap to a higher unifying level of organization. In other words, though his teachings were not mystical they, nevertheless, promoted morality, ethics, and a cooperative social order.

Confucius de-emphasized magic and spirituality and highlighted virtue. Essentially, his program was a conservative focus on tradition. There is a reliance on the *Book of Songs* and the *Book of Documents*, two works from the Chou period. However, his own contribution is contained in the Analects, a collection of brief comments on morals and ethical behavior. He promoted selfless behaviors, courtesy, and loyalty to family and state. He argued that a virtuous man influences others not by force or coercion, but by his ethical behavior and morality. Consider this passage from the Analects: "The truly virtuous man, desiring to be established himself, seeks to establish others; desiring success for himself, he strives to help others succeed. To find in the wishes of one's own heart the principle for his conduct toward others is the method of true virtue."[46] This emphasis on social justice is reminiscent of the Judeo-Christian-Islamic theme of ethical behavior. Thus, early Confucianism is consistent with this aspect of the Perennial Philosophy. Though Confucius himself died without a popular following, his teachings served as an attractor for the next 2000 years, playing a dominant role within the Chinese sociocultural system. Yet, its history is marked by nonlinear interaction with competing philosophical systems.

Several competing schools have developed within Confucianism itself. The two most influential sects centered around the teachings of Mencius and Hsu Tzu. Both of these figures were born approximately 100 years after the death of Confucius. Their teachings have been characterized as being a contrast between the idealism of Mencius and the realism of Hsu Tzu. These two differing perspectives can best be understood by their respective positions in the larger sociocultural system. Mencius developed his philosophy while competing with two schools known as the Utilitarians and the Hedonists. His program emphasized social justice and humanity. Hsu Tzu, for his part, sharpened his rational and rigorous system to compete with several schools. For him, the human mind became the center of the universe.

The Utilitarianism movement was lead by Mo Tzu (479–381 B.C.E.). He rejected authority and antiquity, thus putting his school in conflict with the ruling elite and Confucianism. Though Mohism suffered initially, it was to serve as an attractor for the Christian and Marxist movements roughly two thousand years later. Essentially, emphasis is placed on loving thy neighbor, concern for the needs of many over the few, overall compassion, and self-sacrifice.

Mo Tzu goes further than Confucianism through his emphasis on universal love. Though he denounced emotionalism he advocated for a sort of "mental love."

Suppose that everyone in the world practiced universal love, so that everyone, loved everyone other personas much as he loves himself. Would anyone then be lacking in devotion? If everyone regarded his father, his elder, brother, and his ruler just as he does himself, toward whom could he be lacking devotion? Would there then be anyone who was not affectionate? . . . Could there be any thieves and robbers? If everyone looked upon other men's houses as if they were his own who would steal? . . . Would noble clans contend among themselves? Would states attack each other? . . . If everyone in the world would practice universal love . . . then the whole world would enjoy peace and good order.[47]

While Confucianism focused on the proper functioning of government in the city-states, philosophers in the countryside focused on transcendental experience. This group, later referred to as Taoists, advocated meditation and self-awareness. The interest in shamanism throughout the countryside prior to the development of Taoism was easily incorporated in the new religion. The practical mysticism of Taoism was an attractor for the nonurban populace. This esoteric philosophy emphasized the mystical experience of interconnective flux. On the other hand, early Confucianism, with its exoteric focus on ancestry, tradition, and social ethics, emphasized stability and organizational continuity, which made it popular to the city-state.

The most significant figures in Taoism are Lao Tzu and Chuang Tzu. While Lao Tzu is generally credited with the authorship of one of the great Taoist texts, the *Tao Te Ching*, his historicity is questioned.[48] Chuang Tzu, on the other hand, was an historical figure who lived during the Age of Philosophers. In the *Chuang Tzu*, a text credited with his authorship, he argues through the use of parables that it is impossible to describe mystical truth, as the universe is unified and always in flux. A fundamental premise of Taoism is that all aspects of reality are united into one whole, the Tao. According to Taoist philosophy, all is one. It is not necessary to do anything because non-action is action. Taoist philosophy regards all opposites as different aspects of the same whole.

I have always been touched by the eighty one poems attributed to Lao Tzu, referred to as the *Tao Te Ching*, or Way of Life. This short work sets a tone of gentle quietness and reflection. It is a mysticism of inner balance and outward passivity.

The Taoists advocated a mysticism of nature. While the Judeo-Christian-Islamic mystics advocated a mystical union with God, the Taoists instead argued that one does not have to do anything but *be*. Consider the following passage by Chuang Tzu:

Do the heavens revolve? Does the earth stand still? Do the sun and the moon contend for their positions? Is there some mechanical device that keeps them going automatically? Or do they merely continue to revolve, inevitably, of their own inertia? Do the clouds make rain? Or is it the rain that makes the clouds? What makes it deemed so copiously? Who is it that has the leisure to devote himself, with such abandoned glee, to making these things happen?[49]

By 400 B.C.E. the philosophy promoted by Tsou Yen had gained considerable influence. This school was concerned with broad cosmological issues. Its cyclical view of history incorporated Tsou Yen's proposition that there are five elements: earth, wood, metal, fire, and water. These elements were regarded as being in a constant state of flux caused by tensions between the fundamental opposites, yin and yang. Yang represented the strong and sunny; yin represented the dark and weak. The dynamic interplay among these opposites and the five elements was incorporated into a work of divination that became the *I Ching*. Both Taoism and Confucianism absorbed this cosmology.

With the collapse of the city-states and the advent of the Han dynasty, Confucianism became the state religion. However, Taoism remained strong and the belief in personalized gods, sorcerers, and shamans was pervasive with the masses. By the end of the Han dynasty, institutionalized Taoism had become the "church of salvation." Thus, as the esoteric aspect of Taoism drifted away from its initial mystical position, it moved to absorb the concerns of the masses.[50]

Taoism was also affected by the introduction of Buddhism into China. The challenge of Buddhism led to changes in both religions, so much so that initially Buddhism was regarded as a foreign type of Taoism. As the Han dynasty gave way to a period of chaos, sociocultural conditions created a surge of interest in these new forms of Taoism and Buddhism.

Interestingly, Taoism and Buddhism began with contradictory views. Buddhism denied the existence of the self, while Taoism pursued the concept of the perpetuation of the self through immortality. Yet when Taoism and Buddhism synthesized within the Chinese sociocultural system these differences were obscured. Even the mythologies associated with the major figures of Taoism and Buddhism were fashioned to wed these two theologies. For centuries it was believed that the Buddha had been tutored by Lao Tzu.[51]

When the Mahayana missionaries entered China, they did not strictly adhere to the Buddhist monastic code. During the introduction of Buddhism to the Chinese sociocultural systems, dynasty conditions were far-from-equilibrium and ripe for a new theological message. The Bodhisattvas provided some solace for the downtrodden and disenfranchised.

Eventually Chinese Buddhism became a monastic movement that focused in part on intellectual pursuits. This monastic movement had fallen under the influence of Taoism. Although they continued to subscribe to basic Buddhist doctrine, its members split off to form several distinctly Chinese Buddhist schools. The most closely linked to Taoism was the Ch'an school, which placed strong emphasis on turning inward for instantaneous enlightenment. When Ch'an Buddhism appeared in Japan, it coevolved with Shintoism and became Zen Buddhism. Meditation was the primary methodology employed.

Zen Buddhism incorporated a contemplative form of meditation. A calm and mystical serenity is achieved through the contemplative arts, such as tea ceremonies, flower arranging, and rock gardens. I find the koan the best example of the thoughtful mysticism of Zen. The koan offers a paradoxical and purposively confusing question. The late American philosopher Alan Watts described Zen as follows: "Zen . . . does not confuse spirituality with the thinking about God while peeling potatoes. Zen spirituality is just to peel the potatoes."[52]

In China the so-called "Pure Land" (Ch'ing T'u) Buddhism was founded by Hui-yuan, a former Taoist. He incorporated many Taoist figures of speech into Amitabha forms of Buddhism. The incorporation of the Bodhisattvas broadens the appeal to the masses. In this way people found personal saviors. The best example of such a figure was Kuan-Yin. Originally conceived to be male, this figure became female and was referred to as the "Goddess of Mercy." Kuan-Yin is often prayed to for favors. Again we have an external manifestation of the idea of God—not an internal mysticism to cultivate.

By the Song Dynasty (960–1127 C.E.) a form of Neo-Confucianism developed. The most significant figure in this movement was Zhou Xi, who synthesized Buddhism, Taoism, and elements of Confucianism into a metaphysical perspective. Here "Li" (reason and law) was blended with "Qi." Qi, pronounced "chee," is an energy force similar to the Hindu concept of prana. This new cosmology prescribed behavior that "set heart in the right place and sincerity of mind." All of these concepts were consolidated during a period of sociocultural turbulence.[53]

With economic and sociopolitical chaos during the midtwentieth century some elements of Mohism reemerged in the form of Chinese Marxism. Ancestral worship and reverence for the old established order were suppressed in favor of the needs of the many. In this way famine and economic plunder were averted at the cost of individualism. Only recently have we witnessed a surge of interest in personal liberties.

PERENNIAL PHILOSOPHY AND THE SIGNIFICANCE OF SYMBOLS

There are several similarities between these major sociotheological systems. Though they represent unique sociocultural expressions, many share certain reoccurring themes. The most obvious of these is the belief in a transcendental, unifying principle. This experience of unity is accessible through spiritual discipline, right action, and contemplation. In many cases, the innovative cultural expression of this principle occurred during a period of extreme sociocultural flux.

All of these major religions began during such a period. The attractor in each case was the innovative and reformist philosophy often of an individual who communicated a theme of interconnectivity, compassion, and/or ethical behavior. Many of these individuals did not themselves live to see the sociotheological systems for which they had served as the initial contributor. Rather, they served as archetypal attractors for a later nonlinear transformation of the sociocultural system. It is important to note that the philosophies that derived from the original teaching did not retain the essence of that teaching, though they may have embodied the same general themes. Thus, these religions were, and are, self-organized systems that have evolved within the sociocultural macrosystem. This is why I refer to them as sociotheological systems.

But the mystics themselves were not just reacting to the sociocultural conditions of their respective eras. They were also responding to their own creative and intuitive visions of transcendental unity during periods of social chaos, when unity was difficult to appreciate. Their sensitivity to this unity as a fundamental attractor is a subject that I will discuss at length in Chapters 7 and 8. The important point here is that the sociocultural significance of their mystical revelations further added to the mystics' own power as attractors. Even myths constructed around the lives of these mystics modeled the ideal transformation from mortal existence to reunification with the ultimate macrosystem. For example, Jesus is believed to have been resurrected three days after the crucifixion. This ascension was thought to represent a reunification with his father after a period of semimortal existence.

It is also fascinating to note that many of these religions began during the same era (800–200 B.C.E.), often referred to as the Axial Age. It would seem that the significant attractors emerged during a period of almost nonlocal worldwide connective flux in the evolution of the species. One other consistent theme inherent in all the sociotheological systems of the axial age was compassion. Consider the following passages.[54]

Zoroastrianism: "Do not do unto others all that which is not well for oneself."[55]

Judaism: "What is hateful to you, do not to your fellow man."[56]

Christianity: "Whatsoever ye would that men should do to you, do ye even so to them."[57]

Islam: "No one of you is a believer until he desire for his brother what he desires for himself."[58]

Hinduism: "Do naught unto others which would cause you pain if done to you."[59]

Buddhism: "Hurt not others in ways that you yourself would find hurtful."[60]

Jainism: "In happiness and suffering, in joy and grief, we should regard all creatures as we regard our own self, and should therefore refrain from inflicting upon others such injury as would appear undesirable to us if inflicted upon ourselves."[61]

Confucianism: "Do naught unto others what would not have them do to you."[62]

There are several reoccurring archetypal themes evident in most sociotheological systems. For example, Joseph Campbell has drawn attention to the deification of a hero figure. This hero archetype often experiences a transformation or death and rebirth. Christ, the Buddha, and Lao Tzu are excellent examples of figures who have garnered a complex hero mythology. Christ and the Buddha were said to have been tempted three times. Yet they transcended any interest in worldly gratification to reach spiritual purity. Their heroic focus on global unity allowed them to transcend the immediate concerns of the self.

Campbell and others have pointed out that myths serve multiple functions. At the most basic level they serve to organize societal cohesion. This function is represented in theology by what I have referred to as the meaning of the term sociotheological systems. The more esoteric and transcendental function corresponds to the elements relate that to the so-called perennial philosophy. The bulk of humanity generally experiences the societal/exoteric level. Thus, this level can be thought of as more diverse and literal. The esoteric/perennial philosophical is more subtle and unifying. It is therefore essentially more simple. Given that it unifies, it necessitates broad common metaphors.

Though there has been tension between the exoteric and the esoteric aspects of mythology, without a balance important elements of each cannot evolve. For example, when too much emphasis is placed on the exoteric, myth, as Campbell notes, becomes perverted.[63]

To illustrate these common symbolic themes we will draw on several passages selected by Huxley for his book *Perennial Philosophy*. Huxley states that various themes run from what he referred to as the "bottom," the practice of morality, to the "top," the consideration of metaphysical truths. An example of an overall "metaphysical truth" may be characterized by the theme "Thou art thou," identified by Huxley. On this theme the medieval Christian mystic Eckhart wrote, "The more God is in all things, the more He is outside them. The more He is within, the more He is without."[64]

The same theme of overall unity was expressed from a Chinese perspective by Sen T'sen, "When the Ten Thousand things are viewed in their oneness, we return to the Origin and remain where we have always been."[65] From a medieval Persian/Islamic perspective, Jalala-ad-Din Rum wrote, "The Beloved is in all;

the lover merely veils Him; the Beloved is all that lives, the lover a dead thing."[66] Finally, from a Hinduistic perspective during the ninth century C.E. Shankara taught, "The Atman is that by which the Universe is pervaded, but which nothing pervades; which causes all things to shine."[67]

The importance of ritual and symbols to transcend the immediate personal situation and to appreciate the theological macrosystem perspective is illustrated by the following dialogue found in the Brihad Aranyaka Upanishad:

Aswala: Yajnavalkya, since everything connected with sacrifice is pervaded by death and is subject to death, by what means can the sacrifice overcome death?

Yajnavalkya: By knowledge of the identity between the sacrifice, the fire and the ritual word. For the ritual word is indeed the sacrificer, the ritual word is the fire, and the fire, which is one with Brahman, is the sacrificer. This knowledge leads to liberation. This knowledge leads one beyond death.[68]

The same theme can be seen expressed from other theological perspectives. For example, from the Christian theological/sociocultural system, Stephen Grellet wrote, "I very much doubt whether the Lord by his grace brought me into the faith of his dear Son, I have never broken bread or drunk wine, even in ordinary course of life, without remembrance of and some devout feeling regarding, the broken body and the blood-shedding of dear Lord and Savior." [69]

The significance of symbolic rituals, themes, and archetypes that reflect interconnectivity cannot be overstated. As the foregoing discussion illustrates, symbolism has often transcended periods of chaos and the subsequent theological bifurcations. From this perspective, the transmission of theological systems over time may be seen as a process that incorporates the dominant symbolic themes of a sociocultural system. These symbols both legitimize and vitalize the evolving religion for mass consumption. Symbols also protect what is esoteric from becoming banal; as Jesus put it, "Those who have ears let them hear." Symbols both reveal and hide.

Perhaps more than anyone else this century, C. G. Jung drew attention to the significance of symbols. For him symbolic rituals found throughout most religions permeate all aspects of human consciousness. Jung also demonstrated significance of archetypes and symbols in sociocultural expressions such as in art, fairy tales, literature, and in psychopathology and symptomatology.

An example of this process is provided by the symbolism surrounding the Christian Easter. Since Paleolithic times the spring equinox has symbolized renewal, as growth and new life followed the spring thaw. The myths related to Orpheus, Balder, Tammuz, and Osiris—all of which take place in the spring—represent not only renewal, but also fertility, and often include the Resurrection of a savior. The story of Jesus blends these themes into the story of the Crucifixion and the Resurrection.

SUMMARY

In this chapter I stressed that the major sociotheological systems evolved much like other sociocultural systems. The nonlinear evolution of these systems was punctuated by periods of far-from-equilibrium conditions, chaos, and theological bifurcations. Sociocultural dynamics such as economic, sociopolitical, and competition among the sociotheological systems themselves coevolved to create the diverse theologies seen today. Not only are these theological systems flavored by their macrosystemic sociocultural fields, but within the body of practitioners much diversity exists.

Another variable apparent both within and across religious systems is the utility and significance of symbols. It appears that symbolic themes transcend the immediate message and carry with it archetypal images relevant to a sociocultural system's evolutionary history. On a sociocultural level one should note that symbols and archetypes underlie the fabric of the sociocultural system. These symbols are not static but coevolve with the overall sociocultural system. In terms of their significance within religious systems, they provide a means to transcend personal interests and to appreciate the unifying dimension between people. These symbolic themes are also apparent in the symptomatology of psychopathology.

Not only do sociocultural systems strongly influence perception, cognition, and altered states of consciousness, but there is a complex interrelationship between the evolution of individual consciousness and the evolution of the sociocultural sphere. The evolutionary process occurs in discontinuous leaps to higher levels of organization.

Despite their many differences, the major religions share several dominant themes. One theme is a common thread of the Perennial Philosophy—a general premise that each individual is part of an overall divine macrosystem and that this bond can be experienced. Connectiveness between people is experienced through love. One must ask if there is any support for these concepts from the recent developments of science. To explore these possibilities we shall now turn to physics. Only through an examination of the dynamic properties of physical world can we develop a nondualistic understanding of consciousness.

6

Matter, Fields of Information, and Incompleteness

Common sense is that layer of prejudices laid down in the mind prior to the age eighteen.

Albert Einstein[1]

In the above quote Einstein was commenting on the fact that many of the developments in physics in this century are baffling. Some of these developments appear to defy common sense. We must understand the basis for the physical world even if it defies common sense. This understanding is critical if we are to construct a non-dualistic theory of consciousness.

As I described in the previous chapter, one of the basic tenets of the Perennial Philosophy is that there is an ultimate unity of all aspects of the universe. If this is true then we should expect to find a corresponding support for this premise in physics. Indeed, in recent years there has been a paradigm shift toward the view that there is a connective quality in nature.

From my perspective this paradigm shift is incredibly important to those of us trying to make sense of consciousness. The paradigm shift in physics permits us to heal the dualism that has plagued theories of consciousness.

We must understand the dynamic nature of matter to be able to construct a theory of consciousness. The conceptual changes in physics during the last century highlights the dynamic nature of matter. These changes contradict the view that matter is discrete and fixed, and offer instead the view that matter is composed of fields of information. Understanding this paradigm shift will permit us to have a nondualistic appreciation for how matter and consciousness are interdependent fields of information.

The old view that matter is discrete, dead, and even irrelevant had many proponents. The Judeo-Christian-Islamic sociotheologies viewed the earth as a temporary position for humanity before the Great Judgment Day. Some within this spectrum of theologies have even regarded earthly existence as evil. In the East, Hinduism proposes that earthly existence is a great illusion, or Maya.

In Greek philosophy, which formed the basis for science in the West, there was a view of matter as unchanging and composed of discrete particles. Atomism, as it is now called, conceived of the atom as the irreducible object on earth. The "Atomists" advocated a more mechanistic view of life, arguing that there is no universal mind but unchanging atoms.[2]

This view of matter spawned the mechanical view of the material world. By the time of the Enlightenment, matter was seen as part of an immense universal machine or giant clock directed and set by God. During the seventeenth century a view of the universe developed that formed the basis for science until the early twentieth century. This perspective was articulated best by René Descartes and Isaac Newton. Both had maintained that matter and the universe as a whole were governed by strict mechanical laws. God existed outside this immense clockwork.

To be able to fully understand the paradigm shift of the "new physics" I must first describe how far we have come in our understanding of the physical universe during the past few centuries. I will begin this chapter with a brief sketch of the views of Descartes and Newton.

THE END OF THE CLOCKWORK METAPHOR

When Descartes deduced "I think, therefore I am" (*cogito ergo sum*) he built upon Plato's dualism. He argued that the mind was split off from the body and therefore closer to God. Descartes embarked on his quest for a rationalistic truth by "radical doubt." This involved doubting everything that could be doubted, in a kind of dualistic reductionism. By employing this peeling- away process, he was essentially left with himself. He did not trust his sensory experiences, calling them "secondary qualities." Thus, he was left with only his mind.

He believed that the "thinking thing" (*recogitans*) and the materiality or the "extended thing" (*resextense*) have no common point but through God. He claimed, "There is nothing included in the concept of the body that belongs to the mind and nothing in that of the mind that belongs to the body."

In many ways Descartes' dualism left him safe with the church. By arguing for a split between mind and nature, nature could be seen as God's creation. While plants and animals were regarded as mechanical creations of God, the mind as well as the cosmos maintained progress toward perfection—God. According to Descartes' view, since the mind and body are seen as different entities, they can therefore be studied independent from one another.

I stressed in Chapter 3 the emerging field of psychoneuroimmunology puts an end to this type of primitive dualism. Not only do the body and the brain operate with nonlinear interconnectivity, but emotions and cognitions maintain an interdependent relationship with the body and the brain. Essentially, the matter that composes the body is part of a field of interactions that include emotion and thought. It is fascinating and ironic to note that after Descartes died while on a

trip to Sweden, he was returned to France for burial decapitated. This is the ultimate metaphor for one of the fathers of dualism.

Newton expanded this dualism to include the earth and the known solar system. In his classic *Principia*, he described the interaction of large bodies through
the mathematics he developed (we know now as calculus). He explained that
matter with a great mass exerts a gravitational field in which bodies with a
smaller mass are helpless to resist. The popular illustration of this effect is the
apple that falls to earth instead of floating away.

It is not as if Newtonian physics has been completely overturned, rather it has
been dramatically modified. Though Newton's model has explained various
natural phenomena, it has many limitations.[3] The universe and all of matter in it
was seen as part of an immense clock with gears that move in lockstep. As one
gear moves, the other gears must necessarily move with it. This is a model of
strict determinism. Every change is strictly determined by preceding mechanical
changes.

The Newtonian model embraces linear causality. The billiard ball analogy has
been used to describe this type of causality. For example, one ball collides with
another ball, which then causes that ball to collide with yet another ball. Each
event is the sole causal factor for the succeeding event.

All events are the result of interactions involving attraction, repulsion, and
force. As I noted in Chapter 2, nonlinear dynamics, modern evolutionary theory,
and chaos theory have demonstrated otherwise. Complex adaptive systems
change in much more dynamic ways than do clocks and other mechanical de-
vices.

Newton's mechanistic paradigm promoted many concepts that have since
been discarded. For example, Newton conceived of time and space as absolute
and separate phenomena. Newtonian time is rigid and independent of space.
Further, he adhered to the confusing concept of ether. Ether was thought to occupy the space between large bodies.

Early this century, Albert Einstein put an end to the concepts of absolute
space and time and ether. He found the concept of ether altogether unnecessary.
Einstein demonstrated the fundamental interrelationship between space and time.
We have since referred to space and time as space-time. Einstein published his
first revolutionary paper in 1905. He showed that an observer is affected by his
position in space and time if he attempts to observe another person in a different
position in space and time. According to this "Special Theory of Relativity,"
there is no absolute frame of reference.[4] The only constant is the speed of light.
Relativity basically means that our perception of the world depends on our state
of motion. This runs completely against Newton's physics, which held that there
was a constant objective and absolute frame of reference.

Einstein metaphorically described relativity as the phenomenon that occurs,
"when you are courting a nice young girl; an hour seems like a second, when you
sit on a red-hot cinder, a second seems like an hour—that's relativity."[5] In 1915
Einstein expanded his Relativity Theory to include gravity. In his General Theory of Relativity, he postulated that space can be curved around bodies with

great mass and gravitational fields. Einstein realized that by using geometry he could explain the concept of "force." Since "space" could be "curved" then light could bend in relationship to curved space. We ascribe the deflection to a "force." Curved space can have an effect on the relative flow of time.[6] Based on his seminal work, the next generation of physicists were able to postulate the existence of singularities and black holes.

Thus, Einstein showed that space and time and energy and matter have a unified relationship.[7] That relationship is concisely represented by his famous equation, $E = Mc^2$. Here energy is associated with the amount of matter, times the speed of light, squared. In other words, even a small amount of matter can release an overwhelming amount of energy. A horrifying example of this relationship is an atomic bomb. Thus, matter contains energy. Essentially, mass and energy are the same thing. The curvature of space-time is determined by matter-energy. Matter-energy determines the curvature of space-time.[8]

Space-time curvature is essentially gravity, and is sometimes referred to as gravitational waves. Gravitation is the warping of space-time. Time, therefore, is flexible and coevolves contextually with space or mass.[9] For example, time always runs faster at higher altitudes. In contrast, at lower altitudes it runs slower. On the surface of bodies with large mass (i.e., the sun) time moves slower than on surfaces with less mass (i.e., the earth).

Changes in the relative flow of time also occur with motion. If you were to travel approaching the speed of light, a watch you are wearing would measure a slower flow of time than the watch of an individual standing on the ground. Thus, the flow of time is associated with your relational movement in space.

These phenomena become even more puzzling when you consider that if an object approaches the speed of light its mass increases, thus taking more energy to move it. Only massless objects can move at the speed of light. Approaching the speed of light means time dilation. You and I cannot reach the speed of light because our mass would become too great.

Generally, according to relativity theory there is no absolute frame of reference. This runs in contrast to Newton's physics that held that there was an absolute frame of reference. Yet, Einstein himself maintained high respect for most of the tenets of classic (Newtonian) physics. Later in his life, as we shall see, Einstein remained convinced, despite the advances made in quantum mechanics, that there is an objectivity to be had and that the probabilistic tendencies of quantum theory were misleading. In other words, Einstein remained a determinist. He believed that ultimately all physical processes can be accurately determined or explained.

Relativity physics deals with the very large. It is quantum physics or "Quantum Mechanics" that deals with the very small. Despite its name, Quantum Mechanics describes physical processes that are anything but mechanical. That is, subatomic particles are not "determined" to exist in any particular way. Rather, they have "tendencies to exist" in particular ways.

Two of the early contributions of Quantum Mechanics were the Uncertainty Principle and the Principle of Complimentarity. Both were developed in the late

1920s. Together they form part of what has been referred to as the Copenhagen School, named so because Danish physicist Niels Bohr was its senior member.[10]

The Uncertainty Principle, as proposed by German physicist Werner Heisenberg, drew attention to the difficulty in the identification of a particle's position and velocity.[11] Specifically, an observer can determine the exact position of a particle with accuracy, but not its velocity with accuracy. On the other hand, he can determine its velocity with accuracy but not its position with accuracy. He cannot determine both at the same time.

The uncertainty of values pointed out by the Uncertainty Principle is based on unpredictable fluctuations inherent to all measurable phenomena. In other words, the uncertainty evident at the quantum level suggests that the universe is nondeterministic at the assumed most basic level.[12] This is a fundamental blow to the concept of complete objectivity, inherent to the Newtonian perspective. One cannot separate the observer from the observed. Heisenberg himself noted that quantum theory does not describe nature, but nature subjected to a "method of questioning."

The Principle of Complimentarity was developed by Bohr in an attempt to deal with the confusing phenomenon of "wave-particle duality." This paradoxical phenomenon is based on the fact that light, in the form of photons, sometimes behaves like waves and sometimes like particles. Consider the now famous double slit experiment (see Figure 6.1). When light shines through just one slit, it behaves like particles.[13] The "particulate nature" of the light is illustrated by what results on a light-sensitive panel that is placed on the other side of the plate. There is a neat arrangement of "particulate" impact sites. However, when the plate with one slit is replaced by a plate with two slits, the phenomenon changes entirely. Now the light-sensitive panel appears completely different. What had looked like discrete impact sites appear instead to have been affected by what has been referred to as "interference patterns." These interference patterns are "wavelike" because they interact and ripple in form. Imagine what occurs when you throw two rocks simultaneously into a pool of water. The two series of ripples hit one another and they collectively result in a rough and choppy current in the water.

Bohr argued that the wave/particle duality of light represented the holistic quality of nature. At the heart of Bohr's Principle of Complimentarity is the premise that quantum phenomenon cannot be held to a single description of reality. Physical phenomena are far too complex and paradoxical to limit description of matter to simple statements. From Bohr's point of view the observed and the observer make-up a complete irreducible whole.

Particles, such as electrons, are neither just waves nor just particles, but a mixture of both in appropriate contexts. They are commonly thought to exist in a "wavepack"—a probability wave. Essentially, wave-particle duality means that matter is composed of particles that are located in time and space by a probability wave. In other words, they are thought to "probably exist" in specific locations.

It was Erwin Schrödinger who devised a curious and paradoxical model to illustrate the problem of wave-particle duality. This model is now referred to as "Schrödinger's Cat." Imagine a cat in a sealed box. The cat has no contact with the outside world (see Figure 6.2). Inside the box is an apparatus that when triggered kills the cat. There is a 50–50 chance that the apparatus will be triggered. Yet, there is no way of knowing whether the apparatus will be triggered.[14] The issue is that at some point there will be a "decision" to collapse the "wave function" into a yes or no. For years theorists have argued that since there is no way of knowing whether the cat is either alive or dead, it is both dead and alive. Many have conjectured that it takes consciousness to collapse the wave function. This is analogous to the age-old question "When a tree falls in the forest and no one is there, does it make a sound?" Why wouldn't it make a sound and why can't the wave function collapse without a human being present?

If we were to believe that the collapse of the wave function requires consciousness, we would adhere to a very anthropomorphic view of the universe. In other words, if we embrace this viewpoint we in effect state that without us the universe would not exist. The wave function collapses and trees make sounds with or without the presence of human consciousness.

Though quantum mechanics has brought on a tremendous paradigm shift in the way we examine the physical world at the subatomic level, it is essentially an epistemology. In other words, quantum mechanics sets statistical parameters around what we can know about the quantum level. It does not describe what reality "is"—it is not an ontology.

In general, however, quantum theory dissolves Newtonian determinism, despite the debates about wave/particle duality and the collapse of the wave function. Instead, there is indeterminism. Physicist Paul Davies has clarified this well:

The crucial property of quantum physics is that cause and effect aren't rigidly linked, as they are in classical, common sense physics. There is an indeterminism, which means some events "just occur"—spontaneously, so to speak—without prior cause in the normal meaning of the word. Suddenly, physics became aware of a way for time to "switch itself on"—spontaneously—without being "made to do it."[15]

This does not mean that reductionism need be thrown out entirely. That would be ridiculous. In physics reductionism is balanced by systemic theoretical approaches. We know now through a type of reductionistic process that subatomic particles interact and come into existence through their interactions.

During the last thirty years physicists have employed the use of massive particle accelerators in an effort to explore the basic building blocks of matter. These accelerators smash particles together at great speeds. The debris from these collisions is analyzed and a wide variety of subatomic particles have been taxonomized.

Through the last one hundred years we have come to realize the existence of a wide "family" of subatomic particles. There are protons, neutrons, electrons, and all the way down to quarks. Each particle behaves differently and in curious ways. Physicists have used a variety of metaphors to describe the behavior of particles. Particles have "spin." That is, when measured they appear one-sided or two-sided and so on.

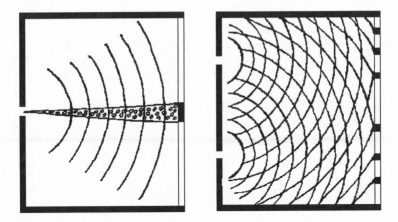

Figure 6.1
The Double Slit Experiment. Note the difference between the panel behind the plate with one slit and the panel behind the plate with two slits. On the former are impact sites that appear particulate in nature. In the other situation the impact sites appear as though "interference patterns" occur.

Figure 6.2
Schrödinger's Cat Box

According to the Pauli Exclusion Principle, two electrons cannot occupy the same state. It is only when two electrons have opposite spins that they can occupy the same state. Fermions (named after the Italian born Enrico Fermi) are particles that respond to the Pauli Exclusion Principle—they cannot occupy the same state with the same spin. In contrast, Bosons (named after the Indian born Sutyendra Bose) can occupy the same state and are not subject to the Pauli Exclusion Principle. They include such particles as photons, gluons, and theoretically gravitons.

This world of subatomic particle sounded rather fanciful. For example, particles have "antiparticles," their complete opposites. Quarks are described as having "color." That is, they exist in particular patterns in relationship to one another (i.e., "top" or "down"). One subatomic particle, referred to as the neutrino, is thought to have no mass. It is believed that the neutrino and its counterpart the antineutrino travel at the speed of light and are not impeded by other forms of matter. In fact, at this moment, a million trillion neutrinos are passing through your head.

Through this analysis of subatomic particles it has been discovered that there are at least four "forces" operative in nature, the strong, the weak, electromagnetic, and gravitational. The strong force glues together subatomic particles, while the weak force causes some subatomic particles to decay. The electromagnetic force is responsible for generating the electricity that powers the lights in your house. Finally, the gravitational force keeps you from floating off in space from where you sit.

Three of the four forces can be theoretically unified. For example, the weak force and the electromagnetic force have been unified into the electroweak force. The inclusion of the strong force into unity has been done by postulating a variety of different quanta that mediate the unity. Such theories are referred to as Grand Unified Theories GUTs.

Unfortunately, gravity is the odd force out. In other words, relativity theory has not been as yet compatible mathematically with quantum mechanics. Unfortunately, the field equations used in relativity theory, which describe gravity, have not worked with the field equations used in quantum mechanics, which describe the other three forces and the subatomic world. Therefore, physics is in a quandary, as relativity and quantum mechanics need unification. To unite the two, one or both need alteration. However, both work quite well by themselves.

In recent years there have been several attempts to unify the physics of the micro universe (quantum mechanics) with those of the macro universe (relativity). To accomplish this feat may involve quantizing gravity. Attempts to develop a quantum theory of gravity are referred to as approaching "supersymmetry." That is, they involve mathematical equations that allow for symmetrical interactions between fermions and bosons.[16] Supergravity theories include a ten-dimensional space.[17] Roger Penrose has proposed a quantum gravity model that may indicate an inherent asymmetrical direction of time at all levels. Theoretically, gravitons have two units of spin and are considered bosons.

Another possible solution to the quantum gravity hypothesis is referred to as

"String Theory." However, much needs to be worked out in String Theory. The theory of hyperspace (String Theory) proposes that there are ten dimensions, instead of the normally conceived 4 dimensions (three of space and one of time). Thus, according to this theory there are six dimensions beyond those generally accounted for. However, we do not currently have the technology necessary to test a ten-dimensional theory.[18]

According to String Theory, strings are the building blocks of matter. They are 100 billion times smaller than protons. Each string vibrates and the specific resonance represents a specific particle. Thus, matter is the result of vibrating strings in hyperspace.[19]

We have come a long way since the Atomism of Democritus. Matter is not discrete and irreducible. According to the "bootstrap" perspective, developed by Geoffrey Chew, one cannot reduce down to a fundamental particle. The investigator is always in a perpetual interrelationship with what he sees. Nobel Laureate Steven Weinburg has noted that particles are "epiphenomena." In other words, particles are the result of fields of interactions, including our investigation of them. We have also come a long way from the classical physics of Newton. Determinism, linear causality, and the premise of objectivity are concepts with limited utility. This is a participatory universe with an open future.[20]

NONLOCALITY AND QUANTUM COHERENCE

A recent and controversial issue emerging in physics involves the phenomenon known as "nonlocality." This development was initially stimulated by Einstein's probing mind. Interestingly, Einstein, who had done so much to put the Newtonian universe into question, was troubled by the lack of determinism in quantum theory.[21] Despite his early contribution to quantum theory, Einstein remained uncomfortable with its lack of "complete" objectivity. For decades, he and Niels Bohr debated about the indeterminant aspects of quantum mechanics. Einstein's major concern regarding quantum theory was expressed in his now famous comment, "God does not play dice," which illustrates Einstein's belief in a deterministic universe, the basis of his subsequent quarrel with Bohr.

During their long-standing debate, Einstein often sent Bohr written rebuttals to Bohr's defense of the indeterminism of quantum theory. One such challenge was to lead to the issue of nonlocality. Through a perplexing thought experiment, Einstein, Boris Podolski, and Nathan Rosen (EPR) attempted to prove that quantum theory was incomplete. They tried to illustrate that hidden variables are operative in the universe.[22] To do this, they explored the theoretical relationship between two electrons that, having emanated from the same locality, maintain a relationship even when they are separated by a great distance. They attempted to explain how a measurement performed on one particle affects the way in which the other particle behaves. In so doing, they demonstrated that the position and momentum of the first particle is correlated with those of the second particle.

In the EPR experiment, Einstein and associates tried to emphasize that particles had a well-defined position in space and time, independent of any observers.

Further, to comply with the rules of quantum theories the particles had to communicate through some process not understood. They argued that this "ghostly action at a distance" was impossible because particles could not communicate instantaneously, thereby breaking the speed-of-light barrier—a fundamental premise of relativity theory.

Since the EPR experiment apparently demanded information transferring faster than the speed of light, they reasoned that quantum mechanics was incomplete. There must be hidden variables not accounted for. Therefore, they argued that the EPR experiment leads to a contradiction.

Thirty years after the EPR thought experiment, John Steward Bell, of CERN, the main European physics lab, developed the theoretical methodology to test nonlocality.[23] He postulated that there is a stronger relationship between particles than can be explained by viewing them as independent entities with locally causal relationships. He showed that all theories that are "local" must satisfy an inequality in many cases.[24] Therefore, the theory (quantum mechanics) could not be replaced by a local theory and reproduce all of the results of EPR. Bell asked whether or not all theories based on additional parameters are nonlocal.[25] Bell's Theorem proposed that an objective universe is inconsistent with the law of local causes. According to Bell, no deterministic theory of physics can exclude faster than light influences. His theorem hypothesizes that the nondeterministic and hidden variables that Einstein had teased Bohr with are actually nonlocal.

Alain Aspect, working outside Paris in the early 1980s, used Bell's Theorem and measured experimentally the nonlocal effects described by Einstein and his associates.[26] [27] He found that nonlocality is a phenomenon operative in nature. This discovery necessitates a fundamental reevaluation of causality and the nature of nonlocal interaction.

What makes these nonlocal effects so puzzling is that, as physicists have pointed out, no information is actually transferred. In other words, these experimental results do not mean that you can actually send information. However, there is a correlation between one result and another. This is a subtle but important point. One event is connected to another event, but it is not "caused" by that event. You cannot know what will be the state of the correlated points in advance. In other words, nonlocal events are nondeterministic.

Several other developments in physics have occurred that reveal nonlocal or what has been called "coherence" effects. For example, the phenomenon of quantum tunneling has presented an interesting paradox with regard to the speed of light. During the puzzling tunneling paradox particles that are projected toward a barrier bounce back. However, some particles appear on the other side of the barrier, as if they somehow have "tunneled" through the barrier.[28] The particle that tunneled through seems to speed up in time. Theoretically, if the barrier is wide enough, the particles that tunneled did so faster than light.[29]

Two other related phenomenon include Bose-Einstein condensates and quantum coherence. As noted earlier, bosons are particles that are massless and are not governed by the Pauli Exclusion Principle. They can, therefore, exist in superposition, or in the same state at once. Bose-Einstein condensates are made up of large numbers of bosons that collectively operate in the same quantum state. A good example of a Bose-Einstein condensate is a laser beam.

Physicist Roger Penrose has described quantum coherence quite clearly:

What is quantum coherence? This phenomenon refers to circumstances when large numbers of particles can collectively cooperate in a single quantum state which remains essentially unentangled with its environment. (The word "coherence" refers, generally to the fact that oscillations at different places beat time with one another. Here quantum coherence, we are conceived with the fact that we are dealing with a single quantum state).[30]

The coherence effect occurs with superconductors. There has been some skepticism regarding whether such coherence effects can occur in warm temperatures. This is because the coherence found in superconductors requires very low temperatures.[31] However, biophysicist Herbert Fröhlich proposed in the late 1960s that in biological membranes there occurs a phenomenon similar to coherence. This occurs with vibration effects within active cells that arise during intensified metabolic drive.[32]

Fröhlich's approach of a "pumped system" involves electrically charged molecules that vibrate when pumped with more energy. These "dipoles" are so named because they are positively charged at one end and negatively charged at the other. When pumped with energy the dipoles within the cell vibrate and emit virtual photons that are electromagnetic vibrations. When enough energy is pumped into the system they vibrate in unison and emit signals of microwave frequency. In so doing, they operate as a whole system. This process resembles that of Bose-Einstein condensates. That is, they are condensed and behave as one system.

Evidently elements in the universe that appear separate are actually "entangled" or interconnected. This interconnectivity is relevant to our efforts to explain consciousness by dealing with the "binding problem" noted in Chapter 1 and various phenomenological experiences. Before I discuss these experiences we must first address the issue of the limits of what we can know.

INCOMPLETENESS

The dramatic discoveries in the fields of relativity and quantum mechanics have been facilitated by the employment of sophisticated mathematical models. Yet during the last century there have been discoveries in the fields of logic and mathematics that have drawn attention to inherent limitations in these fields.[33]

At first glance, the conceptual changes that have occurred in the fields of logic and mathematics may appear irrelevant to our study of consciousness. However, I believe that the implications we can derive from these changes have profound bearing on how we investigate and what we can and cannot say about consciousness.

Let us start with the work of Austrian Logician Kurt Gödel. He began his work during a period in which logicians and mathematicians assumed that there were a finite number of mathematical axioms or fundamental assertions. Many felt that with vigorous work all the mathematical assertions lay waiting to be discovered.[34] Gödel shattered this premise in a twenty five page paper published in 1931.[35][36] Gödel showed that whatever logical system one uses (i.e., mathematics), there will always be truths beyond which can be explained by that system. He also showed that logical systems cannot in advance be free of hidden contradictions. Therefore, logical systems are incomplete. There will always be questions that are beyond the explanatory power of a logical system.

Physicist Roger Penrose pointed out that Gödel's Theorem suggests that computations (i.e., algorithms) cannot necessarily be a means to "truths." In the physical world, there exist phenomena that are noncomputable.[37] The future cannot be deduced algorithmically from the present.

Based on these issues, Penrose has correctly argued that consciousness cannot be replicated through any algorithmic simulation. The point is that the computer models of consciousness can never replicate consciousness. Consciousness is beyond algorithmic activity and is noncomputational in nature.[38] When transpersonal experiences are brought into focus, algorithmic replication is even more inappropriate.

Before returning to the issue of consciousness, I want to note one more development in mathematics that also has profound implications for our efforts to understand consciousness. The recent work of mathematician Gregory Chaiten has dealt with "computational complexity." Specifically, he showed that it is impossible to prove that a sequence of measurements is random, because there will always exist numbers so large as to prove their randomicity. Looked at from a different perspective, there may exist inherent order in the universe, even though it may be impossible to prove. Further, there is increasing computational complexity at transitional states—at the edge of chaos.

The synthesis of multiple patterns of cognition and emotions into a fluctuating field of consciousness cannot be reduced to a logical algorithm. Further, the contention that there is some kind of cognitive/algorithmic process that can be reduced to the "primary truths" regarding consciousness seems to be inconsistent with Gödel's Incompleteness Theorem. This theorem, combined with the implication from Gregory Chaiten's Algorithmic Complexity Theory that there are truths "out there" that can be assumed to exist beyond our grasp, necessitates a leap to a higher level of philosophical speculation. In other words, there may be truth about consciousness that are beyond our ability to describe with mathematical precision. It is in this direction that we turn in the two remaining chapters.

THE BRAIN, FIELDS OF INFORMATION, AND CONSCIOUSNESS

In recent years there have been some attempts to correlate developments in physics with unresolved problems in the description of consciousness. These include three major philosophical issues: 1) the so-called "binding problem"—

described in Chapter 1, whereby sporadic and brain firing patterns are collectively synthesized into a unified sense of self—still requires some explanation, 2) the "hard problem"—the unique subjective sense of self that all of us have—has perplexed many theorists who have attempted to explain consciousness, and 3) the difficulty constructing a nondualistic theory of consciousness remains unresolved and one of the major themes of this book. All of these problems have been addressed piecemeal from the perspective of the new physics.

One such approach has actually promoted a dualistic approach. Though I feel there are some conceptual problems with this approach, it nevertheless deserves mentioning as a reference point. Nobel Laureate and neurophysiologist John Eccles has contended that there are organizational structures in the brain that promote and facilitate a nonmaterial quality to consciousness.

In fact, Eccles' proposal lies in contrast to the Logical Positivism described in Chapter 1. He argues that there is an actual "ghost in the machine." Eccles claims that consciousness "probes" and "scans" the pattern of cerebral excitation.

Eccles suggests that quantum effects occur in the synapses—the gap that exists between the neurons.[39] Because the activity in the synapses is so sensitive and subtle, Eccles suggests that the elements of the synapse are so small that they lie within the range of the Uncertainty Principle. He draws attention to an area of the brain referred to as the supplementary motor area. This area is involved in the voluntary initiation of motor movements. He refers to columns of neurons in this area as "dendrons"—so named because bunches of dendrites are found in pyramidal cells. He then goes on to propose the existence of "psychons" or "mental units" as composed of superpositions of dendrons. The psychons are akin to ideas. Eccles suggests that a psychon can be composed of multiple dendrons that together form a unitary experience. Based on these assumptions, he hypothesizes that psychons give rise to a nonmaterial mind that interacts with the brain but survives the latter's demise.

Such an approach negates the continual importance of the brain. It is ironic that Eccles, a neurophysiologist, relegates the brain to an eventual subordinate role in consciousness. If it is possible to construct a nondualistic theory through the new physics, why jump broadly to the hypothesized psychon. It is my view that more parsimonious descriptions are possible—ones that do not require hypothetical units of consciousness that may not exist.

Another approach that attempts to synthesize quantum effects, neurophysiology, and theories of consciousness has been advanced by physicist Roger Penrose and anesthesiologist Stuart Hameroff. They have proposed that quantum coherence effects occur in the brain. This is an attempt to resolve the binding problem—resulting in a unified sense of self.

Penrose has attempted to correlate many unresolved issues in physics, such as the EPR paradox and the lack of a unified field theory uniting relativity and quantum theory with a theory of consciousness. He argues that just as Gödel's Theorem has implied that noncomputational approaches may be a valid means to approach the "truth" about the natural world, a theory that approaches a solution to the unresolved problems in physics and consciousness must involve noncomputational explanations.

According to Penrose and Hameroff, the brain's noncomputational actions occur at the bridge from the quantum to the classical level. This is the area or gap that is beyond a complete description by physics. Yet, there are possible solutions to this unresolved gap including such phenomena as quantum coherence and nonlocality.

Penrose and Hameroff have drawn attention to a part of the neuron referred to as "microtubules."[40] Microtubules are bundles of tiny tubes that are presumably extremely sensitive to quantum coherence. Each microtubule maintains an interconnective relationship with adjacent microtubules through microtubule associated proteins. Collectively, they are associated with maintaining the strengths of the synapses.[41] The continually subtle effects of the synapses are critical to the nonlinear dynamical quality of the brain.

The totality of microtubules may be involved in global quantum coherence in the brain. This coherence is similar to that described by Fröhlich. These collective quantum oscillations may be associated with brain-wave activity. The global quantum state is thought to occur collectively over large parts of the brain. Penrose proposes that to allow for noncomputible operations to occur, quantum-global coherence must be maintained.

Perhaps the Fröhlich effect is similar to the Bose-Einstein condensate phenomenon in a warm brain. Within the microtubules there exists nothing but perhaps water, which is ideal for quantum fluctuations. As with the Fröhlich effect, quantum coherence happens when metabolic drive is large enough. The microtubules may facilitate the coherence.

Penrose suggests that quantum effects in the brain would explain several interesting phenomena:

If there is no large-scale quantum coherence involved, then there would be no chance of any of the subtle quantum-level effects, such as nonlocality, quantum parallelism (several superposed actions being carried out simultaneously), or effects of counterfactually, having any significance when the classical level of the brain activity is reached. Without adequate shielding of the quantum from its environment, such effects would become immediately lost in the randomness inherent in that environment—i.e., in the random motions of those biological materials and fluid that constitute the bulk of the brain.[42]

Penrose speculates that conscious thinking involves the collapse of wave function, which he calls "R" (for reduction) and smooth development which he terms "U" (for unity). R involves sudden quantum jumps. Each quantum jump is affected by a "choice" or a "decision" which actualizes into a unitary process, or U. He proposes that at the border of U and R there is a yet to be discovered physics that might help us explain consciousness.

Whether or not this theory turns out to be accurate remains to be seen. At this point it has stirred considerable controversy and debate.[43] Nevertheless, it serves as a useful model of how coherence effects may be related to consciousness. It illustrates how the coherent effects can potentially solve the binding problem.

In general it appears that there exist noncausal and noncomputational processes in nature. Given that consciousness is part of nature these processes are relevant to our efforts to explain consciousness. Instead of a deterministic and mechanistic universe in which complete objectivism is possible, we see a fluid and probabilistic universe in which consciousness is a part.

Given that nonlocality is operative in nature it is interesting to speculate whether there are "transpersonal" (i.e., nonlocal) effects on consciousness that occur between people and aspects of the natural world. In other words, we should ask the question; "If quantum coherence and nonlocality effects can occur in individual brains, can such phenomena occur between people and the natural world?" If so, the convergent unity that people have described to have occurred between one another and the universe around them may explain transpersonal experience. It is that direction that we shall turn to in the next chapter.

7

Self-Convergence

We are one.

The Upanishads

So far we have dealt with aspects of consciousness that are relatively easily explained, despite their complexity. In this chapter we move toward the more difficult to explain—transpersonal experiences. I have demonstrated that consciousness is an aspect of, and is affected by, the biophysiological, sociocultural, and self systems. Transpersonal experience transcends, though it still reflects aspects of, these systems.

Consider, for example, the folkloric reports of the so-called "stigmata" phenomenon in which there appears on the body of a person wound-like bleeding assumed to replicate the wounds experienced by Jesus during the Crucifixion. Interestingly, the wounds are said to appear on the hands and the feet—which is where they are traditionally shown in paintings of the Crucifixion—rather than on the wrists and ankles—which is where the nails would actually had been driven.[1] Not only do these individuals identify with the Christ figure so profoundly as to allegedly alter their own biophysiological processes, but the manner in which this is said to occur is profoundly affected by sociocultural context. In fact this may be an example of how folklore develops. These cases involve tales of supernatural downward control over biophysiological processes in a way that conflicts with natural processes, yet reflects images of the sociocultural system.

Individuals within a sociocultural system interpret their own altered-state-of-consciousness experiences within the perspectives of that system. For example, Erika Bourguignon has shown that cultural factors influence the manner in which individuals within a given cultural system organize around culturally relevant rituals and interpret their experience within a cultural context. Subsistence economy, social organization, and theology are interwoven and interdependent. Cultures, such as Native American tribes, that believed in visionary trances but not in possession trances (as Haitians do) were correlated with a subsistence economy of hunting, gathering, and fishing.[2] These cultures also had fewer social stratifications, no slavery, and relatively small populations. Their belief in visionary trances reflects their tendency to promote independence rather than a more hierarchical altered-state condition, such as possession. Cultures that strongly believed in possession trances were correlated with a high dependence on agriculture and pastoralism. These cultures were characterized by high social stratification, inequality between the sexes, slavery, and large populations. Their belief in possession trances mirrored the emphasis on power and hierarchy within their sociocultural system. In other words, there is a profound interaction between one's cultural experience and one's interpretation of subjective experience.

One of the problems that theorists encounter in trying to develop a coherent theory of consciousness is the mythology that has developed in association with transpersonal experiences. The other problem is that the thoughts of emotions of the individual—which are one aspect of the self system, are generally considered to form the boundaries of consciousness.

While materialists have rejected outright the validity of reports of transpersonal experiences, many of those who accept these reports of transpersonal-type phenomena disregard the importance to consciousness of biophysiological, sociocultural, and intrapsychic dynamics. In effect, many transpersonal theorists have not moved past Cartesian Dualism. For example, they adhere to the antiquated belief in the existence of beings without bodies, The materialists, for their part, are limited by their adherence to a linear causality and a reductionistic perspective. They adhere to the antiquated belief that if you cannot hear, see, smell, or touch something it does not exist.

The fundamental interconnectivity implied by reports of transpersonal experience is consistent with what has been referred to as the Perennial Philosophy, the wisdom traditions, or the transcultural belief in the ultimate connectivity of all aspects of the universe. However, a sober assessment of this issue is needed. Consciousness can at times resonate with a universal interconnectivity. But this sense oneness does not reflect a Newtonian world view of determinism with a preconceived order as offered by some theological systems. Rather, consciousness reflects biophysiological and cognitive/emotional processes of each individual and the mythic images of his sociocultural system. In other words, the description of my transpersonal experience will be colored by the context of the sociocultural system I am embedded within and my personal experience. This was one of the main themes of Chapter 5.

The transcendental aspects of consciousness are experienced on an intermittent basis and in a variety of ways. Consciousness is a multilevel process. As conscious human beings we continuously fluctuate between states of consciousness. However, the word "state" in the phrase altered states of consciousness (ASC) is meant as a differentiating term. In other words, one state (dreaming) differs from another state (waking consciousness) in the quality and type of phenomenological experience that it represents.

States of consciousness are the dynamic patterns and active systems of organization. Charles Tart has noted that patterning forces such as negative and positive feedback act on these states to maintain consistent function, stabilization, and identity.[3] In other words, an individual may cultivate an altered state of consciousness that both reinforces and intensifies that experience.[4] One of the most common examples of a methodology that both cultivates and promotes an altered state is meditation. Such methodologies shift consciousness from one state to another. For example, during meditation one is usually able to become more relaxed and focused, in contrast to one's usual active state of consciousness.

A shift in state of consciousness is induced when "disrupting forces" interfere with the psychological or physiological aspects of the self system. The destabilization draws awareness away from the phenomenological experience of the initial state. Thus, the initial state of consciousness is shocked into a state of far-from-equilibrium conditions. Out of the chaos arises a new state. For example, a person may experience a trauma such a near-death experience whereby his usual sense of stability is dramatically disrupted. In Zen Buddhism there is the belief in the importance of the shock occurring when an individual is "ripe" for transformation. An example of a "ripe" shift may be induced after a period of fasting and prayer. Emerging from such a shift in physiology and behavior, the individual may experience an intuitive sense of interconnectivity.

Some altered states of consciousness are not discrete states.[5] Rather, they are by nature inclusive. That is, they include and are affected by intervening variables from other subsystems. Thus, even if altered states of consciousness are conceived of as vertically higher than the biophysiological, sociocultural, and self systems, they still subsume them. In other words, altered states of consciousness can be conceived of as "horizontally" higher.

One can be conscious of the state of consciousness of another person. In other words, consciousness can reach beyond the boundaries of the self system and can feel or be empathetic with another person's emotional state. This experience of shared feeling can occur on many levels. On the most basic level (as I described in Chapters 2 and 3) emotional bonding and connectiveness between individuals is part of a capacity inherited from our mammalian heritage. The paleomammalian cortex (limbic system) facilitates a rich emotional undercurrent of interactions between individuals. This feeling of connectivity with others can also occur on more subtle levels. For example, many people have reported that they have "intuitively" felt that a loved one may be in a particular state (or perhaps even in danger) when the two individuals are in different locations. Can we pass these anecdotal reports off as coincidences? If these experiences are not coincidences how and through what process do they occur? These are some of the perplexing questions that I will address in this chapter.

Many people have argued that such experiences occur because all aspects of the universe are fundamentally interconnected. Is consciousness sensitive to, and so reflects, this interconnectivity? So-called paranormal, or psi, experiences are often regarded as conscious experiences of interconnectivity. These experiences have been reported throughout evolutionary history. Shamanic traditions have a rich history of attempting to incorporate and cultivate these experiences into their overall mythic systems. Elaborate rituals may have included trance-induced dancing with fasting and meditative preparation.

The plea by mystics throughout history to appreciate the interconnectedness of all aspects of life is at issue here. Can the recent research related to psi phenomena and nonlocality argue in favor of this interconnectedness? One is reminded of Einstein's caution that "science without religion is lame and religion without science is blind." One should not simply embrace traditional beliefs just because they are traditional. We must reexamine some of our beliefs about these phenomena.

Almost all of the sociotheological traditions employ various methodologies to achieve an intuitive grasp of this interconnectivity. The often reported transpersonal experiences associated with these methodologies demand this comprehensive and unifying theory of consciousness. To construct a unifying theory of consciousness will necessitate a sober assessment that addresses anomalous transpersonal experiences.

PRAYER AND MEDITATION

As most theological systems describe a transcendent and unifying collective mystical experience, they have developed contemplative methodologies to achieve sensitivity to this all-encompassing interconnectivity. Both prayer and meditation have been employed with varying degrees of intensity by devotees and practitioners of these religious traditions.

The Judeo-Christian practice of prayer reveals many commonalities and dissimilarities with the practice of hypnosis.[6] For example, the state of "Kavanah" described by the Jewish Cabalistic tradition is quite similar to autohypnosis. In the Talmud, Kavanah is characterized by correct intention or motivation and concentration. This state often involves chanting in a relaxed and ritualistic environment with a fixation on an alter or similar image. Often there is a rhythmic rocking of the body back and forth while chanting. Unlike hypnosis there is an attempt to develop transpersonal contact with a being greater than oneself.

In Christianity the practice of prayer is similar to the Judaic prayer without the rhythmic rocking. Both involve contemplation. In Catholicism praying of the rosary is used much like mantras in the East. The basic intent is to communicate or be at one with God. Within the Judeo-Christian-Islamic traditions the practice of prayer may involve fasting and meditation. The individual may attempt to "empty himself" to be able to hear the voice of God.

There have been comparisons of hypnosis and Eastern practices of meditation.[7] In Zen Buddhism, for example, as with hypnosis shifting of attention is important. One Zen technique that aids in shifting attention is referred to as the koan. This is a simple paradoxical statement with no apparent concrete answer (e.g., "The elbow does not bend outward" or the popular "What is the sound of one hand clapping?"). The point is that when one contemplates the paradox there is a leap to an appreciation of the irreducible totality. For example, the Rinzai school of Zen Buddhism utilizes koans for "lightening realization." In Zen Buddhism this process has been referred to as a "train wreck of the mind." The paradoxes presented in the koan force the practitioner to confront reality beyond the usual conceptual format. Once this has been achieved we may say that "disrupting influences" come into play and throw consciousness into far-from-equilibrium conditions and there may occur a subsequent leap to a higher level of organization.

Through the meditative approach of Yoga-Samadhi deep concentration is critical as it is with hypnosis. Several of the variables important in hypnosis are common to most meditative practices such as the general belief in the validity of the practice. This underlies the concept of the utility of suggestion in hypnosis. Other common denominators include expectation, practice, relaxation, and suspension of negative attitudes. Overall both broad methodologies are employed to aid one in achieving liberation of stress. Yet meditation and prayer involve faith in a reality greater than oneself. With many meditation practices there is a belief in the control of oneself and a transpersonal connectivity. In meditation and/or prayer this tenet is perhaps best expressed by Jesus: "If you would only believe you could move mountains."

It has long been contended that a few advanced yogi meditators are able to control general physiological processes. By the early 1970s control of such systems was demonstrated by the use of biofeedback equipment. These results have been demonstrated over such systems as respiration. Though the early research related to meditation produced findings that showed a relaxation effect, the trend during the past twenty years has been to differentiate the various types of meditation and their respective effects. For example, the Tantric yoga technique has been shown to be correlated with an elevation in overall excitation instead of relaxation.[8]

The effect of nasal side activity and activation of hemispherical function has been demonstrated in relationship to yogic meditation[9]—specifically the same-side nasal passage the same-side hemisphere. The electroencephalographic (EEG) readings taken from "passive" meditators (i.e., those practicing Zen and transcendental meditation) has produced evidence of theta wave production. In fact, active meditators were found to produce theta waves as well.[10] Neurophysiologist Karl Pribram has argued that when an individual is engaged in a meditative practice, using an ambiguous stimulus such as a mantra, the part of the brain activated is the frontal-limbic areas. Indeed, Stanley Krippner has noted that in recent years there has been an increase in the literature that implies that fluctuating patterns in the deep temporal lobes may be correlated with transpersonal and psi-type experiences.[11] As I noted in Chapter 3, the temporal lobes are highly correlated with interconnective networks with the limbic system (the paleomammalian cortex) and are thereby associated with emotional processes. This fact will become more significant later in this chapter.

While most meditators assessed with the EEG have been shown to produce alpha waves, Zen meditators have been reported to suspend alpha waves in response to external stimuli. This finding is contrasted by yogi meditators who showed no response to external stimulation. This difference can be attributed to their contrasting philosophical positions.[12] Yogi and Zen meditators have different orientations and practice with different techniques. Specifically, Zen meditators ascribe to a "here and now" perspective in which raw sensory experience is not regarded with disdain as it is in some yoga schools. Yogi meditators, in contrast, abide by a "world denying" attitude. As noted in Chapter 5, the concept of maya ascribed by Hindu-Yogic meditators suggests that the phenomenal world is an illusion. Once again we see multiple subsystems interacting—in this case sociocultural belief systems interacting with intrapsychic process interacting with both ASC and biophysiological processes.

In most religious disciplines prayer and meditative practice have traditionally been associated with spiritual experience. Anecdotally, individuals report feelings of rapture, harmony with the greater whole, ecstasy, peace, and love.

Many mystics caution that extrasensory perception (ESP)-type experiences are common when an individual becomes more focused on the overall unity and the ego attaches itself to these experiences. In such situations an ego-centered position contributes to the delusion that one has a qualitatively more important or greater character. As a result, the insights are lost of the greater whole and one loses the sober humility and knowledge that one is just part of the greater whole. For example, a Vedantic premise is that ESP type experiences are "side effects" associated with meditation. Such experiences are thought to be a distraction from the more fundamental mystical experience.

Throughout history people have prayed for good fortune and health. Only recently has there been research that explores the utility of prayer.[13] For example, in a widely reported study performed at San Francisco General Hospital the effects of prayer were demonstrated in a group unaware that they were being prayed for. One group was prayed for by groups of religious people, while the other was not. This was a double-blind study, meaning that neither the patients nor the medical staff knew which patients were assigned to a particular group. All effects were found to be statistically significant. The prayed-for group were subsequently found to require fewer antibiotics, to be less likely to develop pulmonary edema, and to be less likely to require intubation.[14]

In other prayer studies described by Larry Dossey in his book *Healing Words*, prayer appeared to have an "open ended" effect. In other words, the practitioner of prayer "petitions God" to "let thy will be done" or "may the best thing happen in this particular circumstance."[15] The results of this type of prayer effect appear to be nondeterministic. Dossey argues that this nondeterministic aspect of prayer parallels the EPR phenomenon, in that nonlocal quantum effects cannot be controlled. In other words, just as physicists cannot send specific messages to particles, neither can prayer have a specific effect.

In nonlocal healing it appears that compassion and love toward others has the most dramatic effect. Prayer and nonlocal influences on human events occur only in benevolent circumstances. In other words, aggression and malevolent intent do not seem to occur. This appears to correspond with the overall global process of coevolution. Cooperation rather than strife appears to be the norm.

PSI

As the Empiricist and Positivist perspective has come to dominate thinking in this century, the issue of atypical psychological phenomena has become increasingly controversial. This is probably due to the very nature of the phenomena in question. To accept the existence of such anomalous phenomena would at first glance necessitate a dramatic shift away from the materialist paradigm. In short, it would profoundly disturb our current assumptions regarding the nature of reality. However, as I noted in the previous chapter, these assumptions have already been questioned during the developments of modern physics.

The first rigorous and sustained parapsychological research was conducted by J. B. Rhine at Duke University beginning in the 1930s. It was Rhine who coined the term extrasensory perception to describe phenomena that seem to have no direct causal relationship to normal sensory experience. He employed a variety of techniques to detect ESP, including the use of zener cards. These cards have various geometric designs printed on them. In Rhine's experiments, a sender sitting in a different room than the subject would choose a card at random and attempt to send the image "telepathically" to the subject. Over the next few decades, Rhine and his associates performed numerous such studies, many of which produced statistically significant results.

Most studies that have assessed telepathy have involved these card-guessing tasks. However, several studies at the Stanford Research Institute (now referred to as SRI International) have explored a kind of telepathy known as remote viewing. Here the senders were separated from the subjects by distances of up to several miles. The statistically significant results from these studies indicate that distance does not hinder telepathic communication.

The research using the Ganzfeld procedure in assessing telepathy has been analyzed using meta-analysis statistical procedures.[16] In this procedure, the subject's eyes are covered to prevent visual stimulation, and white noise is used to block auditory stimulation. Subjects were found to pick up the relevant imagery even when sensory input was blocked by means of the Ganzfeld procedure. The results indicate a strong statistical significance.[17][18] The effect of physical shielding and/or spatial distance on both clairvoyance and telepathy has been found to be negligible.[19] These findings are consistent with the phenomenon of nonlocal interconnectivity. In other words, they seem to indicate that individuals who experience telepathy are either utilizing or are sensitive to a fundamental interconnectivity that apparently can occur between individuals who are not in physical proximity to one another.

In addition to telepathy, various other forms of ESP, now referred to as psi phenomena, have been researched. These include precognition, clairvoyance, and psychokinesis (PK). Princeton engineering professor Robert Jahn studied PK using random number generators (RNGs).[20] A RNG is an electronic instrument that produces statistically random numbers occurring in binary forms (e.g., 1, 2, 1, 2, 3, and so on). A subject is asked to influence the production of numbers "by will" in a prescribed direction. Jahn found that subjects who expressed a strong desire to do well produced more statistically significant results than other subjects. Additionally, when pairs of individuals were asked to act in concert to influence the RNG it was found that "emotionally bonded" couples demonstrated the most significant effect. Again we find that there is a connection between emotional connections and psi-type experiences.

These findings may also reflect a connection between the wave functions of matter and consciousness. Not only does consciousness interact with the quantum world but it is also a creative force within it. Many of the PK experiments, especially those utilizing random number generators, reportedly succeed in demonstrating a connection between consciousness and matter. Perhaps this success is due to the "micro-PK" processes associated with the probabilistic laws of quantum theory.[21] In the absence of a steady state, the quantum process allows subtle fluctuations to occur. I will return to this issue in Chapter 8. My point here is that an exchange of information appears to take place, perhaps at the quantum level. Consciousness may play an active role in generating these subtle fluctuations.

However, the issue of enduring forms of transcendence has been indiscriminately applied to a variety of beliefs in psi phenomena. Take, for example, the belief in reincarnation. This belief occurs cross-culturally throughout the world; it attains almost doctrinal status in Hinduism, most forms of Buddhism, and Shiite Islam. The theologies of some African, Native American, and Australian tribes include a form of belief in reincarnation.

In the case of reincarnation, the proposed phenomena contradict the belief—subscribed to by all mystical traditions and advanced in this book—that all beings and aspects of the universe are ultimately interconnected in holistic and nonlocal relationships. In other words, to conceive of spiritual beings that do not merge and evolve with the totality—but rather somehow their individuality is sealed off and they change bodies as one changes clothes—is a kind of philosophical narcissism.

Furthermore, the research investigations of reincarnation have produced inconclusive results. Studies using memories of past lives supposedly retrieved during hypnosis are fraught with complications. A review of the literature on hypnosis and reincarnation reveals frequent inaccuracies.[22] For example, the identification of a specific individual past life has either been an inaccurate portrayal or the individual was not clearly identified. Research to date suggests that the issue is at best inconclusive. We are left with anecdotal and difficult-to-verify reports.

People who believe that they intuit images from their own past lives may actually be picking up on enduring forms of information from the lives of others who lived in the past. Since this information is collectively dispersed, it may be blended with other forms of information, making it difficult to identify the source. The assumption, then, is that information is collective, and that due to the fundamental interconnectivity of all aspects of life, it can be intuited.

Overall, the research related to telepathy and clairvoyance over the years has been reported to have reports of statistical, albeit controversial, support for the validity of both.[23][24] However, this has been a troubling critique of one the most influential studies. Susan Blackmore has reported that one of the series of studies included in the meta-analysis was flawed with tampering.[25] This controversy has fueled a debate whereby Bem and Honorton have argued that if the contaminated studies were taken out of their meta-analysis the result would still be statistically significant. On the other hand, Blackmore has countered that if there was such a gross distortion in one series of studies, perhaps there is reason to doubt the validity of other studies.

With regard to the research on precognition results have been consistently weak. In fact, when research related to present-time psi phenomena is compared to research related to precognition, the results of the former are ten times more statistically significant.[26]

Perhaps precognition involves the sensitive perception of initial conditions (the present) and the projection of these conditions and potentialities into the future, rather than moving as it were into the future itself. From this point of view the precognitive experience can be thought of as the intuitive perception and projection of possibilities. Such a perception of the future is colored by current belief structures. This may explain why parapsychological research related to precognition has produced fewer convincing results than research related to telepathy and clairvoyance. This view leaves room for free will, evolutionary processes, and the asymmetry of time.

To return to our discussion of psi phenomena in general—the preponderance of evidence suggests that *some* of these reports may be valid. Though reports of some psi phenomena are questionable, others have been supported by rigorous research.

Contrary to popular belief, people who have been demonstrated to have experienced psi phenomena in parapsychological experiments are not disturbed individuals with closed self systems. On the contrary, successful performance in parapsychological experiments is associated with a variety of personality variables. Subjects who believe that they have experienced psi phenomena tend to be more successful than those who do not. Subjects who have practiced meditation, biofeedback, or some other similar discipline also perform well. Interestingly, a review of sixty different studies on the relationship between personality and psi experience revealed that extroverts performed better on parapsychological experiments than introverts.[27] This is a curious finding. It suggests that individuals who invest less energy in self absorption and more energy engaged in interrelationships with others may have more psi-like experiences. Introversion must be balanced with the ability to experience connectivity with others to achieve transpersonal experience.

It is plausible to hypothesize that any measurement of psi phenomena is inherently limited by the experimental process. At first glance, entertaining such a hypothesis sounds conveniently evasive. In other words, critics of the field of parapsychology may say, "If you cannot produce consistent and verifiable results in tightly constructed studies 100 percent of the time where is the validity for psi phenomena?"

On the other hand, the experimental process is a very contrived and sterile process. It may be difficult to expect that one can produce a consistent psi-type skill in a consistent manner devoid of the contextual aspects in which these experiences have anecdotally have been reported. For example, many psi-type experiences have been reported to have been embedded within the context of significant life transitions and emotionally laden interactions between people emotionally bonded. I will return to this issue later in this chapter.

NEAR-DEATH EXPERIENCE

Another curious and often reported phenomenon that relates to the issue of interconnectivity is the so-called near death experience (NDE). This experience, which occurs when an individual clinically dies and then is revived, has been the subject of only recent research.[28] What is particularly interesting about the NDE is that it involves compassion, euphoria, and the subjective sense of inclusiveness. That is, the experience of compassion and a euphoric sense of unity between self and deceased love ones is quite provocative and deserves some explanation.

Though each NDE has unique characteristics, and no NDE report yields a standard format, several commonalities are reported. There is often an initial feeling of extreme peace, joy, and sometimes ecstasy. There is often an out-of-body experience in which vision and awareness are heightened as the individuals view from above whatever heroic attempts are made to resuscitate them.[29]

In the next phase, they feel as though they were being swept through a dark tunnel at extremely high speed, moving toward a bright light at the end.[30] Although the light is brighter than anything they have ever seen, they can nevertheless look at it, and they feel an irresistible urge to be absorbed by it. During this process they experience a vivid review of their entire past life.

At some point, many NDE survivors are met by deceased loved ones. They experience this reunion as joyful and warm. As they feel increasingly embraced by the light, they may experience the presence of a powerful loving being. They communicate with this entity by means of telepathy. They experience a sense of homecoming and belonging as if they are being reunited with their source. Many report feeling an energized sense of the purpose of life. Above all, they feel bathed in a powerful experience of love and acceptance.

At another point along the way it occurs to them that they are going to have to decide whether or not to return to life. Eventually they are asked or told to consider doing so, either to accomplish something or to be with people who still need them. Sometimes they make this decision for themselves. On the other hand, they are sometimes told, "Your time has not come," or "You have things to accomplish."

There is evidence of sociocultural patterning in NDEs. For example, the typical Western report outlined above is modified, in India, by the image of black figures taking the body away to the land of death.[31] Thus, it appears that the imagery experienced during the NDE is interconnected with the sociocultural system of the individual. Once again we see the interaction among sociocultural systems, self systems, and transpersonal experience.

The imagery that occurs during a NDE is metaphoric and the discontinuities in the NDE are reminiscent of the dreaming process. Both often include comments such as "The next thing I knew was" and "The next thing that happened was." In fact, there are some similarities between lucid dreaming and NDE.[32]

Some theorists have argued that the NDE phenomenon is the result of physiological change that occurs during death. But can NDEs be dismissed as the result of oxygen deprivation or some other biophysiological toxic reaction? Neurotoxic effects do not generally include the vividness and pleasure that characterize the NDE. Furthermore, neurotoxic and metabolic imbalances usually entail a spectrum of disoriented and confused reactions. For example, if a person is exposed to chemical solvents or deprived of B vitamins he or she may experience memory and concentration problems. However, brief periods of oxygen deprivation and cerebral blood flow irregularities may be a factor worth investigating.

James Whinney has pointed out that NDE has many similarities to what occurs when there is an alteration in blood flow to the brain. In research he conducted with pilots experiencing inflight acceleration (+Gz) he found that many of the symptoms associated with NDE can be compared with what occurs when blood flow changes during centrifugation. He and his co-workers have argued that the entire symptom complex and associated psychophysiological alterations produced by +Gz stress can be described as a +Gz induced loss of consciousness—(or G-Loc). In the extreme the G-Loc experiences have many symptoms that overlap with NDE. For example, he reports,

1. Tunnel vision/bright light
2. Floating
3. Autoscopy
4. Out-of-body experience
5. Not wanting to be disturbed
6. Paralysis
7. Vivid dreamlike/beautiful places
8. Pleasurable experience and euphoria
9. Friends and family inclusion
10. Prior memories /thought inclusion
11. Confabulation
12. Strong urge to understand the experience[33]

These are profound findings. They suggest that the NDE have neurophysiological causes and that the folkloric buildup around the reports of NDE is a distortion. Further, when considering the phenomenon of oxygen deprivation, discussed in the next section, we must consider carefully how we understand the NDE.

On the other hand, even though it appears that the NDE reports may be correlated with cerebral blood flow irregularities and brief periods of oxygen deprivation, we should not dismiss the possibility that they represent a transpersonal experience. It appears that the NDE is associated with a subjective sense of a transpersonal psi-type experience. That is, it involves a subjective sense of interconnectivity to others, especially those remembered as significant figures in one's life. Yet the NDE does not necessarily imply dualism. In other words, the NDE experience need not be interpreted as a confirmation that the soul lives on as an independent entity.

Interestingly, NDE survivors are often profoundly affected by their experience. They may become more patient, loving, understanding, and accepting of others and even of themselves. They often report that they focus less now on material values and personal gain and more on collective gain and spirituality.[34] Such a dramatic shift in one's overall perspective of life can be seen as a leap to a higher level of organization following the most extreme far-from-equilibrium conditions that the self system can experience. Because NDEs have such a catalyzing affect, they may serve as a powerful experience of interconnectivity that promotes the evolution of the species toward unification with totality—the light (or God).[35]

At the very least, the NDE phenomenon suggests that the individual is subjectively experiencing a euphoric blending with the greater whole. Perhaps this is why individuals who have NDEs experience joyful reunions with long-lost loved ones and feel an irresistible urge to merge with the light, from which emanates a powerful sense of love. In this respect, NDEs are related to other transpersonal experiences all of which involve an intuitive sense of overall unity. Perhaps the brain has evolved in such a manner that at death we are comforted by profound experiences of convergence. The transpersonal nature of these experiences implies that there is an all-inclusive macrosystem. This implication makes it necessary to develop a coherent evolutionary transpersonal psychology.

TRANSPERSONAL PSYCHOLOGY

Historically, shamanic traditions and the major theological systems have attempted to explain, and indeed induce, paranormal experiences. Few attempts have been made to develop a comprehensive transpersonal psychology outside of the sociotheological systems.[36]

Ken Wilber has developed a transpersonal schema that attempts to synthesize Vendantic theology and developmental psychology. He calls his model the Spectrum of Consciousness.[37][38] Wilber conceives of consciousness as multilevel and stratified.[39] The development of a human being entails the movement from subconsciousness to self-consciousness, in what Wilber terms the "outward arc." He calls the first stage of development "pleromatic." In this stage the infant is undifferentiated from his or her surroundings. Wilber bases this premise on a theoretical position taken by some psychoanalytic writers. This premise of an undifferentiated state is now seen as questionable by developmental psychologists. As noted in Chapter 3, the infant interacts with others and is a "self"-organizing system during the first few weeks of life. The second—or "uroboric"—stage corresponds to Freud's oral stage; it has to do with the relationship between the infant and the caregiver. The third stage ("typhonic") encompasses Freud's anal and phallic stages; it involves differentiation from the caregiver and the development of a coherent self. All of the developmental and corresponding cognitive milestones, such as the use of language, are encompassed in the fourth, or "verbal-membership," stage. Higher cognitive skills, such as the utilization of linear thinking and the development of a self-concept, emerge in the fifth, or "mental-egoic," stage. Finally, in the "centauric" stage body, persona, ego, and shadow are fully integrated into a whole individual.[40]

Beyond the "centauric" stage, consciousness evolves into the transpersonal realm. On the first, or "lower subtle," level, all of the psi phenomena noted earlier are operative. This is because one is operating from the "astral body," which enables one to transcend the basic body-mind and have out-of-body experiences. Religious or mystical intuition and archetypal visions occur on the second, or "higher subtle," level. The third level in this schema, which is called the "causal realm," has two sublevels. The first one is the source of the archetypes and divine consciousness; the second and higher is without boundaries and form.

As psychologist Allan Combs notes, Wilber misunderstands Jung's concept of archetypes. For Jung archetypes are grounded in the evolutionary history of the species, whereas for Wilber they are "highly advanced structures lying in the high-subtle and low-causal planes." In fact, he regards "angelic beings" and other hypothesized dhyana-buddhas as "simply high archetypal beings." This sort of stratified old paradigm perspective I take issue with. Why slap together antiquated concepts including non-material beings with a layer-cake model of existence? As I noted earlier, Whitehead had cautioned that we have the unfortunate tendency to repeat the problem he described as "the fallacy of misplaced concreteness." Do we really need to repeat the unsubstantiated belief in various angels, and "high archetypal beings."

By adhering to the "structures" of consciousness, Wilber misses the fact that transcendental experience is so colored by sociocultural context. As I made clear Erica Bourguignon's work clearly illustrates the impact of cultural context on the type of altered states of consciousness experienced. With regards to the levels as "structures" of consciousness, the term structure is misused. I have made clear in Chapters 2 and 3 that structure and function coevolve.

Wilber uses Aristotle's Great Chain of Being to conceptualize a generally linear schema into a set of concentric circles, each of which represents a "realm" or "holon" of reality.[41] These begin with matter, or physics, which is subsumed by biology, which is further subsumed by psychology, followed by theology, then mysticism, and finally spirit. Each realm is transcended by the one above it but does not violate the principles of the one below it.[42]

Even though Wilber makes brief reference to evolution, he does not seem to understand the phenomena of bidirectional causality. Both top-down and bottom-up causation occur. The "lower" systems get reorganized and restructured and have a profound effect on "higher" levels of organization. These are the lessons of chaos theory and the sciences of complexity. Thus, there is bi-directional causation, not, as Wilber has maintained, "higher" levels having primary control over the lower. Self-organizing systems evolve with complex nonlinear processes and therefore involve *all* of the elements of a holistic system.

Wilber has been widely criticized for his emphasis on "hierarchies" or levels of existence. I think that many have misunderstood the concept of hierarchies. If we replace the term hierarchy with the phrase "levels of organization," perhaps more people could appreciate Wilber's concept of hierarchies.[43] Wilber, therefore, has offered an important contribution. The levels of organization that I have emphasized throughout this book are irreducible to the sum of their parts. Yet there are bidirectional interactions among the subsystems.

An Existentialist perspective—one in which transcendence does not dissolve the self but includes it—is proposed by Michael Washburn, who advocates the "spiral-to-integration" view.[44] Here transcendence is achieved by making a reversal or "U-turn" to one's origins, followed by reintegration and transformation. This is in contrast to the straight ascent of the Vedantic "ladder-to-oneness." The U-turn paradigm is associated with the Western theologies of Judaism and Christianity. It is exemplified by the Judeo-Christian sequence of paradise–fall–redemption–salvation. The U-turn paradigm is also associated with the hero odyssey. In a hero's odyssey, for example, the protagonist must descend to the underworld before being transformed into superhuman form. There he or she may be tested, or his or her lower self may be tempted, before he or she transcends his or her former existence. The U-turn model may be understood as a process in which the self is put into far-from-equilibrium conditions and emerges transformed from this state of self-organized criticality.

The classic example of this motif is the story of Jesus entering the wilderness and resisting temptation. After forty days and forty nights of fasting he was tempted with great wealth and pleasure, but managed instead to emerge with an epic sense of mission.

A sociocultural U-turn to transcendence is offered by the book of Revelation. Here civilization is prophesied as experiencing great upheaval in wars and natural disasters and the fate of the world is threatened. Just when it appears that such an event would happen, God "saves" and subsequently transformed the world into the "New Jerusalem" or the "Kingdom of God." In other words, the old world ends and a new world is created.

Washburn's approach highlights the individual's interaction with life. He uses the terms "ego" and "dynamic ground" to highlight this interaction. He advocates for a kind of developmental theory of transpersonal psychology. By dividing up three principal states he terms the "pre-egoic," "egoic," and "trans-egoic," he emphasizes the emergence of the individual and transcendence. The reunification with the dynamic ground involves self-transcendence and spiritual awakening. Washburn contrasts his model to that of Wilber by calling his "dynamic-dialectical" and Wilber's "structural-hierarchical." This dialectical emphasis perhaps over-emphasizes the "bipolar" concept. That is, Washburn's model emphasizes thesis, antithesis, and antithesis that requires the "poles" making them opposites.[45]

Unfortunately, like Wilber, he uses very outdated developmental psychology. While Wilber relies on a Piagetian and to a lesser degree Freudian model, Washburn adheres to a generally early psychoanalytic model. Nevertheless, Washburn's emphasis on psychodynamic influence is important. We can broaden this motif with the self-organizing model outlined in Chapter 3 and the biopsychosocial influences on consciousness.

Along the same lines as the existential approach, Stan Grof placed great emphasis on birth and death, the two most dramatic transitions in life.[46] Grof attempted to explore the birth process with subjects who had taken LSD, or who used the "holotropic" breathing technique, which is similar to a rhythmic hyperventilation. Grof reports that practitioners of this technique often describe what he has referred to as "perinatal" experiences. These experiences were clustered around the recollection of specific stages of childbirth, or "basic perinatal matrices" (BPMS). Each of these stages corresponds to metaphorical experiences such as being "engulfed" or "trapped." Grof theorized that if one has experienced disturbances in utero or during the birth process, reexperiencing these disturbances in a therapeutic environment and working through their negative influences permits one to leap to a higher level of organization. My question is, are these really transpersonal experiences or imagistic phenomena generalized to everyone? Nevertheless, this theory resembles the U-turn model because one reexperiences, or goes back before, experiencing a transformation.

The general idea is that through the destabilizing influence of hyperventilation one breaks into an altered state of consciousness. Grof hypothesizes four levels in what an individual can experience. These are: the sensory barrier, individual unconsciousness, the perinatal level or the level death, and finally the transpersonal level.[47] The similarities between the effects of holotropic breathing and NDE are interesting. Perhaps the early part of the holotropic effect is a prelude to the more euphoric effects of NDE when oxygen is more profoundly disrupted.

Generally, the straight-ascent (latter-to-oneness) model overemphasizes linear movement and does not fully appreciate nonlinear multidimensional movement. The U-turn model involves a self in far-from-equilibrium conditions; Washburn and Grof emphasize the existential struggle including the underworld and regression. A combination of these two perspectives is called for. Such a combined perspective will be sensitive to the coevolution of multiple micro- and macrosystems.

Allan Combs offers a "soft" connection between the various levels of being noted by the theorists noted above.[48] In so doing he acknowledges the need for degrees of movement between the levels of personal growth and species evolution. Like Combs I argue the need to incorporate a nonlinear dynamical approach to the evolution of consciousness. I am receptive to the idea of attractors affecting consciousness, but unlike Combs, I am not convinced that the "structures" most theorists describe are not just overemphasizing sociotheological motifs.

An interconnective transpersonal model must also include the synthesis of unconscious and conscious aspects of transcendence. Jung defined the "transcendental function" as a bridging of unconscious and conscious processes. From an evolutionary perspective, the Jungian concept of the Collective Unconscious is relevant here. Archetypes can be seen as universal predispositions that arise in consciousness.[49] According to this view, a given set of circumstances resonates with an archetypal pattern. These archetypal patterns act as an attractor for consciousness. For example, the U-turn and the ladder-to-oneness models can be considered archetypal patterns. They can influence consciousness to evolve through a U-turn or a ladder-to-oneness pattern. In other words, we may at times respond to the ladder-to-oneness archetypal motif during periods of little flux in one's life. Alternatively, during particularly turbulent times in which we feel ourselves threatened, the U-turn archetypal motif may be more relevant.

Since personally significant symbols are encoded in state-dependent form, they are fused with emotion. Symbols also reflect several dimensions of cognitive experience and act as attractors for sociocultural systems. Thus an individual can derive meaning from symbols and metaphors on many dimensions simultaneously.

Archetypes and personally significant symbols resonate with emotional meaning[50]—in other words, when there is a conversion of strong emotional feeling and meaning intuition occurs. Consider again the frontal-limbic and temporal lobe correlations with meditation and psi experiences. This convergence synthesizes cognition with emotion. The congruence of cognition and emotion allows one a leap to a horizontally higher level of consciousness (see Figure 7.1). This balance of emotion and cognition can be associated with feelings of unity with others and the inclusive feeling of oneness with all in existence. Compassion and the discernment of interdependence while in an altered state of consciousness is perhaps the clearest meaning of spirituality.

One experiences any altered state of consciousness in the context of one's sociocultural system. Yet perhaps this is only one level of mystical experience. While the character and form of mystical experience may vary, at a deeper level that experience "may be cross-culturally identical."[51] The broader the perception of interconnective relationships, the less differentiating particulars are apparent. From this perspective, interconnectivity is more obvious on a macro level than it is on a micro level.

We might call this broader and deeper level of mystical experience an example of "convergence evolution." This metaphor is useful because such experiences transcend both the self and the sociocultural system in which the self is embedded. In fact, one common denominator of most of the sociotheological systems is that as the individual lets go of personal pettiness in the form of "earthly concerns," desire, or attachments, when this is achieved the self is experienced as part of one convergent reality.

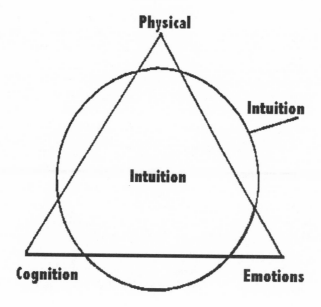

Figure 7.1
The Balance of Cognition and Emotion with Biophysiological Processes and the Inclusive Experience of Intuition

Each individual is potentially able to experience the convergence directly. These important transcendental experiences act as catalysts in one's life, allowing one to leap beyond one's own self system. Individuals consumed with their own psychic entropy close themselves off from such experiences. They are closed self systems with little consciousness of interdependence. But compassionate openness and awareness of interdependence allows one to converge with the larger whole. It is the simple message of love and compassion that transcends, sensitizes, and allows one to achieve self convergence.

SUMMARY

Consciousness is sensitivity to a field of interrelationships. It is also provocative and anticipatory processes. Consciousness is a participatory phenomenon that can be aware of macrosystems beyond its own self system. The transpersonal properties of consciousness reflect the individual participation in a universe in which he or she exists. Infrequent experiences and sensitivity to global interconnectivity are at times marked by synchronicities that follow periods of flux. One individual may intuit another's experience during such a period of shared flux and coevolution.

One's consciousness coevolves interconnectively and fluidly with that of others. Therefore, various aspects of the self system, such as emotion and cognition, may help individuals to intuit one another's experience. We have the capacity to empathize and support one another emotionally. Further, because love and compassion are inclusive emotional experiences, they may help to facilitate the leap to higher levels of interconnectivity. The bond between individuals generates shared resonance.

A radical shift from one state of consciousness to another can precipitate a dramatic self-transcendence. This is especially evident when the shift is to a so-called higher state of consciousness. To revert to the terminology that I employed in earlier chapters, such a shift simplifies the "noise" of complexity into a unified order. The mystical experience of oneness between self and other may be viewed as one such dramatic shift in consciousness. Such an experience can produce profound and ongoing transformations.

Mystical experiences, psi, NDEs, and perceptions of synchronicities can be regarded as leaps beyond the microsystem of the self to perception of the macrosystem. All such experiences have this one thing in common. They are only brief glimpses of one's overall unity with the systems within which they are embedded. This is what differentiates these experiences from experiences in which one is synchronized with the biophysical, sociocultural, and self systems described in previous chapters. All of these systems are subsumed by the leap to convergent unity.

Therefore, the phenomena noted in this chapter, together with the implications of those phenomena, require a unifying paradigm. In Chapter 8 I will discuss such a paradigm, and we will attempt to make it relevant to the evolution of consciousness.

8

An Evolving Unity

In the preceding chapters I stressed that not only do the biophysical, sociocultural, and self system dimensions coevolve, but also within each system there are multiple subsystems affecting consciousness, all evolving with a high degree of nonlinearity. All these systems and subsystems are part of a single macrosystem which is constantly changing—this macrosytem is better thought of as a verb than as a noun. The subsystems are profoundly interconnected at levels and can be experienced transpersonally. This being the case, the fundamental attractor of consciousness is the capacity to see unity in ever-changing diversity.

Because the variables that affect the individual are multifaceted, if not infinite, any change in the overall system, however seemingly remote, can potentially have a nonlinear effect on that individual. A useful analogy is provided by the game of chess. The movement of a single pawn has potential ramifications throughout the entire chessboard. But life and consciousness are more fluid and more complex than a game of chess. Any individual is part of an evolving species; is part of a sociocultural system, is composed of his or her own self-system dynamics, and is interconnected with others in nonlocal transpersonal fields.

As I have demonstrated throughout this book, there exists no one way to explain consciousness. Each individual self system reflects an infinite number of fractal microsystems and is interconnected at every level with other aspects of the biosphere. In other words, the interconnectivity affecting all aspects of consciousness prohibits any reductionistic description of consciousness. Rather, consciousness reflects and thrives on interconnective relationships.

Consciousness must be understood from an evolving open-systems paradigm. The evolution of consciousness is facilitated not only by an open system but also by self-convergence—the transpersonal experience of being within an interdependent macrosystem.

If all systems occur simultaneously, and each system is composed of an infinite number of subsystems, transpersonal perception is not simply a higher level of consciousness but the perception of multiple systems simultaneously. Humans are not necessarily "higher" vertically than other organisms. Rather, they are higher horizontally; that is, they can be sensitive to multiple levels of life at once.

Some people achieve, at best, only brief mystical glimpses of the all-inclusiveness of the universe. When one has one of these brief experiences it is colored by the sociocultural system the individual is embedded within and his unique self-system perspective within that sociocultural system. In other words, though colored by a Western sociocultural system, and having exposure to Eastern perspectives, I am also composed of my own particular cognitive/emotional tendencies that differentiate me from others within the same cultural system.

Moving beyond the boundaries of one's own self system to become sensitive to macrosystems stimulates growth, and thereby intuition. The perception of the interrelatedness of all phenomena is the essence of all mystical traditions. The intermediate experiences, such as peak experiences, psi phenomena, and flashes of intuition—are but brief, enticing reminders of the larger whole.

To reconcile the natural sciences, psi phenomena, and the Perennial Philosophy, the issue of nonlocality and fundamental interconnectiveness must be addressed. One's consciousness can reflect sensitivity to nonlinear change, multidimensionality, and nonlocal interconnectiveness. Therefore, to fully understand consciousness the findings of the natural sciences and relevant aspects of the Perennial Philosophy should be unified. Without such a unification, we are doomed to repeat the dualism of the past.

A completely nondualistic theory of consciousness necessitates an appreciation of our place in the universe. A few theorists have advocated for what has been referred to as the "strong anthropomorphic principle," which suggests that the laws of nature include some place/time for consciousness. In other words, nature has organized itself toward self-awareness. John Wheeler has noted that we are in a participatory universe. We are part of the universe looking back on itself (see Figure 8.1). In fact, given that we are an aspect of an evolving universe, not only has the universe become conscious of itself but it has also become aware of its unity.

However, some have erroneously proposed that we as conscious beings are an irreplaceable part of the universe. For example, according to John Wheeler and Eugene Wigner, the collapse of the wave function (described in Chapter 6) is the result of the crucial ingredient of consciousness. I feel that this perspective is grossly anthropomorphic and tends toward dualism. Before the emergence of humanity what was around to collapse the wave function? Taking such a position emphasizes primarily anthropomorphic top-down causation. We, as conscious beings, are not the cause of everything. As I have made clear earlier, both top-down and bottom-up causation occur. Humans have an influence on, as well as have been caused by, the natural world. We are participants in an expanding universe and not independent from it.

Figure 8.1
The Universe Looking Back on Itself. Based on John Wheeler's original illustration.

INTERCONNECTIVITY AND NONLOCALITY

The contribution of physics to the understanding of consciousness is in many ways highly theoretical. Yet how can one hope to understand transpersonal phenomena if one cannot explain the nonlocal connectiveness that these phenomena imply? The fact that all systems are part of one macrosystem likewise cries out for a unified theory.

As I have demonstrated throughout this book, determinism, reductionism, and dualism cannot provide the explanations we seek. To explain the transpersonal aspects of consciousness, a nondeterministic and nondualistic model of the connectiveness between matter and consciousness is called for. To construct such a model, we must move away from linear causality toward an appreciation of self-organization, bidirectional causality, and nonlocality.

A visual and graphic illustration of nonlocality was offered by Roger Penrose through the use of "tiles" (Figure 8.2).[1] From this perspective the tiles are globally self-organized into a pattern of interconnected relationships. To construct these tiles, one necessarily has to examine the state of the pattern away from the position of assembly. The point of Penrose's tiles is that the position of each tile is determined not by the adjacent tiles, but by the pattern as a whole. The phenomenon of nonlocality is the most dramatic example of the interconnectiveness of all systems. Nothing is separate from, and independent of, the whole.

In quantum theory the work of the late David Bohm has relevance to the issue of nonlocality. Bohm and his colleague Basil Hiley note that quantum mechanics is an epistemotology—a theory of knowing how we know what we know. They argue that quantum theory must also offer an ontology—a theory of what is. Their ontological interpretation of quantum theory emphasizes nonlocal connectivity in which particles are seen as part of an undivided wholeness. According to this theory, all observations of the quantum dimension constitute a complementary part of the fundamental whole. Essentially, it is not possible for a quantum object to have an independent existence apart from the greater whole.

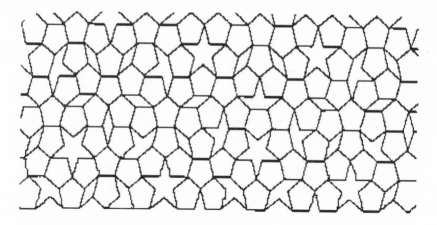

Figure 8.2
The Penrose Tiles, with the Fivefold Symmetry

Bohm and Hiley propose that nonlocality is the result of what Bohm has called "quantum potential." According to this model "pools of information" guide particles to act in a nonlocal manner.[2] Quantum potential connects distant particles.[3]

Essentially, the "form" contains a small amount of active information, which affects the larger system by creating a greater energy flow. Order is context-dependent and is in a fluid state of transition.[4] Therefore, according to the concept of quantum potential, action depends on form, not just the magnitude of the forces between particles. This is a perspective that appreciates the environmental context of the quantum state of the whole system, including time. Thus, the interaction between particles is nonlinear and nonlocal.[5]

For consciousness, these subtle fluctuations can take place on many levels. As discussed in Chapter 6, the convergence of significant life events and psi-type experiences represents both the fluidity and interconnectivity of consciousness. These convergent points are context dependent. From this perspective, consciousness and quantum theory have the implicate order in common.[6] To illustrate how consciousness and the implicate order are connected Bohm and Hiley use the metaphor of listening to music. At any given moment one can identify a note; however, previous notes are "reverberating" in consciousness. Simultaneously, one can anticipate how the movement of the notes will unfold. We appreciate music in its entirety. Some musical geniuses such as Mozart could hear an entire symphony in their mind before writing it down.

Language also provides a cognitive perception of order, and its meaning is dependent upon context. Given the fundamental interconnectiveness of all aspects of the universe, everything that happens has some sort of order and some sort of significance. While many events appear in isolation, they appear to have meaning when considered in the context of the macrosystem. Bohm argues that in Western culture there is a perceptual compulsion to fragment the whole.[7] As Semanticist Alfred Korzybski has also noted, using nouns such as "rain" or "waves" tends to bind cognition to breaks or fragments. Using the verb instead of the noun more accurately describes the process of flux.[8]

Chaos can therefore be seen as a subtle type of order within the broader context of what Bohm referred to as the "holomovement." The concept of holomovement seeks to explain a dynamic interrelationship between matter and mind. Both are reflections of mutually enfolding aspects of the evolving universe.

Bohm differentiates between two types of order. He defines explicate order as the surface structure of parts, and implicate order as the underlying and interconnected whole. The latter is "enfolded" and preexistent within the former.[9] That is, it is the fundamental reality.[10] Bohm used the hologram to illustrate the concept of enfoldment. A hologram is comprised of many discrete photographic images. Each of these explicate parts are unfolded within the overall image made by the collective composition of all of the discrete images. This concept is analogous to the Gestalt concept of the whole being greater than the sum of its parts.

Bohm postulates the existence of a still more subtle form of order, "superimplicate order." To understand superimplicate order, one must dispel the notion that particles are the fundamental reality and instead think in terms of fields of potential. Superquantum potential underlies the movement of these fields, "informing" them through the enfolding process. Superquantum potential "will sweep in energy from the whole field," thereby exhibiting nonlocality.[11]

On a neuronal system level, Karl Pribram's "Holonomic" theory of brain functioning compliments Bohm's "implicate" holism.[12] Just as Bohm has proposed that the metaphor of a hologram constitutes the larger infinite holographic universe, so Pribram has proposed that memory is contained holographically on a nonlocal basis in the brain.[13]

In Pribram's model, the explicate order in the Bohmian sense, corresponding to things visually sensed, is conceived of as reflecting local and causal interactions. Thus, it is consistent with Newtonian dynamics. The implicate order, corresponding to holistic forms, supersedes and encompasses all subsystems. Thus, it is characterized by quantum nonlocality.

From this perspective, thoughts can be regarded as explicit forms. Accordingly, a single element in space-time contains a reflection of the implicate order. Given the overlap between cognitive/emotional processes and objective events in one's life, synchronicities are associated with major transitions in one's life. Synchronicities most often occur when one is highly focused on change or is engaged in a deeply meaningful activity.[14] These situations are highly organized patterns of convergent subjective and objective life experiences.

For example, if one makes a major move or gets married, he or she may coincidentally hear from an old friend who was once a lover just prior to the marriage. Or just prior to a move he or she may receive a letter inviting the person to apply for a position in a different locality.

Synchronicities are "internal restructuring" occurrences that "produce external resonance."[15] The significance of these occurrences may resonate on many levels simultaneously. In this sense, there is a perception of order harmonized on many levels. Synchronicities illustrate how macrosystem dynamics "unfold," or are expressed, in individual situations. Seen from another point of view, the macrosystem is enfolded within the microsystem. A synchronicity is a unification of objective events and subjective experience. In other words, neither kind of experience causes the other; both are unified patterns of creation. They are different aspects of the same process.

Converging interactions can be seen as an aspect of evolutionary processes. Interestingly, the discovery of the use of fire by *Homo erectus* appears to have occurred simultaneously throughout the inhabited world, from Africa to China. This anomaly is probably not attributed to trade or shared culture. Another broad synchronicity is the simultaneous appearance of the "golden age" philosophies in Greece, India, and China. These converging patterns are nonlocal aspects of the evolution of our species.

To deal with such anomalies, Rupert Sheldrake differentiates between what he terms "energetic causation" and "formative causation."[16] Energetic causation is local. It takes place in a manner in which the causal interactions are relatively easy to identify. Energetic causation is an attribute of traditional science which values quantitative relationships. Formative causation is nonlocal. It can occur in regions irrespective of location. Formative causation involves qualitative relationships.

Sheldrake proposed the concept of the "morphogenetic field" to account for what appear to be noncausal relationships. A morphogenetic field is a nonlocal evolving form. Within this field, information is stored that relates to the form of the organism, and development is determined by this information. It is "morphogenetic resonance" that makes possible the same type of organismic development noncausally along a given pathway.

Sheldrake often uses the example of the historic behavior of a species of bird called the blue tit. Reportedly, prior to World War II in England, the blue tit had developed the practice of tearing off the foil cap on milk bottles. To the frustration of many, the birds got to the milk bottles right after delivery in the morning. However, the war halted deliveries. When the deliveries were resumed in the late 1940s all of the birds that were alive before the war had died. Yet, somehow the practice of taking caps off the milk bottles reappeared relatively quickly. Sheldrake claims that no learning could have taken place and the practice resonated within the species' morphogenetic field.

However, there is an element of dualism in the concept of morphogenetic fields and this concept implies one-directional causality. But in fact, causality is bidirectional, multidimensional, and nonlinear. Nor can the concept of morphogenetic fields explain how organisms evolve. Formative causation cannot account for evolutionary processes, because it relies exclusively on species memory and pure resonance without involving energy.[17] In other words, formative causation is thought of as an immaterial process. Since matter contains energy there is no room for an exploration of how matter/energy evolves.

Nevertheless, Bohm's concept of quantum potential is similar to Sheldrake's concept of morphogenetic fields. Therefore, both have heuristic value. Quantum potential and morphogenetic fields both act, in effect, like "guide waves" which inform and affect motion.[18] Since the information potential is extremely complex, the resulting movement appears indeterministic and chaotic.

To account for the convergent phenomena in evolution, there needs to be "creative feedback" and memory. The field concept, with its holographic pattern-conserving properties, allows for self-consistency. System theorist Ervin Laszlo has proposed that the new emerging paradigm emphasizes "unified interactive dynamics."[19] This is an attempt to unify physics, biology, and consciousness. The unresolved problems in the physical sciences—such as the EPR paradox, wave/particle duality, Pauli's Antisymmetry Principle, the problem of recurring forms in evolution, and the issue of psi phenomena—are all aspects of unified interactive dynamics and of interconnectivity.

Laszlo proposed that the unified interactive dynamics occur in the quantum vacuum, which lies at the very root of the universe. The quantum vacuum is named so paradoxically because far from an empty space, it is filled with "virtual" particles. In quantum field theory the quantum vacuum is thought to be filled with energy fluctuations that result in actual particles. Laszlo hypothesizes that the quantum vacuum is an energy-filled pleunum where potential energies interact. Because the interactions are so sensitive, extremely subtle fluctuations can cause a nonlinear change in the interdependent systems.[20] Since humans are part of the interdependent systems that make up the biosphere we can be conscious of these interactions.

According to Laszlo's model the brain may enlarge the bandwidth during altered states of consciousness, which would allow for indiscriminate sensitivity. Support for this view comes from recent research that shows electroencephalograph (EEG) measurements of both hemispheres to be more synchronized during some altered states of consciousness. Furthermore, synchronization often occurs between individuals. As their respective individual EEG patterns are synchronized, the two patterns also become synchronized with each other.[21]

The action potentials of neurons may be affected by fluctuations in the quantum vacuum. Owing to the extreme sensitivity and chaotic nature of the brain, these fluctuations alter the firing patterns of groups of neurons and create a butterfly effect that alters the state of consciousness. This may explain how the brain can be sensitive to nonlocal sensitivity, such as has been described as transpersonal experiences.

Transpersonal sensitivity implies that aspects of the universe are subtly interconnected. As I noted in Chapters 4 and 6, mystics throughout history have experienced this interconnectivity directly. How and through what neurophysiological process does this occur?

The spiritual nature of consciousness may be facilitated by dendritic microprocessing in the frontolimbic forebrain. Stimulation of this system may result in an intuitive experience of the holographic nature of the universe.[22] This might explain why telepathy is frequently facilitated by an emotional bond between people. The cognitive, emotional, and frontolimbic aspects of the brain are harmonized, increasing one's sensitivity to higher levels of transpersonal organization and interconnectivity.

There also appears to be some kind of process that involves coherence effects akin to the Fröhlich phenomena, Bose-Einstein condensates, and general nonlocal effects described in Chapter 6. In the wet, warm, and chaotic brain this nonlocal sensitivity results from the conscious experience of "global coherence"—the feeling of being at one with the biosphere.

To retrace the steps taken in earlier chapters, the experience of a cohesive sense of self is the collective result of a synthesis of multiple subsystems (i.e., biophysiological and intrapsychic). This self system is a dynamic and self-organizing higher level of organization than its constituent subsystems. Just as water is a different level of organization than one part of oxygen and two parts of hydrogen, so is the self system on a higher level of organization than the sum total of the firing patterns in the brain. Just as water interacts with other natural forces in the biosphere, so too does the self system interact with others and the environment in which they thrive.

Though this cohesive sense of self allows for individual subjective experience, the self system is still a part of a larger biosphere with interdependent bidirectional interactions. The self system therefore is a field of self-referential information that not only provides a cohesive sense of self but can also be sensitive to systems outside of oneself.

Given that we have an uncanny ability to sense the emotional state in another individual, and experience the result of that interaction, intermittent nonlocal transpersonal experience may also occur, especially during periods of emotional significance to both individuals. Our sensitivity to our interconnectiveness is this crux of transpersonal experience.

THE ARROW OF TIME

The illusive issue of time has rarely been addressed in theories of consciousness. This is a serious omission. Time in a broad sense needs to be addressed when making an attempt to understand our experience of time and how consciousness evolves in time.

Throughout history we have developed a variety of concepts of time. The cyclical concept of time was inherent to most prescientific societies. This concept involved the belief in an "eternal return"—the return to the roots of creation. This belief made current life experiences relevant to the unity of the society in the context of the creation myth—the concept of historical time that pulled the frame of reference away from an eternal return. Whereas the concept of eternal return allowed earlier societies to develop rituals to reenact the return to creation, the concept of historic time implied movement progressively away from primitive conditions. In Judeo-Christian-Islamic societies historical time had an end point—heaven or hell. In this sense there is a continual adherence to the concept of eternal return—to God. Also, because of the unfortunate concept of original sin, theologians needed to resolve the problem that this concept created. To ameliorate the problem they incorporated the archetypal myths of rebirth. In the Christian world the concept of Christmas and Easter allowed for a reverence for the "rebirth" or "resurrection"—the archetypal theme of eternal return.

In the sciences the residual concept of cyclical time was converted into the notion of time reversibility.[23] The time symmetry or reversibility is fundamental to Newtonian dynamics, relativity theory, and early quantum theory. Time reversibility is also consistent with determinism and linear causality. In other words, if you move back the clock all the "mechanics" would reverse. However, living beings are not mechanical and time is asymmetrical—it moves toward the future. Living beings change irreversibly. Time asymmetry, therefore, conflicts with the notions of determinism and linear causality. The future is not predetermined—we have a hand to play in the making of our own future.

Up to this point, I have discussed the importance of viewing consciousness from a nondeterministic perspective. Consciousness is the result of bidirectional causality, and a reflection of systemic nonlocal field phenomena. The picture emerging is one in which individuals can be conscious of nonlocal and nonlinear change.

As I noted in Chapter 1, Alfred North Whitehead has argued that Western philosophy has been marked by "the fallacy of misplaced concreteness." Process Philosophy has emphasized that time and temporality are the "ultimate features of reality."[24] Therefore, according to Process Philosophy, concreteness has a temporal reality; yet in the world of explicate forms, things exist only during specific periods of time. John Wheeler noted that time is nature's way of keeping everything from happening at once. Furthermore, as space-time configurations evolve, living systems, such as ourselves, actualize our potential. Evolution cannot occur without time.

Ilya Prigogine has proposed that time is the "forgotten dimension," for the arrow of time "carries, pushes, or pulls" all phenomena toward higher and higher levels of organization.[25] This process is especially evident in matter and energy far-from-equilibrium, in which open systems are able to seek out ever-higher levels of organization. Without time coevolution is not possible. In fact, nonlinear reactions can be globalized and can have interdependent nonlocal effects.[26] In other words, coevolving living systems, such as ourselves, can have nonlocal relationships.

Given that aspects of the universe are interconnected, time reflects this interconnectivity. It follows that, because consciousness is also an aspect of the evolving universe, it is fundamentally interconnected with time. The asymmetry of time implies a fundamental directional movement in the evolution of consciousness. Our species will never again replicate the consciousness of *Homo habilis*.

Since the expansion of the universe and the increase in entropy are associated with the arrow of time, the "entropy barrier" makes it impossible to move backward in time.[27] The evolution of the universe prevents us from reversing time. For example, in the case of hypnotic age regression, we find that while one can remember earlier experiences, these memories are colored by one's subsequent experiences. It is not possible to move backward in time as if in a bubble sealed off from the present. The fundamental issue here is whether one can disconnect from, and operate independently of, one's position in space-time and one's inter-connectivity with the rest of the universe. In other words, if all aspects of the universe are interconnected in an ultimate holomovement, how can one simulta-neously be a part of and apart from this totality? The available evidence suggests that one cannot. Stephen Hawking once joked that time machines must not be possible because we have not been invaded by tourists from the future.

But if one cannot move backward in time, does this preclude perceiving events in the future? That is, does it preclude so-called precognition? As we have seen, the research related to precognition has been inconsistent and inconclusive at best. However, there have been *some* positive results. Anecdotally, people have reported intuitively feeling something specific were to happen before in fact it does happen. One can regard these infrequent positive results as reflecting the sensitive perception of initial macrosystem conditions and the projection of the evolution of these systems into the future through the arrow of time. In other words, one may be so conscious of interconnections that she may also sense po-tential results of the coevolution of the interconnections. Being conscious of the interconnective potential of events in the future is not the same as moving into the future and reporting back in the present what one had seen.

From the perspective of this new paradigm, time is inherently asymmetrical. In other words, the arrow of time moves inherently toward the future. Accord-ingly, from this perspective we can conceive of a nonlocally unified time-asymmetric universe.

This has important implications for consciousness. The lack of the restriction inherent in determinism permits conscious self-organization, or free will. From this perspective, one "participates" in determining one's own future. But the new paradigm has still broader implications. It offers us the opportunity to reconcile useful aspects of the Perennial Philosophy and contemporary developments in the natural sciences. We can now shift to a nonlinear evolutionary perspective— one in which time asymmetry and nonlocality are seen as factors affecting con-sciousness.

EVOLUTIONARY THEOLOGY

No theology, Eastern or Western, offers a coherent description of the process of change *and* an evolutionary perspective. Without such a balanced perspective we are unable to understand consciousness. Approximately half a century ago, Einstein commented that "science without religion is lame, and religion without science is blind." The two must be reconciled to give overall meaning to the evolution of consciousness. Indeed, this reconciliation hinges on the evolution-ary process.

One theorist who attempted a synthesis of religion and evolutionary science was Pierre Teilhard de Chardin. In mid-1930s, Teilhard de Chardin, a Jesuit priest and anthropologist, was involved in the *Homo erectus* finds at Chouk-outein, China. As a result of this "blasphemous" work, the Catholic Church forbade him to publish. However, at the highest levels the evolutionary perspective was not opposed, as they did not want to repeat the Galileo debacle.[28]

In his *Phenomenon of Man*, published posthumously, Teilhard de Chardin speculated how evolutionary theory and theology might be synthesized into an overall philosophy. This inspiring work is highly relevant to our view of the evolution of consciousness.[29] Though his technical understanding of the evolutionary process is dated, the general premise is metaphorically appealing. According to this view, the biophysical aspects of evolution have been superseded by a dramatic leap toward self-consciousness on the part of human beings. As a result of this leap, we humans have a conscious role to play in our own evolution.

From Teilhard de Chardin's perspective, all evolution is directed toward the convergence of consciousness at the transcendental "omega point" where spirit and matter are one.[30] He equates this convergence with the final communion with God. Though it is not his view, I view God, or the omega point, as the totality of the universe itself. Rather than the God of Spinoza, or some deterministic theological conception of "timelessness and stillness" or a "void," the universe that we are part of is an evolving universe. Though we experience it as stillness and timelessness, this may be an illusion perpetuated by our position in space-time. In other words, that which is greater than ourselves only appears timeless, owing to our preoccupation with our own evolution.

Look up at the night sky. There are perhaps 200 billion stars in our galaxy and as many as 100 billion galaxies in the universe. We are but a minute speck on a planet, in a solar system, in an average size galaxy, and in an immense universe. Thus, the conscious experience of stillness is relative to our limited experience within the immense totality.

Ultimately all aspects of nature are directed toward an evolutionary process enfolded in God, the omega point, Brahman, or the implicate order. Therefore, the earth, living systems, and matter have a sacramental quality. This is because the fundamental interconnectivity inherent in the universe demands the recognition of interdependence and respect.

If all is in a state of flux, viewing transitional phenomena—such as things or thoughts—as independent entities merely serves to fragment consciousness. Since all is in flux, it is the evolutionary process itself that binds all phenomena in a fundamental interdependence. The only fundamental reality is the evolving totality. This absolute can be regarded as God, Brahman, or the universe, and all of the particulars in transition, including ourselves, can be regarded merely as evolving aspects of God, Brahman, or the universe.

Attempts to differentiate oneself from this process fragment experience and move one toward a closed self system. On the other hand, attempts to become sensitive to interconnectivity move one in the other direction, toward openness, and toward closer to harmony with God. Christ and the Buddha best exemplify this latter process.

We are at the stage in our evolution in which consciousness can reach out beyond the self system and embrace with compassion living systems and the universe as a whole. So spirituality is the transpersonal experience of compassionate connectivity. Spirituality is the energetic unity between individuals and the bio-sphere. It is love and compassion that facilitate unity—a love and compassion uncomplicated by possessiveness, but rather marked by selflessness and open-ness to the collective whole.

In the early Christian, rather than the later Christian, system of thought (I re-fer to it as Churchianity), the injunctions to love thy neighbor, turn the other cheek, and care for the poor and disadvantaged provide theorems for a higher level of organization. Not only is caring for others and promoting resolution adaptive, but it makes possible a leap to a higher level of existence. Empathetic openness to others allows one to transcend one's own self system and merge with the greater whole. Such transpersonal consciousness coevolves with macrosys-tems and the enhancement systems at all levels. From this perspective, sin can be regarded as the act of assaulting the macrosystem in which one is embedded. In other words, behaving with pathological narcissism and exploiting others ulti-mately causes suffering for our species. Thus, behaving selfishly reaps poor species Karma. Collectively, we have to pay the price (Karma) of these "sins" through crime, war, and pollution.

The religious mystics whose philosophies have served as attractors for socio-theological systems responded to this principal attractor of consciousness—interconnectivity. Their mystical experiences involved the compassionate per-ception of interdependence.

An evolutionary theology takes all aspects of evolution into account. It takes into account the biophysical, sociocultural, and self systems as well as the sub-suming transpersonal dynamics. Because the arrow of time permits evolution at all levels, the appreciation of universal interconnectiveness enhances and defines the evolutionary theology.

In Einstein's rebuttal to the fundamental unpredictability of quantum theory, he argued that "God does not play dice." Roughly a century before him Ralph Waldo Emerson wrote, "The dice of God is always loaded."[31] Perhaps the "loaded" quality of the "dice" for us is the hidden effect of free will, balanced by the systemic and interdependent conditions we find ourselves within. Each indi-vidual is born into his or her unique existential position, or initial conditions. But though each individual's consciousness reflects the turbulence within each of our lives, we have the free will and responsibility to act as part of an interdependent whole.

Since there is a nonlocal connecting fabric that binds all beings within the larger macrosystem, we are subsumed by it at death. Actually, we are never apart from the cosmic matrix that produces us. But perhaps at death our attachment to biophysical, sociocultural, and self systems is shaken, and the resulting chaos precipitates a leap to a higher level of consciousness. Perhaps this inclusive sensitivity, in turn, precipitates a leap to a higher level of awareness—an aware-ness of our real place in the universe—our interdependence. Such an awareness has been described as an aspect of the near-death experience. In such far-from-equilibrium speculation, one might even ask whether different individuals have different "spiritual evolutionary" histories. If so, perhaps the energy of highly evolved individuals, such as Christ and the Buddha, is widely absorbed into the consciousness of others. It is possible that this attracting interconnective energy may promote evolution at all levels.

Notes

CHAPTER 1: THEN AND NOW

1. Kuhn, 1967.

2. Arden, 1996.

3. The term "transpersonal" has a variety of definitions depending on the context and the author. What I mean by the term transpersonal in this context refers to an experience that the individual cannot identify as having caused by himself. This experience would conceivably be beyond the normal sensory processes. I will elaborate on this issue later in the book.

4. Nevertheless, it is interesting to note that the earth-centered model was initially proposed by the Greeks almost two thousand years earlier. For several centuries and through the Middle Ages, Greek thought had not been widely accessible in Western Europe. In contrast, the Arab world had embraced Greek thought and had flourished in science, philosophy, and medicine. Unfortunately, the Arab world incurred an invasion by the Turks. As a result, much of the cultural fertility became neutralized. The European Renaissance was partly fueled by the reintroduction of Greek thought.

5. What makes the Church's initial intransigence even more intriguing was that neither Jesus nor any other prophet had argued for an earth centered model. The Church adopted the model because it fit well with its creation myth as presented in the book of Genesis. This dogmatic intransigence exemplifies how belief systems rigidify and themselves become susceptible to sudden change.

6. In the Greek city of Ephesus, Heraclitus (500 B.C.E.) expounded his philosophy of infinite flux, and Parmenides lived in Elea in what is now southern Italy around 475 B.C.E.

7. Quoted in Hyland, 1973, p. 156.

8. Parmenides argued that nothing can change into something it is not. The concept of becoming was alien to him. From this we can surmise that for him time was irrelevant and an illusion.

9. Because Plato adhered to the concept of the unchanging reality introduced by Parmenides, his concept of ideal forms was static. From this perspective there is no room for an evolutionary emphasis.

10. If we take the concept of Plato's ideal forms and modify it by an evolutionary perspective we can appreciate the concept of levels of organization. I will expand on this concept in Chapter 2 when discussing advances in evolutionary theory.

11. Whitehead, 1925.

12. Idealism, realism, correspondence theory, and coherence theory can also be referred back to Plato (Mahoney, 1991).

13. In some ways it is unfortunate that Plato and Socrates took issue with the Sophist view of relativism. By doing so they overemphasized objectivism.

14. Aristotle, like Plato, split off "reason" from emotions. In his *On the Soul, Sense and Sensbila, On Memory and Recollection,* and *On Sleep and Waking* he argued that reason is autonomous. Yet reason (*nous*) affects the heart. According to Aristotle the heart, not the brain, was the site of mental phenomena. Within the heart there can occur a fusion of thought and emotion. Aristotle also differed from Plato with respect to the concept of the soul. He argued that the soul is tied to the body. In contrast, Plato was a dualist.

15. Ryle, 1949.

16. Dennett, 1991.

17. Husserl (1931) is often regarded as one of the founders of phenomenology. Like Freud and James, he studied for a time under Franz Brentano. In many ways, Brentano's ideas supported phenomenology as he regarded introspection and personal experience as crucially important. Husserl himself was also influenced by Descartes' emphasis on radical self-doubt and introspection.

18. Heidegger actually denied being an existentialist himself. The term "existentialist" was coined by Jean-Paul Sartre. Heidegger probably wanted to be remembered as an advocate of a unique philosophy. Heidegger and Sartre shared the view that each individual inherits a unique set of circumstances over which he or she has no control. It is each person's responsibility to make the best of those circumstances. Therefore, free will is available and if one does not exercise it constructively, one sentences oneself to a bleak existence. It is interesting to note that when it came to ethical responsibility, unfortunately Heidegger himself became associated with the Nazi regime in Germany. He did not move to distance himself from their oppression. In fact, he assumed Husserl's university teaching position after the latter had been let go because of Jewish heritage.

19. Heidegger takes Husserl's phenomenology and introduces the concept of "dasein." He defined dasein as representing one's "being in the world." He charges Plato and the other Greek philosophers with being the original advocates of the split from the source of "being" to focus on "beings out there." For example, Heidegger (1927) proposed that each person is "thrown into the world at a unique place and time"—our dasein or "being there." Also important is what he refers to as *umwelt* or "being in the world." It is our responsibility to work within the constraints of our actual condition and make the best of it. Not doing so leads to falling into existential despair or disappointment with oneself. In his now classic *Being and Time* he proposed that the transcendental capacity is associated with our ability to project into the future. This temporal openness allows for a sense of being. Heidegger argued that Western consciousness had moved away from a sense of wonder and "awe" of our existence in the world. He stressed that the "isness" or being had been ignored in awareness because of the "chatter" and the "busyness" of our daily lives. Such shallow lives are thought to be inauthentic.

20. The French structuralist perspective has brought attention to the significance between "signs" and the variety of meanings that can be represented. The context dependent theme of the Post-Modernism of Ferdinand de Saussure has emphasized the signified and the signifier as important variables. This "difference" is dependent on a variety of other signs. The distinction between the signified and the signifier is represented by the S/S

initials. For example, the letters in these words are the signifiers and the signified corresponding to the meaning of words represented in the mind. The variety of meanings corresponding to the variety of contexts. Derrida stresses the importance of "the process of differentiation," or "difference." Accordingly, difference is an "eternal activity" of nature. His "critique of the presence" corresponds to the play of the differences. Synthesis and referral allow there to be experience of the present. Each element functions as a sign which is referred to as a trace of "linkage to the other elements."

21. In fact, Whitehead argued that the world is internally determined and externally free. He maintained that our choices are "self-determined" because conditioning or influence takes place. There is no strict determinism. Turning to Einstein for inspiration, Whitehead postulated that within a four dimensional universe one can perceive reality from different spatial and temporal positions. Therefore, one can describe reality only from a relativistic position. In 1925 he proposed that every "actual entity" should be seen as organically related to its own environment. Whitehead has argued that there is a creative movement of the universe toward an endless development of new syntheses.

22. Actually, Whitehead noted that these two varieties of monists (those that put mind inside matter and those that put matter inside mind) produce confusion.

23. This is what Whitehead (1929) called the "fallacy of simple location."

24. Like Friedrich Hegel before him, Whitehead postulates a philosophy of unity. Yet, Hegel's system was too all-inclusive for its time. Without current scientific insights now available it was inevitably incomplete. Unlike Hegel, however, he does not point to dialectic conflict but rather to "process" as the dynamic of change. Here Whitehead points to the interaction between God and the world, flux and permanence, subjective and objective, conceiving the relationship between these mutually indispensable aspects of reality as a single totality, a single reality. In his review of both philosophers Immanuel Kant and David Hume, Whitehead argues that they have a limited, one-dimensional view of perception. He called their model "presentational immediacy." I put the emphasis on the word *"immediacy"* because this mode in many ways is materialistic, sterile, and lacking dimension. Whitehead offers what he refers to as "causal efficacy" to describe the gray areas of dreaming fantasy and nonordinary states of consciousness as well as ordinary states. Whitehead's view of consciousness is most consistent with the nonlinear perspective outlined in this book.

CHAPTER 2: EVOLUTION AND CHAOS

1. Benjamin Disraeli, speech—on November 25, 1864, at the Diocesan Conference, Oxford.

2. Darwin had proposed, for example, that evolution occurs on a gradual basis. Perhaps he needed to adhere to the zeitgeist of "progressive gradualism" associated with the Industrial Revolution. This term described technological advances as the result of steady technological innovations gradually accumulated.

3. In biology the metaphors often used include: fitness, emergence, survival, struggle, and effort. Goodwin points out that there is a move underway in biology to incorporate metaphors from modern physics. These metaphors include; least action, interaction, and least effort. Even the concept of equilibrium is now in question. These metaphors are in contrast to the Newtonian/Cartesian clockwork dynamics and perhaps the Judeo-Christian concept of a preconceived order. In the new physics (as described in Chapter 6) particles are not seen as discrete objects that are acted upon by forces but rather parts of an interconnected process. In this sense, the new paradigm involves physics looking more like biology and biology looking more like physics. The emphasis is on interaction,

emergence, interdependence, and organization.

4. To achieve maximum growth and development organisms must cooperate in addition to competing. Organisms are organized as cohesive evolving forms. It is the relational order and the way that the parts cooperate that is of issue here, not just random selection of various genes.

5. Goodwin has noted that the selfish gene approach is similar to the metaphors offered by the Christian fundamentalists. For example, in many Christian fundamentalist traditions humanity is seen as condemned to a life of conflict and perpetual toil; it nevertheless possesses a selfish spirit.

6. In a recent letter Brian Goodwin suggested that I include this clarification of the relationship of genes to evolution.

7. Goodwin, 1994, p. xxi.

8. Stephen Jay Gould also argues that we should "put this concept of the organism back into evolutionary biology" (Gould, 1982, p. 144, in Brockman, 1995).

9. Stuart Kauffman (1993) has described the rich source of relational order within living systems that aids in their evolution as coming from the species itself. This is a different approach than the natural selection model offers. According to the natural selection model organisms adapt to changes in the environment as if they are "survival machines." Within the new model, organisms are seen as having intrinsic order. This order is emergent from the complex interactions between the elements of an organism. In other words, there are intrinsic and complex dynamics within each organism that allow it to reproduce and self-organize. For example, how can some organisms regenerate a missing limb or a tail without this intrinsic order?

10. Maturana and Varela, 1987, p. 47.

11. Von Bertalanffy, 1968.

12. Many authors have referred to the amount of order in a system as "negentropy."

13. Prigogine and Stengers, 1984.

14. One of the initial contributors to chaos theory, Mitchell Feigenbaum of Los Alamos Laboratory, found that two numbers occurred over and over again in his mathematical calculations. He discovered that 4.669201 and 2.5029 were found frequently (quoted in Gleick, 1987).

15. Story told in Gleick, 1987.

16. Chaos theory is now a subset of complexity theory. Kauffman notes that with the evolution of complex systems there is convergent flow as well as divergent flow. Complex systems have learned to balance convergence and divergence. Borrowing a phrase from chaos theorist Norman Packard, Kauffman and Goodwin note that complex system are "poised between order and chaos."

17. Gell-Mann, quoted in Lewin, 1994, p. 14.

18. Gell-Mann, 1994.

19. Quoted in Lewin, 1994

20. Ibid.

21. Goodwin, 1994.

22. Jantsch, 1980.

23. Mammals emerged during the period of a single land-mass known as Pangaea. This occurred after the development of monotremes and marsupials, but placentas developed after Australia broke off from the larger land-mass. This resulted in the overwhelming preponderance of monotremes and marsupials without placentas in Australia.

24. Donald, 1991.

25. All evidence suggests that hominids (human-like species) emerged in Africa. The Great Rift Valley has provided the wealth of the hominid fossils. It was formed as the result of the collision between the Eurasian and the African continents. This upturning of

land exposed several layers of geological history.

26. The term "hominid" is a derivative of "hominidae," which includes all earlier human-like subspecies.

27. Savich and Wilson, 1967.

28. It was Gordon Gallup (1970) who first noted that chimpanzees are capable of recognizing themselves in mirrors and using the image to explore parts of their bodies. This is in contrast to various species of monkeys and other apes that are unable to demonstrate this capacity. Gallup (1977) went on to propose that this ability demonstrates that chimpanzees are capable of a certain level of self-awareness, and that this ability to perceive themselves allows them to infer what similar experience might be like in other organisms. As Povinelli (1993) has pointed out, the relationship that Gallup has made between chimpanzees' ability for self-recognition and the developmental process of humans in childhood to do the same relates to the later development of social communication. For example, children aged eighteen to twenty months are capable of self-recognition but are not yet apparently cognizant of the mental experiences of others. Interestingly, chimpanzees do not show the ability for self-recognition until age six. Self-representation has incredible adaptive value. It allows for a flexible problem-solving approach and permits planning and foresight.

29. White, 1994.

30. Johanson and Edey, 1981.

31. *Australopithecus boisei* appears to have specialized to such a degree on a diet of coarse vegetation that it developed a sagittal crest, or bony ridge on the top of its head, to attach the massive jaw muscles needed to chew the roughage.

32. Shipman, 1986.

33. Corballis, 1991.

34. Fagan (1990) notes that the tools manufactured and used by *erectus* have been referred to as "Acheulian" based on the site in St. Acheul, France where the characteristic hand axes were first discovered. The Acheulian tool culture disappeared with the disappearance of *erectus* 100,000 years ago.

35. The Sahara Desert served as a barrier between Europe, the Levant, and sub-Saharan Africa. Yet during the interglacial periods to the north the Sahara was grassland periodically and as recently as 8000 years ago. The Sahara can be thought of as a pump that pulled various animal species and hominids during the wetter cyclical climate and pushed them out during the more arid periods. It may have aided *Homo erectus* 900,000 years ago in the initial mass migration out of Africa and then perhaps 90,000 years ago with *Homo sapien sapiens* (Fagan, 1990).

36. The *Homo erectus* find at Choukoutein in China dates to approximately 500,000 years ago, while the *erectus* find in Java dates to approximately 700,000 years ago. We know that at least at the Choukoutein site fire was utilized and perhaps cannibalism was practiced. At this site over forty skulls were found that indicated some type of heavy blow to the head was incurred by the victims. Also, it appears that the large bones were broken presumably to get at the bone marrow. In one skull it was found that the foramen magnum at the base of the skull was broken presumably to get at the brain.

37. Donald, 1991.

38. The Neanderthal cranium included a "bun shape" toward the rear of the head. Neanderthals also had a sloping forehead. It appears that their skeletal structure allowed for a robust musculature. They were capable of withstanding the cold climate as it appears that they were structured to contain warmth.

39. William Howells differentiated between two theoretical clusters that attempt to describe the emergence of *Homo sapien sapiens*. He called them: the Candelabra and the Noah's Ark Hypothesis. The Candelabra approach envisions all of the subspecies of

hominids as being a linearly arranged evolutionary sequence of stages resulting ultimately in *Homo sapien sapiens*. This evolutionary sequence occurred in parallel in the three continents of the Eastern Hemisphere, Africa, Europe, and Asia. In contrast the Noah's Ark model envisions there being an explosion in colonization of *Homo sapien sapiens* from Africa. Because it was more advanced it succeeded in a more successful adaptation than the more specialized subspecies of Neanderthals and *Homo sapien sapiens*.

40. Donald, 1991.
41. Arden, 1996.

CHAPTER 3: THE SELF SYSTEM

1. Quoted in *Life* magazine, August 21, 1961.
2. A few decades ago the philosopher Karl Popper drew attention to three different dimensions of understanding. He regarded these three "worlds" as levels of existence. The first world represents the physical world. The second world represents states of consciousness of individuals. Finally, the third world knowledge is derived from historical and sociocultural influences. He suggested that there is a dynamic interaction between the individual (world 2) and the sociocultural system (world 3). In this chapter I will demonstrate that this is in fact the case. However, the so-called world 1 of physical objects and biophysiological systems also has an indispensable influence on consciousness. Without these three dimensions the one unified world of human consciousness would not exist. As an individual accesses the resources in culture (world 3) he or she becomes enriched, just as he or she contributes to that culture. There is a dynamic and inextricable interaction between the two. Humans make up the elements of culture and that culture is reflected in the consciousness of individuals. Further, as demonstrated in Chapter 2 we are emergent from biophysiological/evolutionary processes that have occurred in the biosphere. We are biological beings. Yet these three worlds have a coevolutionary relationship.

The "Three world" perspective of Karl Popper is relevant to sociocultural evolution. While world 1 is materially based Worlds 2 and 3 are beyond materiality. A summary of this schema is represented below:

World 1. Physical Objective States
–Inorganic
–Biological
–Artifacts

World 2. States of Consciousness
–thinking
–feeling
–imagination
–perception

World 3. Knowledge in a Subjective Sense
–historical
–philosophical
–theological
–scientific and theoretical

3. The olfactory bulbs are very primitive structures. They are evolutionarily associated with our mammalian species. In fact, some mammals such as dogs rely on such keen sense of smell that their snouts evolved elongated to allow for this exceptional ability.

4. Lieberman (1991) has argued that the major factor influencing the enlargement of the brain was the capacity for rapid communication. He suggests that it was language that made possible hominids' expanded cognitive capacity and thereby "moral progress."

5. It is interesting to note that patients who have suffered neurological damage to the left hemisphere have been described as having a "catastrophic reaction"—they are profoundly more depressed than are right-hemisphere-damaged patients. This is because the hemisphere that is not damaged becomes the dominant hemisphere. Patients with right-hemisphere damage are unable to reflect voluntary facial expressions on the left side of the face, but spontaneously to emotion they are able to reflect expression on the left side of the face. The left hemisphere manages voluntary facial movements through the right-brain brain stem nucleus and thus to the right lower facial muscles. But also these signals are sent from the left hemisphere through the corpus callosum to the right hemisphere and subsequently to the left facial nucleus and the left side of the face. Yet, spontaneous facial expression can be triggered by either hemisphere.

6. The lateralization of language functions to the left hemisphere coevolved with the increasing ability to produce speech with rule-governed syntax. These structural aspects paralleled the ability to communicate with complex thoughts.

The lateralization of speech functions to the left hemisphere has been thought to correlate with handedness. Specifically, Kimura (1979) has argued that handedness evolved in association with the need for more skilled hand movements, permitting the later development of tool use.

It appears that lateralization for manual dexterity was evident at least by the rise of *Homo erectus*. For example, Annett's (1985) genetic theory of handedness postulates that there is a uniquely human right-hand preference found in no other species than our own. In an extensive review of the related literature he concludes that right-handedness was dominant with *Homo habilis*. He speculates that the australopithecines may also have been predominantly right-handed. However, he suggests that it is more probable that tool use may have been the dominant factor in the evolution of right-hand preference.

7. Luria, 1966.

8. Karl Pribram (1991) has noted that the frontal lobes go through three developmental epochs. The first epoch deals with motor movements, the second with the ability to direct behavior toward the completion of tasks, and the last epoch (occurring as late as ages 17 to 21) involves the development of values and a philosophical perspective.

9. Men generally perform more efficiently in spatial tasks. For example, Doreen Kimura (1992) has shown that men are more accomplished at performing tasks in psychological testing that involve rotating an object or form in one's mind and mathematical tasks. They are also more accomplished at targeted motor tasks, as measured by their ability in guiding and interpreting projectiles. In contrast, women are more accomplished at matching items, verbal fluency, and word finding tasks. For example, when asked to find words that begin with a specific letter women perform this task swiftly and accurately when compared to men.

10. It has long been noted that women are afflicted by depression more readily than are men. Glantz and Pearce (1989) have suggested that this is in part related to the differences in stress responses between men and women that stem from our hunter-gatherer ancestry. Men had to respond to stress factors as hunters by dealing with immediate dangerous situations by generating active responses. Women, in contrast, functioned more readily as nurturers and responded to interpersonal stress by conserving energy and simultaneously maintaining sensitivity to those around them. Of course, hormonal differ-

ences paralleled these tendencies as testosterone promoted more aggression thereby re-leasing tension toward a target outside oneself.

11. Interestingly, there are tremendous overlap and extensive feedback loops between neurons. There are perhaps as many as a million billion connections between neurons in the brain. Each neuron can make as many as 50,000 synaptic connections with other neurons. Neurons need at least 1,000 connections to stay active.

12. The action potential involves the movement of positively charged sodium ions across the surface membrane. The positive charge enters the axon in one or two millimeters and then dissipates across the axon. They are measured at 100 milliseconds. There are two types of synaptic transmission, normal and neuromodular. Normal transmission takes place in approximately one second. Neuromodular transmission takes place over several hours. Normal synaptic transmission involves the release of neurotransmitters from the synaptic vesicle on a "presynaptic" site. The neurotransmitter travels across the synaptic gap to a receiving neuron and attaches itself to a receptor site on a "postsynaptic" neuron. It binds onto special proteins that induce a conformational change in the protein. This results in a pore opening—resulting in an electrical current or action potential. Neuromodular transmission involves "second-messenger systems" that change the protein in the cell and modify the mode of operation of that protein. This process creates changes in the strength of synaptic transmission—resulting in the relative strength or weakness of synapses.

13. Shatz, 1992.

14. Edelman (1992) has noted that genetic instructions can only provide constraints on the process of selection, not specific instructions. Given the sheer multitude of geno-types, genetics can be seen as providing the boundaries of biological expression at any one period, not the predictor of specific behavior. Certainly, in recent years epidemiol-ogical and genetic studies have shown that individuals may be predisposed to specific disorders but the hard-wired one-to-one linear causality researchers had hoped for is not necessarily apparent. Though the regions of the brain are specialized through genetic influence, there is tremendous self-organization within broad constraints. There is a feed-back loop between neurons and genes. Once a neuron becomes electrically active it can influence genes which in turn influence how the nerve develops (Gazzaniga, 1992).

15. Connectionism has a long history. Beginning in the late 1940s Donald Hebb (1949) had proposed in his *Organization of Behavior* a form of connectionism from a neurophysiological perspective. Hebb's contribution involved the description of the adaptive process of synaptic connections. Specifically, he proposed that synaptic connec-tions are developed and change as the individual learns new information. In this way, there is a kind of positive feedback process that develops as the more the individual or-ganizes his or her experience and behavior in a particular manner, the stronger the syn-aptic connections that support that behavior. In contrast, unused synaptic connections would be atrophied or pruned back. The strong synaptic connections over time will de-velop "cell assemblies" or clusters of neurons that fire together and all correspond to particular experiences. Each of these cell assemblies can include one to ten thousand neurons, with each neuron having thousands of synaptic connections with other neurons. The cortex is approximately three to four millimeters thick. To conserve on the length and the amount of axons but maximize the number of connections between neurons the cortex is arranged in columns. The neurons in the columns are further composed of co-lumnar "modules," similar to what Hebb had referred to as cell assemblies. The columns are composed of approximately five thousand neurons (Szentagothai and Erdi, 1989). The focus on modules in recent years is part of an outgrowth of the localization school of thought. These modules are thought to be specialized neuronal circuits that have specific functions. It is undeniable at this point that there are specialized areas but the phenomena

of plasticity and critical periods suggest that the brain is far more malleable early in life.

16. The self-organizing process of the neuronal system was described well by Szentagothai and Erdi (1989), who noted, "The essence of the neuronal organization is—at its very basis and its ultimate origin—self organization of spontaneous (random) neuronal noise into spatial-temporal patterns of activity. Everything else is secondary: viz. Establishment of connections with the environment over receptors, epigenetic selection and selective stabilization of appropriate functional chains of genetically not preprogrammed neuron connections, and gradual integration with the primary activity patterns of various kinds of flows of information [including eventually those carrying mental (psychic, cognitive, etc.) phenomena]. The idea that we are trying to bring across is but to show that the old paradigm of the neural as a 'reflex machine' is hopelessly outdated and has to yield to the new paradigm being now built around the central concept of self organization" (p. 381).

17. Freeman, 1991.

18. Larry Vandervert (1990) has advocated for a "neurological positivist" approach to the study of consciousness. He has argued that the "transformational rules" connect the world of the brain and the mind because there is "reciprocal projection" of neurological order of the environment on the brain. According to this perspective there is an "algorithmic organization" of the brain that follows chaotic/fractal energetic systems. Vandervert has maintained that the algorithmic organization follows chaotic/fractal dynamics according to the maximum power principle. According to this principle the lowest or least amount of energy is maximized in a high degree of complex neuronal processing. As he has pointed out, the energy efficiency of the brain (which operates at approximately ten watts) has not been able to be matched by AI researchers, who have not even been able to match the energetic complexity of the brain of a fly.

19. Memories are associated with the strength of specific synaptic connections. However, memories are not static. They involve the enduring modification of synaptic connections. The brain is in a constant state of reorganization. The synaptic arrangements are organized through function. That is, through experience the brain eliminates superfluous synaptic connections and establishes and/or strengthens new connections. The "long term potentiation" of synaptic connections is enhanced and made more efficient through stimulation.

20. Pribram, 1991.

21. From Roger Sperry's perspective, "downward causation" (top-down) occurs when one's consciousness determines the flow of cerebral excitation. This may sound dualistic, but consider the mediator or a person engaging in relaxation exercises. Cerebral excitation is almost always slowed down.

22. Sperry's (1988) concept of "emergent interactionalism" suggests that "upward" or "micro-determinism" interacts with "downward" or "macro-determinism." He suggests that there is a mind-brain interaction in which conscious mental states are emergent from the brain. They can also interact on their "own level" and exert downward control over brain physiology in a "supervient sense" (p. 607).

23. Arden, 1996.

24. The basic structures of the immune system include: the lymph nodes, spleen, thymus gland, and hypothalamus. Through the multiplication of lymphocyte cells, which bear the antibodies (of which there exist forty million), the immune system is braced for a potential further threat from similar antigens. In other words, the immune system develops a memory of previous assaults as it prepares to fight off attacks.

The macrophages, an immune system cell produced by monocytes, destroy bacteria by consuming it. The monocytes receive signals from neuropeptides. In this way neuropeptides direct the immune system's search-and-destroy system for bacteria. Candice Pert has referred to areas in the brain with especially high concentrations of neuropeptides receptors as "nodal points or hot spots."

It appears that glucocorticoids are involved during periods of stress, and help activate muscles and the heart to respond to potential threats. This occurs through the hypothalamus-pituitary tract, which triggers the adrenal cortex to produce this chemical. Yet prolonged stress can feed back and lead to glucocorticoids promoting cell death in the hippocampus, thus leading to the deterioration of the system.

25. Solomon, 1990a.

26. Natural killer (NK) cell activity is suppressed with uncontrollable stress and loneliness.

27. Solomon, 1990b.

28. Kobasa, 1990.

29. That is not to say that physiology is not important—of course it is, as I made clear in the preceding section. Broadly speaking, cultural systems themselves, like other systems, adapt to circadian rhythms, from prokaryotes and eukaryotes. Though humans have adapted social systems to conform with circadian rhythms we have to a degree emancipated ourselves with major limitations.

30. Early in the eighteenth century, Giambattista Vico from Naples, had proposed a constructivist theory of historical and sociocultural evolution. His theories pointed out the importance of mythology as the first real rigorous attempt to construct a semblance of order. This initial "age of the gods" stage was regarded by Vico as one of three cyclic ages of the evolution of human consciousness. The next major age was referred to as the "age of heroes." Here individual historical figures were glorified by superhuman myths of almost impossible accomplishments. The next and current "age of men" ushered in the acknowledgment of human attributes such as reason and personal accomplishments.

Vico's major contribution was put forth in his *New Science* (*Scienza Nuova*), published in 1744. He was critical of the ahistorical emphasis of Descartes. Vico proposed that people create history. He viewed the process of consciousness not as dualistic, as Descartes had proposed, but rather proposed that body and mind are intertwined.

Two hundred years later both Freud and Jung proposed a phylogenetic approach to mythology. However, they differ significantly in their approach. Whereas Freud (1961) regarded religious mythology as regressive (i.e., *The Future of the Illusion*), Jung regarded mythology as transpersonal, archetypal, and instinctual.

Following in the tradition of Emil Durkheim, Claude Levi-Strauss suggested that myth serves as a structure or system through which members of a society are led to understand their world. This "structure" is much like an "infrastructure" that models thoughts. He analogizes music as a totality that we don't understand until we hear the whole piece. Myth, like music, cannot be understood without understanding the whole story. He bypassed the psychological theories and suggested that the structure is inherent in the brain without the need for an intermediate entity. The structuralist view of Levi-Strauss is somewhat ahistorical. In other words, sociocultural systems are viewed as static, unchanging structures.

Levi-Strauss delineated two forms of structures, the "clockworks" and "steam engines." The former are historyless sociocultural systems that may be regarded as closed systems due to his suggestion that they are in relative equilibrium. In contrast, his steam engine cultures are dynamically ripe for evolution. It is perhaps much easier to view these latter types of societies as being driven toward evolution because the variables affecting them are more obviously nonlinear and multidimensional. But it would be a mistake to view the former as being societies in closed systems as the comparison between the two is only relative.

Within the model referred to as "cultural pluralism" many fluctuations would influence the evolutionary effect of overall human sociocultural evolution without there being an easily definable fabric. Cultural pluralism promotes "gliding mechanisms" providing smoother transitions. So the strengthening of subsystems and the breakup of dogmatic social control hierarchies are prerequisites for non-destructive cultural transitions. Ethics, which is most powerful at multilevels, is the behavioral code promoting a "tuning in" with evolution.

31. Societies can increase in complexity or devolve to a lower state prior to later emerging to a higher state. Extended periods of stability will lead to increased internal entropy in the form of bureaucracy and, societal rigidity develops as sociocultural norms that serve as stabilizing attractors gradually lose hold and nonequilibrium conditions develop. Thus, the sociocultural systems desperately look for attracting (stabilizing) symbols. The bifurcating influence of new and novel symbols and ideas allows for a leap to a another level of organization (Laszlo, 1993).

32. Milgram, 1963.

33. Donald, 1991.

34. Marshack (1991) has argued that the "storied" categories in Paleolithic culture involved a rich assortment of ceremonies, ritual, history, and religion. Stories and myths essentially amount to ways of explaining changing relationships in time.

35. The "collective representations" described by Emil Durkheim were akin to self-referential cognitive maps that a sociocultural system uses to reflect itself through negative feedback. This is a form of self-perpetuating stabilizations.

36. Claude Levi-Strauss, *The Raw and the Cooked*, "Overture" Section 1 (1963).

37. Myths and rituals for rites of initiation and passage in many cultures provide for a functionally symbolic transition from one stage of life to another. The most common example is the transition occurring during puberty. Modern Western culture does not ritualize this transition anymore, while adolescence in Western culture is marked by role confusion and more acting out than in most non-Western cultures. Nevertheless, this transition and the period of adolescence that follows is a powerful period enculturation. The individual is driven to develop an identity in a social context. To assimilate and not stand out he or she conforms to the cultural environment. Though there is a high degree of variation in sex roles across cultures for adolescent and adult groups, Whiting and Whiting (1975) found a fairly constant theme differentiating the play of three- to five-year-old boys and girls. Though the boys and girls are equally nurturing, boys are more aggressive and more prone to horseplay, while girls seek out and touch one another more often. Interestingly, latency age children were found to be bossy and self-righteous across cultures.

38. Jakobson, who eventually taught at Harvard after beginning his career in Prague, proposed that all languages are composed of common features. It is the latter modification of these innate hardwired capacities that results in an individual's characteristic expression of his or her respective sociocultural system. Beginning in the 1950s Noam Chomsky provided an explanation of why commonalities are found between all languages. These "deep structure" characteristics are perhaps genetically anchored. Chomsky argued that a "language acquisition device" provides this deep structure. He argued that syntax could be studied independently of semantics. He proposed through his "transformational grammar" that the syntax or logical connections between words could be understood without focusing on semantics, or the actual meaning of the words.

Semantics and phonology are subsumed by grammar. From Chomsky's perspective this organization is referred to as "universal grammar." Thus, it is assumed that all languages have the same properties. Yet, he maintained that syntax is independent from semantics and is part of the underlying and hard-wired organization patterns that our species uses to communicate with language. All of the other aspects of language are considered surface patterns.

Phonemes are the individual sound units. When assembled they comprise of morphemes, which are words. Syntax is actually the grammar and the admissible combination of words. The lexicon of a language involves the assortment of words, while semantics involves the corresponding meaning of the phrases, sentences, and words. Prosody is the vocal intonation of the language which can modify the meaning. Discourse involves the linking of the sentences, thereby the narrative. It is generally believed that the first language a person learns is more closely associated with consciousness than are second languages. It has become evident that bilingual children are more capable of various cognitive skills than are monolingual children. This has especially been apparent in areas such as categorization and the use of symbols. However, monolingual children eventually catch up (Lieberman, 1991).

In an effort to assess whether people in illiterate cultures reason in the same manner as literate individuals, Cole and Scribner (1974) reassessed several previous studies. Making many methodological changes, they denounced the popular assumption that the illiterate culture differed in cognitive capacity evaporated especially when familiar materials were used by the people in the culture being assessed. This study and others have contributed to a movement toward "universalism." This paradigm suggests that ultimately all humans use the same fundamental cognitive structures to operate and interpret the environment. Superimposed on the structures are idiosyncratic ethnocultural styles of adaptation.

39. Throughout his extensive studies of attachment using monkeys, Harry Harlow had shown that separation between infant and mother creates a "separation anxiety." This distress signaled to other potential females that the infant needed nurturing and as a result elicited that response.

40. Daniel Stern (1985) developed a concept which he referred to as the "evoked companion," in many ways is similar to the self-object concept of Object Relations Theory. Children can only rely on the evoked companion when playing alone as if they are playing with someone they previously played with.

41. Just as Winnicott (1958) had proposed that a child uses transitional objects (e.g., teddy bears) as a bridge between unreality and outer reality, he also proposed that later in life one uses culture as the potential space between the individual and the environment.

42. The structural division of the psyche as outlined by Freud reflects the mechanistic perspective of his era. The terms "work" and "force" were of critical importance to the physics of Freud's era. The scientific paradigm that served as a backdrop to Freud's era included the Newtonian-Maxwellian "force-field" concept. Just as Newton had explained the influence of gravity, James Maxwell by the mid 1800s had explained the combined influence of electromagnetism as a force-field. On a human level Freud was to incorporate instinctual drives into this motif. Yet the twin drives of aggression and sexuality blended a thermodynamics and early evolutionary theory emphasis into his metapsychology. Those psychodynamics theorists to follow Freud offered major advances to Freud's original model. For example, both Jung and Adler contributed an important emphasis on teleology. In this way the determinism advocated by Freud was abandoned while the psychodynamic emphasis was retained.

43. Arden, 1996.

44. Ibid.

45. On the extreme of the Connectionist perspective are those such as philosopher Daniel Dennett (1991) who has argued that these modules are an "army of idiots" and that any illusion of consciousness actually existing is just a "Cartesian Theater." He argues that there is no self. As I noted in Chapter 1 and elsewhere, this position is best described as reductio ad absurdum and an outgrowth of Logical Positivism.

Another popular model of Connectionism has emerged form the field of Artificial Intelligence (AI). AI researchers try to simulate the mind by circuits and neural networks that operate in parallel. The functioning of this information-processing network is measured by the "weight" of the connections. The AI model has been controversial despite the fact that researchers have yet to replicate anything remotely resembling consciousness.

The AI model can be regarded as deterministic while the actual neuronal system is not restricted by such "preprogramming." Rather, the neuronal system is an open system as are all living systems. In fact, the so-called "programming" is an ongoing process that is open-ended, fluid, and coevolves with environmental demands. Certainly there are some limitations just as humans cannot fly or stay underwater for long periods of time. Yet the creative process allows for the development of means to accomplish such feats as submarine technology.

Because of the emphasis on digital functioning and the reliance on perceived "programs" AI has not been able to shed reductionism and determinism which have a long history in American psychology. Because American psychology has been so influenced by the British paradigm of Associationalism and the concept of tabula rasa originating with Locke, it has been more focused on the content of thought rather than the manner in which information is known. Therefore, stimulus variables and their "determined" responses predominate. In this manner a paradox was unknowingly developed where the focus of interest became a linearly perceived environment, while the individual was seen as a one-dimensional organism.

46. Piaget had postulated that children play an active role in their own learning. In this sense he can be considered a Constructivist.

47. Rogers (1980), Jung (1964), and Maslow (1968) were all proponents of the concept of self-actualization.

48. Rosenbaum and Dyckman, 1995.

49. James established his psychology laboratory at Harvard a year before Wilhelm Wundt had in Leipzig in 1878—though the later is often referred to as the founder of the first psychology laboratory.

CHAPTER 4: NOCTURNAL CONSCIOUSNESS: THE NATURE OF DREAMS

1. Over twenty-five years ago Webb (1969) had noted that REM deprivation results in hyperresponsiveness, while Stage 4 deprivation results in hypo-responsiveness. Non-REM dreaming emerges later in development after five years of age, while REM type dreaming emerges after age three.

2. Roschke and Aldenhoff, 1991.

3. Hobson and McCarley, 1977.

4. The co-author of the activation-synthesis model, Robert McCarley, has attempted to explain the alternation between REM and non-REM sleep. McCarley and Massaquoi (1985) have proposed a "limit cycle" model, which involves two different neuronal systems. Those neurons that activate the REM cycle are found in the pontine reticular formation and are associated with cholinergic neurotransmitters. The cessation of the REM cycle is associated with the locus ceruleus and the dorsal raphe nucleus and involves noradrenergic neurons. This latter system is generally active in waking consciousness.

5. Hobson, 1988.

6. Winson, 1991.

7. Perhaps the main reason the theta rhythm did not evolve with primates is that vision replaced olfaction as the dominant sense. Winson has detected the theta rhythm in

mammalian brains specifically located in the hippocampus (the triynatic circuit). This area apparently processes information from the endorhinal cortex, which receives information dispersed throughout the sensory cortex. Once received by the trynatic circuit, information is sent throughout the limbic system as well as the thalamus and the prefrontal cortex. During theta rhythm activity this route is not operative. Interestingly, this occurs during REM sleep—in other words, when the route noted above is blocked. According to Winson this permits the brain during REM sleep to process information received throughout the day.

8. Hall and Domhoff, 1963.

9. Foulkes, 1987.

10. Hall and Van de Castle, 1966.

11. Pregnant women dream more of architectural objects. Interestingly, when the dreams of working mothers were compared with those of nonworking mothers it was found that working mothers experienced more unpleasant emotions and male characters in their dreams (Lortie-Lussier, Schwab, and DeKornick, 1985).

12. Kramer, Kinny, and Scharf, 1983.

13. An assessment of the dreams of male transsexuals revealed that like other males they rarely dreamed of the indoors, but unlike other males they dreamed less about the streets and money, and more about clothes (Krippner et al. 1974).

14. Krippner and Rubenstein, 1990.

15. Hall and Van de Castle, 1966.

16. Van de Castle, 1994.

17. LeVine, 1966.

18. Though the actual term "dreamtime" was coined by Englishmen approximately one hundred years ago, the concept is important to Australian Aboriginals.

19. Degarrod, 1989.

20. Van de Castle, 1994.

21. Arden, 1996.

22. Basso (1987) suggested that the Kalapalo explanation of the process of dreaming as the wandering self could be taken as a metaphor for the goalsearching of the self.

23. Hunt (1989) has argued that the cognitively inspired dream theories have overemphasized memory process, to the exclusion of the more bizarre and intense imagery of sexuality, aggression, dreams of flying, and so on that do not have roots in the personal memory of the dreamer.

24. By the eighth century Tibetan Buddhists actively pursued cultivating the ability to produce lucid dreams.

25. Dentan, 1987.

26. Tart, 1964.

27. Tart, 1965.

28. Tart, 1970.

29. Gackenbush, 1990.

30. Galvin, 1989.

31. The Taoist text Lie-tseu defines and describes several classes of dreams. In Chinese Buddhism, Kwan Hiu was said to have prayed that he might envision the saintly figure of Arhat. In the Vedas several favorable and unfavorable dreams were described. In the Brhadaranyaka Upanishad two types of dreams were described. One type was thought to depict inner personal desires. The other type involved the tendency of the soul to travel through dreams.

32. Alexander's dream was interpreted by Aristander, a seer from Telemessos. Aritander had proposed that Alexander's dream involving a satyr (a demigod who lived in wooded areas) was significant because the Greek word "satyros" could be divided into sa

and Tyros. Based on this analysis he suggested the dream meant "Tyre is yours."

33. Krippner, 1990.

34. Through an analysis of dream reports from the Cuna Indians of Panama, Van de Castle (1994) reported a relationship between reduced regression expressed in dreams and ESP ability. Specifically, he regarded dreams that were longer, having more animal and more direct sexual and aggression behaviors as indicators of less repression.

35. Rhine, 1961.

36. Van de Castle, 1974.

37. Hunt, 1989.

38. In fact even Freud (1953) had once remarked that sleep creates favorable conditions for telepathy.

39. Hunt, 1989.

40. Rhine, 1961.

CHAPTER 5: PERENNIAL PHILOSOPHY AND SOCIOTHE-OLOGICAL SYSTEMS

1. Huxley, 1948.

2. Donald, 1991.

3. Campbell, 1987, p. 377.

4. Solecki, 1977

5. Campbell, 1987, p. 331.

6. The earliest known cave paintings are associated with the so-called Cro-Magnons, after the area in France where they were found. Many of the paintings we are aware of were found in France and Spain. They date as early as 30,000 years ago. Though most of the paintings are depictions of various game species such as bison and reindeer, they appear to represent a ritualistic observance of the importance of these species in hunter-societies.

During the last 15,000 years there has been an increasing interest in lunar and general astronomical events. For example, initially notched bones found in various parts of Europe apparently reference lunar events. Later, during the Neolithic period, there was increasing reference to astronomical cycles that correspond to seasonal information.

7. Many of the female/Goddess images are represented as pregnant. They are almost all depicted as naked. At Laugerie Basse the image of a pregnant human female lying below a bull and the phallus of the bull was engraved on reindeer bone.

8. Campbell, 1987, p. 331.

9. The invading Indo-European tribes possessed more advanced technologies. Specifically, the dual influence of the "T-bifurcating" innovations of more advanced metals and the use of horses for transportation was profound. These invaders were more primitive in their social relationships (i.e., oriented toward domination instead of cooperation) (Gimbutas, 1982, and Eisler, 1987).

10. Many of the Indo-European cultures to develop later were to preserve the myth of the final battle in which the protagonist fights an evil opponent (Mallory, 1989). We can see this theme played out in the Hindu epic of the Mahabharata and the Judeo-Christian Armageddon.

11. One of the earliest written expressions of human rights was the Sumerian "Code of Ur-Nammu." It was a blend of theological pronouncements which were generally interpreted by priests. It is assumed that these priests held powerful positions within the Sumerian sociocultural system.

12. Similarly, there was a great flood myth in Egypt. Ra was warned by his father that

the earth had grown too wicked. Hathor went to earth and slew masses of humans until the Nile overflowed with blood. There was also a great flood myth in ancient Greece. Zeus was angry about the state of the world. In anger, he sent a great flood. After nine days and nights of rain Dericalion and his wife Pyrrha had been warned of the flood by Prometheus. They were placed in a large wooden chest and managed to survive, eventually landing on Mount Parnassus.

13. Of course this date is highly speculative. This assumes that Abraham was an actual historical figure. In fact, most commentators suggest a blurring of folklore and myth with history.

14. Armstrong, 1993, p. 14.

15. The initial creation myth embraced by the early Hebrews was referred to as Elohist, associated with the Canaanite God El. God for the early Hebrews was referred to as Elohim, which is a plural form. It is only later (post Moses) that God was referred to as Yahweh.

16. We see a transition in Judaism from the Pagan belief in many Gods to monotheism through the faith and allegiance that Abraham and later Jacob paid the God El. This faith evolved into an allegiance to one God.

17. The appearance of the Egyptian god Osiris took many forms in Egyptian mythology. Initially tied to agriculture in the Nile Valley, he later became the supreme god and was associated with the sun. Osiris, in fact, became one in a long line of gods of resurrection, such as Mithras, Balder, Tammuz, and later Christ. This tradition, played over and over again, has reinforced the concept of immortality.

18. Parrinder, 1971.

19. Isa. 46:1.

20. Exod. 3:5–6.

21. Berry, 1957.

22. Zoroastrianism depicted Ahura Mayda as the lord of wisdom and the principal deity. He had a helper who was referred to as Mithras, or light. These two figures on the side of the good were thought to be in conflict with Aingra Mainyu, who was referred to as the Lie Demon. The Jews later translated this figure into Satan. The main premise of Zoroastrianism was that one could not compromise between good and evil. Rather, one must take a position. It was thought that one's fate on the Judgment Day was influenced by which position was taken. Zoroastrianism was basically a monotheistic religion with heaven and hell as the possible end points in one's life.

23. Grant, 1977.

24. The Essenes believed that the temple in Jerusalem had become corrupt. They rejected the animal sacrifice and the focus on the temple itself as a holy place. Instead, they advocated for the concept of "temple of spirit."

25. Grant, 1977.

26. Matt. 27:11.

27. Grant, 1977.

28. Actually, January sixth was the original date that marked the birth of Jesus by Matthew and Luke. The celebration of the birth of Jesus on December twenty-fifth was a reflection of the Roman influence. Another Roman ritual involved the god Saturnalia. Taking place just after the winter solstice on December twenty-fifth, this festival involved many rituals, such as candle lighting, feasting, forgiveness of debts, and gift giving. The Roman Christians absorbed many of these rituals, including the date, thereby enabling them to practice their faith during a period of great persecution.

The Roman Emperor Diocletian seemed to understand how to manipulate the symbolic significance of such dates. He proclaimed himself a Sun God and chose December 25 as his birthday. The persecuted Christians practiced their faith by pretending to observe his birthday. Here we see a multi-layer overlap of sociocultural dynamics.

Mithras, of Zoroastrian myth, became an important cult figure throughout Europe. This figure was also thought to have been born of a virgin birth and brought up to the status of a god by Mayda. One popular myth depicted Mithras fighting the forces of evil in a great bull fight. Mithras slayed the bull, repressed evil, and thereby saved the earth. The practitioners of this cult thought that nonbelievers would perish. This is an interesting parallel to present-day Christian fundamentalism, which suggests that non-Christians will not be saved.

Sunday was held as a day sacred to those practicing the cult of Mirthas due to his status as a Sun God. On December 25 practitioners celebrated Mithras by singing hymns, lighting candles, and giving gifts. Also sacraments of bread and water were given. The period from this date until the spring equinox became the mystical forty days (later called Lent) until Black Friday. Then Mithras was said to slay a bull in a great fight. Worn from the battles he was placed in a rock tomb, only to rise three days later.

In Rome the popularity of Mithraism was so strong that the Emperor Aurelian proclaimed it the official state religion. The December 25 date became an attractor for several competing sociocultural belief systems. For Mithraism, it was the "Birthday of the Invincible Sun God" ("Natis Solis Invicti"). It is obvious that the early Christian Church coevolved with these sociocultural systems. Within this nonlinear sociocultural macrosystem it is difficult and perhaps senseless to separate out which group originated some of these rituals. Nevertheless, it is quite obvious that the Christian and Mithraic Easter coevolved with and emerged in this complex context. When these myths were combined and introduced in Northern Europe several centuries later, the tree so symbolic to the Druids was combined with the Christmas holiday.

29. Gnosticism is a general term that applied to several contrasting streams of thought. However, the generality I have employed here is useful heuristically.

30. The concept of "original sin" was largely a contribution of St. Augustine.

31. Armstrong, 1993.

32. Koran 112.

33. With the Mongol invasions disrupting the Arab Empire the populace needed an experience with God that was more personal and comforting. Sufism became more popular and the Faylasufs less influential. The Sufi tradition has been translated into Western practice by Gurdjieff. Here there is a strong focus on "self-remembering." The practitioner notes to him/herself that "I am now in this place chopping wood."

34. In another example of how bifurcations are not always to a higher qualitative level of organization, the Protestants argued that the previously allegorical interpretation of the Bible was not pious. However, the Protestants were not part of a unified movement. They varied widely between sects, cultures, and historical periods. Some protested that the Bible should be read literally. Thus, instead of regarding Adam and Eve as representative of the early humans, they were thought to be actual individuals. During the early sixteenth century Martin Luther went so far as to insist on 4000 B.C.E. as the date of creation. Further, he argued, like the Catholic Church, that Copernicus was wrong to propose that the earth revolved around the sun. He also believed in witchcraft, thereby being one of the contributors to the Inquisition, which erupted later that century. Today the same line of thought is operative when fundamentalists insist that the concept of evolution is wrong.

Like Luther, John Calvin in the mid sixteenth century offered another literalist Christian perspective. Calvin was a strong believer in predestination and the belief in being "chosen." Calvinism was exported to England as Puritanism then exported again to America. The wide variety of Protestant faiths have been important in the United States. In the United States the affliction of Puritanism and has been transformed into a neofundamentalism where Churchianity is characterized by judgment of others, social exclusivity, and political extremism. In a subtle way this theology promote "hate thy neighbor" rather than "love thy neighbor." Therefore, neofundamentalists have become Anti-Christians in Christian clothing.

35. Mallory, 1989.

36. The real difference is the notion of "an-atta," um-self—as part of "anucia"—impermanence.

37. The Bhagavad Gita.

38. Vahamana became Mahavira. He had been a Charvin.

39. It is ironic that the Buddha, who regarded himself as simply "awake," should be deified by his followers. In fact, he recommended that after enlightenment "people should return to the market place and practice compassion to all living beings."

40. Parrinder, 1971.

41. Anguttara-Nikaya IV: 13–14.

42. In Tibetan Mayayana Buddhism the term "Dharmadata" refers to the unity of forms and emptiness. This paradoxical dual nature is metaphorically similar to the dual nature of "wave-particle duality," discussed in the next chapter.

43. Parrinder, 1971.

44. The Buddhist monasteries were destroyed by the Muslim invaders. As a result Jainism, which did not have monasteries, survived in India, while Buddhism was pushed out.

45. Jiayin, 1992.

46. Analects 6:28.

47. Mei Yi-poa, *The Ethical and Political Works of Motse* p. 79–80.

48. Parrinder, 1971.

49. The Writings of Kwang-zze, I:345

50. Parrinder, 1971

51. Ibid.

52. Watts, 1957, The Way of Zen Part 2, Chapter 2.

53. After the peasant rebellion that was followed by the Ming Dynasty (1368–1644) external exploitation was ceased and the Chinese system closed down. Even after the invasion from Manchuria and the subsequent Qing Dynasty (1636–1911) the Chinese remained a closed system making it ripe for exploitation from the Europeans (Jiayin, 1992).

54. Compiled by John White (1996) in *Toward a Transpersonal America.*

55. Dadistan-I-Dinik 94:5.

56. Talmud, Shabbat 31a.

57. Matt. 7:12.

58. Sunnab.

59. Mahabharata 5:1517.

60. Udana-Varga 5:18.

61. 24th Tirthankara

62. Analects 15:23.

63. Adherence to mythology without science and a coherent knowledge of interdependence leads to regression. Witness the outbreak of fundamentalism throughout the world. There is a rejection of sensibility, therefore, professed Christians lose the basis for Christianity. They no longer embrace the tenets; love thy neighbor, turn the other cheek, and care for the sick and the needy. Without an evolutionary perspective and an acknowledgment of our common emergence, divisions and separateness are intensified.

64. Huxley, 1948, p. 2.

65. Ibid. p. 14.

66. Ibid. p. 15.
67. Ibid. p. 5.
68. Ibid. p. 262.
69. Ibid. p. 271.

CHAPTER 6: MATTER, FIELDS OF INFORMATION, AND IN-COMPLETENESS

1. Quoted in Davies (1991).

2. Democritus and Leucippus were contemporaries of both Socrates and Plato.

3. The world of Descartes and Newton was actually quite revolutionary for its time. Prior to that time and not since the era of the classical Greeks was there such an emphasis on reason and analysis—the basis of scientific investigation.

4. The designation of "Special" in the Special Theory of Relativity is used to denote those special situations in which gravity is not a factor.

5. Einstein quoted in the *News Chronicle,* March 14, 1949.

6. Bruce Boghosian of Boston University clarified for me that light travels along a straight (geodesic) path in curved space. The concept of force is thus the discrepancy between the concept of straightness in natural geometry of space-time and Euclidean geometry on which we try impose space-time. Some people refer to space-time as warped. Yet Einstein himself preferred to refer to space-time as curved.

7. In physics the amount of energy influences the rate of time—no energy, no time (Davies, 1995).

8. Kuku, 1994.

9. According to the Theory of General Relativity, time is a particular choice of coordinates in the description of the location of a space-time event. The physicist's space-time description does not single out "time" as flowing (Penrose, 1994).

10. Quantum Mechanics and by and large the main emphasis of the Copenhagen School was on epistemotology—on how we know what we know. This lies in contrast to an ontological approach that places an emphasis on what is.

11. David Hilbert developed a theory of infinite-dimensional spaces. The quantum theorists used this methodology in developing quantum mechanics.

12. Davies, 1992.

13. It was Einstein who combined Newton's concept of the particular (he referred to it as "corpuscles") and James Clerk Maxwell's wave description of light and discovered that light (now called "photons") sometimes behaves like particles and sometimes like waves. He noted that light behaves like a particle in the photoelectric effect and behaves like a wave when it "interferes with itself" (Thorne, 1994). In fact, when Einstein won the Nobel Prize in 1922, it was not for Relativity Theory but for his contribution to the developing field of Quantum Mechanics. It was during the mid 1920s that Louis de Broglie noted that electrons and protons also have wave-particle duality.

14. The apparatus can be conceived of as a sealed-off steel box that contains one radioactive atom. The atom has a half-life of almost one hour. After one hour there is a 50-50 chance that the atom has decayed and emitted radiation in the box. If this happens, the atom strikes a photocell, which trips a circuit that allows a poisonous gas to fill the box.

15. Davies, 1995, p. 188.

16. As one appreciates progressively inclusive theoretical perspective, each new perspective is actually more simple, or to use a metaphor often used by physicists elegant. According to theoretical physicist Peter Freund, central contributor to string theory, "The laws of nature become simpler and elegant when express in high dimensions" (quoted in

Kuku, 1994, p. 12).

17. Kuku, 1994.

18. Ibid.

19. The theory of hyperspace is sometimes referred to as the Kaluza-Klien Theory, and "supergravity" denotes the efforts of these two theorists and others to account for gravity with the other three quantum forces (i.e., the strong, the weak, and electromagnetism). During the 1980s the theory of hyperspace reached new plateaus as Superstring Theory. The current speculation is that initially after the big bang the universe split into four and six dimensions.

20. It was John Wheeler who coined the phrase "participatory universe."

21. In fact, from Newton's perspective nonlocality was a "philosophical absurdity." All physical action were seen as the result of attractions and repulsions on a local basis (Newton, *Principia*, London: Ed. Mothe-Cajor, 1713, quoted in Bohm and Hiley, 1993). From Einstein's perspective, as we shall see nonlocality could put the speed-of-light barrier in theoretical jeopardy. However, this is not necessarily the case.

22. Einstein, Podelsky, and Rosen, 1935.

23. Bell, 1964.

24. In his 1964 paper Bell argued that there can be certain mathematical relationships, which have since been referred to as Bell's inequalities. Specifically, the probabilities of joint probabilities of various spin measurements that may be made on particles would be the consequences of their being separate objects (Penrose, 1994). Bell had shown that this relationship could be violated. Bell's Theorem was, therefore, framed as inequalities that established that any deterministic theory of hidden variables to which the locality condition applied could be experimentally distinguished from quantum mechanics. In effect the thrust of Bell's Theorem stressed that if any experiment violated the inequality in a manner predicted by quantum mechanics, local hidden variable theories would have to be ruled out as explaining the effect. This would leave only nonlocal hidden variable theories.

25. Hiley, 1994.

26. Aspect, 1983.

27. Alain Aspect, working at the Institut d'Uptique Theoretique at Appliqull in Orsay, France, experimentally demonstrated nonlocal effects. The results of three experiments conducted between 1980 and 1982 violated Bell's inequalities and were in agreement with quantum mechanics. Bruce Boghosian stressed to me that "Aspect's results are not at all at odds with relativity. Relativity precludes sending 'messages' faster than light. When you measure the state of one of two widely separated spins in Aspect's experiment, it 'affects' measurements of the state of the other one, even though those measurements may be space-like separated (so that it is not possible to say which happens first). There is, however, no way to send a message using this mechanism. You might imagine a time sequence of such EPR spin pairs, with person A measuring one spin of the sequence each time. When he gets the result +1(-1), person B measuring the other spin far away will get -1(+1). But note that person A has no advance knowledge or control over the sequence of results that he is going to get, so he cannot convey any information to person B this way."

28. This phenomenon is illustrated by an electron that encounters a massive barrier. Somehow there is a statistically significant probability that it will appear on the other side of the barrier.

29. Davies, 1995.

30. Penrose, 1994 , p. 351.

31. Brian Josephson won the Nobel Prize in 1973 for his superconducting loops. He showed that a switchover process occurs that takes a condensate from low-energy quan-

tum states to high energy classical states. These "Josephson Junctions" are illustrations of the interplay between the quantum (microscopic) dimension and the classical (macroscopic) dimension.

32. Penrose, 1994.

33. Actually, early this century Bertrand Russell critiqued dicodomistic thinking through his now famous paradoxes. Black and white logical categories are inadequate. So another chip was taken away from Aristotelian logic.

34. Stephen Hawking a few years ago made a comment he probably wished he had not made. He said that by the end of the century physicists will probably have discovered all the laws of nature. This premise is obviously now doubtful.

35. Gödel had shown that the dream of the "Formalists," spearheaded by mathematical greats such as David Hibert, was flawed. No formal system can be consistent and complete.

36. Gödel, 1931.

37. Penrose (1994) combines the argument made by philosopher John Searles (the Chinese Room) regarding the necessity of consciousness with the implications of Gödel's Incompleteness Theorem to argue that consciousness necessarily must be noncomputational in nature. In other words, consciousness (understanding) must lie beyond the ability of any computational device such as a computer. Creativity and the experience of "quali" are not "rule based." Gödel's Theorem suggests that there are Platonic mathematical truths that lie beyond human computational procedures. However, these same truths are accessible through human insight. In other words, consciousness is beyond that which can be achieved through computational operations.

38. Penrose points out that when you move from the quantum level to the classical level you get randomness. It is in the process of magnification that randomness comes to play. He argues that it is actually a noncomputational problem, not randomness, that is involved. The term "noncomputational" does not mean "incomprehensible."

39. John Eccles (1994) has proposed that quantum effects occur in synaptic actions. This is thought to occur to the presynaptic vesicle grid, which is a paracrystalline hexagonal lattice in the pyramidal cells. Put another way, Eccles suggests that the mass of the synaptic vesicles is not so great as to lie outside of the range of the Uncertainty Principle. In this "microsite" description of neuronal processes, Eccles claims that synaptic mechanisms respond neither to mass nor to action, but rather to probability fields of quantum mechanics. Further, Eccles points to the proposal by Margenau (1984) that regards the mind as a nonmaterial field analogous to a probability field.

40. A protein substance called tubulin forms interpenetrating spiral arrangements which constitute the tubes. The tubulin molecule can have two states of electrical polarization. The microtubulin may be a possible location for quantum-oscillation activities.

41. The microtubes seemed to be involved in controlling the strengths between different neurons. Neurotransmitter molecules are transported along microtubes.

42. Penrose, 1994, p. 135.

43. At a recent conference in Tucson, Arizona, entitled "Towards a Science of Consciousness," physicists, neurophysiologists, philosophers, and psychologists from throughout the world gathered to discuss many of the current theories of consciousness. The Penrose/Hameroff theory was one of those most widely debated.

CHAPTER 7: SELF-CONVERGENCE

1. Murphy, 1992.
2. Bourguignon, 1978.

3. Tart, 1975.

4. According to Tart, loading stabilization involves behaviors that help maintain a consistent state of consciousness. Another concept is similar to the cybernetic mechanism of negative feedback whereby the individual makes adjustments to bring awareness back to the desired state. Positive feedback involves the cultivation of a new and perhaps even an altered state of consciousness. One may meditate to cultivate a relaxed and centered state of consciousness. Finally, limiting stabilization involves the exclusion of other states by enhancing one state to such a degree that other states incompatible with it are not as possible. For example, while one is in a meditative state an anxious state of mind is less possible because one's heart rate and pace of breathing have slowed.

5. Tart maintains that consciousness occurs in discrete states, rather than as a continuous spectrum. In other words, sleep, relaxation, and dreaming all represent discrete states of consciousness.

6. Kroger, 1976.

7. Ibid.

8. Elson, Harris and Cunis, 1977.

9. Werntz et al., 1982.

10. Corby et al., 1978.

11. Krippner et al., 1996.

12. Tart, 1969.

13. In a broad survey of the healing literature, Daniel Benor (1993) reported that of the 131 controlled trials 56 produced statistically significant results at the <.01 level. An additional 21 were significant at the <.02 to the <.05 levels. These studies were performed with a wide variety of biological organisms (reviewed in Dossey, 1993).

14. Dossey, 1993.

15. People who have been well respected for their spiritual advancement apparently did not pray for health or did not benefit from their own prayers. For example, many of the people who have been regarded as saints and mystics have died of cancer and various other serious illnesses Krishnamurti, Suzuki Roshi, and Saint Bernadette all died of various types of cancer. Perhaps they had so focused on the transpersonal aspects of existence that they did not find it necessarily important if they lived or died (Dossey, 1993, p. 85).

16. In a comprehensive meta-analysis of the parapsychological research, Radin and Nelson (1989) reviewed 832 studies from sixty-eight researchers. They found that 38 percent of the studies produced statistically significant results. They noted that the studies with the most rigorous research methodology produced more statistically significant results. They argued against there being a "file drawer effect." Yet, a major problem troubling this type of research is that psi phenomena suffers from repeatability failure (Irwin, 1989).

17. Honorton, 1991.

18. In a major meta-analysis of the Ganzfeld research, Bem and Honorton (1994) have found statistically significant results that suggest general confirmation of psi effects. However, they also found significant differences in selection rates for "popular" images when they were the actual target. Ray Hyman (1994) has argued in his response to the Bem and Honorton study that the hit rates may have involved experimenter prompting and a "Goodfellow Effect."

19. Tart, 1991.

20. Jahn, 1990.

21. Broughton, 1991.

22. Perry et al., 1986.

23. Honorton and Schechner, 1986.

24. Bem and Honorton, 1994.

25. Blackmore, 1996.

26. Tart, 1991.

27. Sargent, 1981.

28. Overall, Ring (1980) speculates that perhaps 35 to 40 percent of all individuals who come close to death have a NDE. Sabom (1982) reports that NDEs are more common among patients who have suffered long-term illnesses than with sudden accidents and with patients who have been unconscious for at least thirty minutes and had been resuscitated medically. This of course suggests that there has been some preparatory meditation. In other words, the patient has had time to think about the possibility of death prior to the NDE.

29. Ring, 1980.

30. Kubler-Ross (1991) writes that her patients who have experienced the NDE have reported that after the tunnel they are "embraced by the light." This light is described as "whiter than white" and as the individual approaches the light he or she feels a sense of "indescribable, unconditional love" (p. 16).

Ring (1980) has reported these individuals often experience a distortion in time and space. Typically, after rising above their body and observing themselves below seemingly dead they are pulled through a tunnel faster than the speed of light. At the end of this tunnel is a light brighter than the brightest light ever seen. However, unlike other lights they are able to look at it directly. There is an increasingly strong feeling of love and joy.

Hunt (1995) has pointed out that the "white light" experience often described by mystics is related to synesthesias. Tying in Indian mythology, he argues that chakra experiences one "sensed and embodiments" that distinguishes these experiences from merely sensory experiences.

31. Parrich and Stevenson, 1986.

32. Gackenbush and Bosveld (1989) have reported that there has been found to be a correlation between having had a NDE and the frequency of lucid dreaming.

33. Whinney, 1996.

34. Ring, 1985.

35. In fact, Elizabeth Kubler-Ross (1991) analogized the dying process to a "butterfly emerging form its cocoon" (p. 10). Further, she compares the dying process to the experience of birth. Ring speculates that NDEs are related to the concept of kundalini, in that they both involve a powerful energy source that is often associated with mystical experience.

36. Abraham Maslow was a major contributor to the concept of Transpersonal Psychology. He regarded human beings as biologically endowed with the capacity for spiritual experience. These experiences he called "peak experiences." Even Freud was receptive to the validity of some transpersonal experiences. Despite his break with Jung, which can be partly attributed to Jung's frustration with Freud's one-dimensional (sex and aggression) psychology, Freud actually did believe that telepathy was a viable process.

37. Wilber, 1977.

38. Wilber, 1995.

39. Wilber depends heavily on Piagetian developmental psychology, Abraham Maslow's hierarchy of needs, and Lawrence Kohlberg's stages of morality. He weaves these influences into a Ventantic schema. For example, each individual is thought to be surrounded by "Koshas," or sheaths of reality. They include the food sheath—governing the physical body; the energy sheath—governing the pranic body, the mental sheath—governing the mental body; the intellectual sheath—governing the subtle body; and finally the sheath of bliss—governing the causal body.

40. Both Combs (1996) and Wilber have been quite influenced by Jean Gerbser, a

Polish-born theorist who eventually settled in Paris. Gerbser argues that there exist "structures of consciousness" that are discrete jumps in levels of consciousness. These include the archaic, magic, mythical, mental, and integral levels. He argued that each structure is a knowledge or noetic process. Gerbser argues that these structures emerge as a mutation to denote the abrupt transition from a previous form. Wilber, in fact, attached his terms to Gerbser's with a hyphen to acknowledge his contribution. Wilber's stages are generally the same as Gerbser's. For example, the mythic-membership epoch involves the mythic "structure" of consciousness. Wilber and Gerbser regard the mental-egoic mode as the predominant trend today. Both regard the simplistic focus of ego concerns as the main reason so many people today feel so alienated. I agree with Comb's critique that Wilber's effort to line up Gerbser's structures with the Vendantic planes as full blown structures of consciousness is problematic. Wilber's stage theory depicts a linear arrangement of $A> B> C>$ etc.

41. Just as Aristotle misunderstood the concept of change offered by Eurepecles, so to does Wilber seem to have a difficult time with the same. In this sense Wilber is an Aristotelian.

42. Wilber's simplistic schema conforms to a rigid hierarchical approach. There is little room for coevolution. He incorrectly states, "The reason physics can't explain biology is precisely because the bios is not in the cosmos" (Wilber, 1984, p. 93). Then what is it part of? If he advocates for a holistic perspective why promote dualism?

43. Wilber does correctly point out that hierarchy leads to wholeness. In other words, if we can appreciate the multiple levels of hierarchies ("levels of organization" from my point of view) the levels of organization progressively subsume multiple subsystems.

44. Washburn, 1988.

45. Washburn refers to his model as "dynamic, triphasic and dialectic." His focus is on how the ego has a dynamic life within the Dynamic Ground. He regards the ego as going through three stages or phases—thus the term "triphasic." Specifically, the pre-egoic stage is correlated to early infancy. The egoic phase is so named because the ego establishes itself as an independent system. However, there is a cost of the original repression of the "non-ego pole" of the personality. He feels, and I agree, that few people leave this plane. Finally, according to Washburn the trans-egoic phase involves the "U-turn" experience. Namely, there is a "regression in the service of transcendence." As the ego losses control through this chaos and disorientation, one emerges with more sensitivity of the dynamic ground. This is a dialectical model—thesis, antithesis, synthesis.

46. Grof, 1985.

47. According to Grof, within the personal unconscious there exist systems of condensed experience (COEX systems). These are condensed memories of potent life experiences. Grof's concept of COEX suggests that people maintain emotional predispositions, often resulting from birth trauma.

48. Combs is right to point out that Gerbser-like structures represent more of a historical sequence than actual states of consciousness.

49. Archetypes are in some ways associated with Platonic Forms. However, with archetypes, the images take on a metaphoric and thematic character. Jung referred to them as patterns of instinctual behavior. He felt that they represent primordial images. These images have a dynamic effect on the experience of numinosity. They are the dynamic organizer of ideas and images. In this way they help focus one's attention.

Not only does Plato's concept of ideal form a precursor to Jung's archetypes, but we also see Giambattista Vico in the mid eighteenth century advance the concept of a shared physical metaphor. In his *New Science* (1744) he argued for the concept of common "ideas" among all people that are unknown to all but have a common origin.

50. Jung had thought that myth was an intermediate stage between consciousness and

unconsciousness.
51. Smith, 1987.

CHAPTER 8: AN EVOLVING UNITY

1. Penrose, 1989.
2. Bohm built on the concept of "guide waves" introduced by Louis de Broglie in the 1920s. Bohm, in fact, consulted with de Broglie when developing his idea of quantum potential.
3. Bohm and another colleague, David Peat, have argued that nonlocality is consistent with Bohm's Causal Interpretation, which results in "nonlocal quantum potential" that connects distant particles. According to the Causal Interpretation of quantum phenomena, information contained within quantum potential will have an inherent effect on the actual outcome of the quantum process (Bohm and Peat, 1987, and Bohm, 1980).
4. Bohm and Peat, 1987.
5. The interaction of particles becomes highly unstable near bifurcation points, according to Bohm and Hiley (1993). Because of this nonlinearity and nonlocality, energy is "swept in" from the entire wave packet so that on the atom there is a single quantum of energy" (p. 231).

According to Bohm and Hiley, a particle need not travel in a straight line. It can behave like a wave. In the double slit experiment a particle can only go through one slit at a time—a wave can go through both. On the other side of the slits the waves interferes with one another to produce quantum potential. Yet, if we project two particles through each of the two slits each particle informs the other particle of its position and momentum. The result of this exchange of "active" information is that the particles behave like waves— they interact.

Particles projected can be strongly affected by the presence of the slits in the distance. But the slits are ignored once the particles pass through. Perhaps there is a nonlocal interaction of the slit and the electron. Bohm and Hiley have argued that a particle, such as an electron, can be described accurately by both its position and its momentum. The particle is profoundly affected by a wave that it accompanies. Yet the precision with which the particle can be observed affects limitations set by the Uncertainty Principle. The particle is conceived to be a sequence of incoming and outgoing waves. Any measurement of the quantum dimension alters the wave function. Heisenberg had argued that the wave function does not represent actual reality by a set of potentialities. Bohm and Hiley regard the field qualities as "beables."

They have shown that if particles collide with other systems, there is a constant narrowing down of the "domain in which the wave function can significantly affect the quantum potential at the location of the particles. From this it follows that the channel entered by particles eventually becomes irreversibly fixed, so it cannot be undone" (p. 95).

They note that between the shortest distances now measurable (ten to sixteen centimeters) and the shortest distances relevant to the current notions of spacetime probability, there is great degree of undiscovered structure. They point out that this undiscovered area is comparable to the range between our size and an elementary particle. They point out that "since vacuum is generally regarded as full with an immense energy of fluctuation . . . it may be further suggested that ultimately the energy of a particle comes from this source" (p. 38).
6. Why is it that nonlocal phenomena are not more obvious? Perhaps there is a need to converge energy, symbolic significance, and personal significance. Bohm and Hiley

(1993) note that "with massive bosons the energies required for such a classical situation are so high that these do not play a significant role in the manifest world of ordinary experience" (p. 288).

7. Bohm, 1980.

8. Korzybinski, 1958.

9. Quantum potential originates in the implicate order. It is considered a "pilot wave" that influences the movement of quanta. Bohm and Hiley propose that "as in particle theory, the implicate order manifests in the activity of the particle through the quantum potential. It is clear then that in field theory there is a superimplicate order that manifests in the field beables" (p. 380).

10. Bohm and Hiley (1993) propose that there could be high levels of implicate order. "The third level would organize the second which would become nonlinear" (p. 380). The infinitely large set of fields Bohm refers to as the "holomovement," to emphasize the unbroken wholeness. Everything in our common experience (i.e., the explicate order) is enfolded in the holomovement. By being both a part of it and yet having freewill we participate in the holomovement. Everything follows from this deepest level of universal order. Bohm even notes that time is context dependent and proposes that randomness is a type of order. Ultimately the implicate order lies outside of space-time.

11. Bohm and Peat, 1987.

12. Pribram, 1991.

13. Holographic processing in the brain occurs because information is globally but unevenly dispersed. The dendritic microprocessing networks are distributed throughout the brain and systematized in a global ordering process. Pribram proposes that this distribution acts on a nonlocal basis and is facilitated by electron tunneling (Pribram, 1991). Support for Pribram's view has been provided in the earlier research of DeValois, DeValois, and Yund, who showed that the brain converts visual information by means of clusters of specialized neurons called "feature detectors" (DeValois, DeValois, and Yund, 1979). This was demonstrated by the use of Fourier Transforms of the original visual patterns.

Almost two hundred years ago, Fourier had developed mathematical equations that can now be used to convert a pattern of images into a wave function and back again. Dennis Gabor used Fourier Transforms to develop holographic technology (Gabor, 1948). This technology converts patterns into wave forms of various densities which are blended in the spectral side into a hologram.

Pribram made use of Fourier Transforms and of Gabor's contributions to describe the neuronal processing of visual information. According to Pribram's model, the brain essentially functions as a visual frequency analyzer. In other words, the brain synthesizes and converts images into a dynamic holistic form.

14. Jung, 1955.

15. Peat, 1987.

16. Sheldrake, 1988

17. Laszlo, 1993.

18. Peat, 1987.

19. In the quantum vacuum the potential energies and vectoral energies interact. When symmetry is broken a large amount of energy floods into the vacuum. These dynamics "inform" the configurations of universal constants. According to Laszlo, this acts as a holographic medium that registers and conserves "scalar wave transforms."

Laszlo proposes that the observed anomalies in psi and quantum phenomena are due to the "psi effect"—which can be regarded as the "fifth field." The psi effect is the interconnectivity. This effect is produced by the totality of information that is fed back in the wave pattern through the vacuum. The problem of form is dealt with by the interconnectivity that takes place in the psi field, which is hypothesized to operate on multiple dimensions. There are continuous read-ins and read-outs in the multidimensional wave pattern from the field. In this sense Laszlo has conjectured that the psi field is an extrasensory memory bank. In other words, holographic information is not necessarily stored in the brain but is accessible to it (Laszlo, 1993, p. 182).

20. There appear to be "zero-point" energies in the quantum vacuum. In other words, it is highly sensitive to very subtle fluctuations. These energies seem to be interconnected, which may explain synchronistic arrangements. Laszlo speculates that observed nonlocal phenomena results from the vacuum-transmitted feedback of one particle state or field to another. It is therefore incorrect to think that one particle "knows" what the quantum state of the other is, and responds out of that "knowledge." Rather, the two particles are connected by a continuous, instantly transmitting field.

21. Quoted in Laszlo, 1993.

22. The motion of quanta triggers secondary waves (Pribram, 1991). The phenomena of secondary wavefronts encode their evolutionary trajectories, and in this way matter keeps a record of its own evolution. The process of encoding the wavefronts produced by the trajectories of material objects is carried out in the quantum vacuum, and is translated forward in a kind of Fourier-Transform into the spectral domain. The forward transform creates a kind of imprint or memory.

23. In the mechanistic Newtonian model time reversibility was a mainstay. In 1945 Wheeler and Feynman proposed that the laws of electrodynamics permit radiation as time reversed. They argued that radiation was emitted in both directions in time.

24. Griffin, 1986.

25. Prigogine and Stengers, 1984.

26. Ibid.

27. According to the big bang theory, space-time and the universe are one and began together. So at very high temperatures all particles and forces were fused. The cooling down of the universe contributed to the variation we see today. If the rate of expansion and the emergence of large gravitational masses influence the rate of time, may time be slowing?

28. Teilhard de Chardin was forbidden to teach at the Catholic Institute in Paris because his ideas about evolution were found objectionable by the Church. Though his major work, *The Phenomenon of Man*, was finished in 1938 he was forbidden to publish it. It was finally published in 1955.

29. De Chardin envisioned various levels of evolution. To begin with he refers to the initial web of evolutionary dynamics as forming the "biosphere." The web of inner life or the mind forms the "noosphere." Finally, the convergence and goal of life is to reach the "omega point." De Chardin describes a type of energy he referred to as "radial energy" that radiates out from the organism itself. It is radial energy that evolves to increasing complexity.

30. De Chardin envisioned the evolutionary process as the transformation of matter to spirit to personality to God. He argued against the anthropomorphic view of Christ and preferred to consider Christ at one with the omega point. The term omega point is derived from the Greek letter *O*. He added "mega" to denote greatness. De Chardin proposed that planetary consciousness forms the "omega point." This process occurs with the experience of love. It is the deepest experience one can have "in themselves."

31. In the Emerson essays "*Compensations*," 1st section, 1840.

Glossary

Algorithm: A well-defined sequence of operations or calculation procedures of some kind, such as computations.

Attractor: An organizing principle or "basin." Several types of attractors are evident, such as a "periodic" attractor occurring during a cycle, a "static" attractor occurring when a system is at rest, and a "chaotic" attractor, which offers a new organizing principle following periods of chaos.

Autopoiesis: The term used by Chilean biologist Humberto Maturana, which is derived from the Greek for "self-protection." Autopoietic systems have organizational closure, as they renew themselves and maintain organizational continuity. Yet they are also open systems, as they feed on outside information or energy for life.

Bifurcation: An instantaneous branching or forking in new development, often following a period of far-from-equilibrium conditions during which the previous organization was shattered.

Bottom-up process: A description of the process by which micro components are presumed to have a causal relationship to a macro or higher organization.

Chaos: Unpredictability and indeterminacy. Sometimes chaos is referred to as an extreme form of irregularity. According to chaos theory small changes can result in large differences.

Coevolution: The joint evolution of living systems and the environment.

Complexity: The study of complex systems. Such systems spontaneously self-organize. They are not passive, and they turn whatever happens to their advantage. Living systems, by nature, are complex.

Cybernetics: An information theory developed by Norbert Weiner in the late 1940s. Though generally a description of mechanical processes, it introduced such concepts as negative and positive feedback loops.

Dissipative structure: A leap to a higher level of organization following a bifurcation point. Dissipative structures are novel and result from a reorganization.

Dualism: The concept that there are two or more levels of reality that generally do not coevolve or have influence on one another. However, some dualists feel that there is top-down causation.

Entropy: A measure of the increasing disorder in a system. Entropy is often used in conjunction with the thermodynamic description of disorder, such as "heat death."

Far-from-equilibrium: The condition in which a system such as an organism is destabilized. It is during far-from-equilibrium conditions that systems may reorganize to adjust or deal more effectively with the environmental changes.

Fractal: A term invented by Benoit Mandelbrot to denote self-similar geometric shapes of infinite detail. According to Mandelbrot the coast of Britain could never be accurately measured because of the infinite amount of detail of every curve and rock.

Function: The activity, behavioral qualities, or adaptive pattern of a living system.

Morphogenesis: The development of complex pattern formations, such as the process by which a fertilized egg grows into an adult organism.

Noncomputable: A number that cannot be generated by finitely defined mechanical procedures. Noncompatibility implies that there is no algorithm or procedure to explain consciousness through the use of a computer. This is because computers rely on well-defined computations.

Nonlinear: Subject to changes that are not linear because multiple variables or factors interact to produce abrupt reorganization. In nonlinear systems reductionism has little utility, as the evolution of the whole system cannot be reduced to the sum of its parts.

Process: Change in an organism or other system through which it naturally evolves.

Psychoneuroimmunology: The study of the relationship between the immune system, the brain, and the mind. Researchers in this field have demonstrated a strong connection between one's characteristic emotional states and/or thought patterns and the relative strength of the immune system.

Self-organization: The holistic quality of a system that contributes to emergent properties and attempts to reorganize itself in ever more complex structures despite apparent obstacles.

Self-referential: The process by which a living system refers back to itself as well as to the environment for direction in its evolution or development, in contrast to nonliving systems, which refer only to the environment.

Structure: The biophysiological organization of an organ system or species.

Top-down process: A description of a process by which a higher-order organization has a causal relationship to a bottom-level organization, such as macroprocesses affecting microprocesses.

References

Abraham, R., & Shaw, C. (1984). *Dynamics: The Geometry of Behavior, Parts I and II.* Santa Cruz, CA: Aerial Press.

Annett, M. (1985). *Left, Right, Hand and Brain: The Right Shift Theory.* London: Erlbaum.

Arden, J. (1996). *Consiousness, Dreams, and Self: A Transdisciplinary Approach.* Madison, CT: Psychosocial Press/International Universities Press.

Armstrong, K. (1993). *The History of God.* New York: Ballantine Books.

Aserinsky, E., & Kleitman, N. (1953). "Regularly occurring periods of eye motility and concomitant phenomena during sleep." *Science* 118, 273–74.

Aspect, A. (1983). "Experimental realization of Einstein-Podolsky-Rosen-Bohm-Gedanken experiment: A new violation of Bell's inequalities." *Physics Review Letters* 48, 91–94.

Babloyantz, A. (1988). "Chaotic dynamics in brain activity." In E. Basar (Ed.), *Dynamics of Sensory and Cognitive Processing by the Brain.* Berlin: Springer, 196–202.

Barnaby, K., & D'Acierno, P. (Eds.). (1990). *C. G. Jung and the Humanities: Toward a Hermeneutics of Culture.* Princeton, NJ: Princeton University Press.

Basso, E. (1987). "The implications of a progressive theory of dreaming." In B. Tedlock (Ed.). *Dreaming: Anthropological and Psychological Interpretations.* Santa Fe, NM: School of American Research Press.

Bell, J. S. (1964). "On the Einstein Podolsky Rosen Paradox." *Physics* 1, 195–200.

Bem, D. J. & Honorton, C. (1994). "Does psi exist? Replicable evidence for an anomalous process of information transfer." *Psychological Bulletin* 115; 4–18.

Benor, D. J. (1993). *Healing Research.* Munich: Helix Verlag Gmbh.

Berry, G. L. (1957). *Religions of the World.* New York: Barnes & Noble.

Bertalanffy L. Von (1968). *General System Theory.* Allen Lane/Penguin, Harmondsworth.

———. (1972). *Problems of Life.* New York: Wiley.

Blackmore, S. (1996). "Why psi tells us nothing about consciousness." Paper presented at the "Toward a Science of Consciousness" conference in Tucson, AZ, April 8–13.

Bohm, D. (1980). *Wholeness and the Implicate Order*. New York: Routledge & Kegan Paul.

Bohm, D., & Hiley, B. (1993). *The Undivided Universe: An Ontological Interpretation of Quantum Theory*. New York: Routledge & Kegan Paul.

Bohm, D., & Peat, F. D. (1987). *Science, Order, and Creativity*. New York: Bantam Books.

Bourguignon, E. (1978). "Spirit possession and altered states of consciousness: The evolution of an inquiry." In G. Spindler (Ed.). *The Making of Psychological Anthropology*. Berkeley: University of California Press.

———. (1979). *Psychological Anthropology*, New York: Holt, Rinehart & Winston.

Bowlby, J. (1988). *A Secure Base*. New York: Basic Books.

Breger, L., Hunter, I., & Lane, R. (1971). "The effect of stress on dreams." *Psychological Issues Monograph* 27 (7, Suppl. 3).

Brockman, J. (1995). *The Third Culture: Beyond the Scientific Rrevolution*. New York: Simon & Schuster.

Broughton, R. S. (1991). *Parapsychology: The Controversial Science*. New York: Ballantine Books.

Brown, B. (1970). "Recognition of aspects of consciousness through association with EEG alpha activity represented by a light signal." *Psychophysiology* 6:442.

Brown, P. (1991). *The Hypnotic Brain: Hypnotherapy and Social Communication*. New Haven, CT: Yale University Press.

Byre, R. (1988). "Positive effects of intercessory prayer in a coronary care unit population." *Southern Medical Journal* (July) 81: 7, 826–29.

Campbell, J. (1974). *The Mythic Image*. Princeton, NJ: Princeton University Press.

———. (1987a). *Occidental Mythology*. New York: Penguin Books.

———. (1987b). *Primative Mythology*. New York: Penguin Books.

Cann, R. L. (1987). "In search of Eve." *The Sciences* 27, 30–37.

Cannon, W. (1957). "Voodoo death." *Psychosomatic Medicine* 19, 182.

Cole, M., & Scribner, (1974). *Culture and Thought: A Psychological Introduction*. New York: Wiley.

Combs, A. (1996). *The Radiance of Being: Complexity, Chaos, and the Evolution of Consciousness*. New York: Paragon Press.

Convey, P., & Highfield, R. (1990). *The Arrow of Time: A Voyage Through Science to Solve Time's Greatest Mystery*. New York: Fawcett Columbine Books.

Corballis, M.C. (1991). *The Lopsided Ape: Evolution of the Generative Mind*, New York: Oxford University Press.

Corby, J., et al. (1978). "Psychophysiological correlates of the practice of tantric yoga meditation." *Archives of General Psychiatry* 35, 571–77.

D'Andrade, R. (1961). "Anthropological studies of dreams." *Psychological Anthropology* April, 73–81.

Davies, P. (1988). *The Cosmic Blueprint, New Discoveries in Nature's Creative Ability to Order the Universe*, Touchstone. New York: Simon & Schuster.

———. (1992). *The Mind of God: The Scientific Basis for a Rational World*. New York: Simon & Schuster.

———. (1995). *About Time: Einstein's Unfinished Revolution*. New York: Simon & Schuster.

Degarrod, L. N. (1989). "Coping with stress: Dream interpretation in the Mapuch family." Paper presented at the 6th Annual Conference of the Association for Study of Dreams, London.

Dennett, D. C. (1991). *Consciousness Explained*. Boston: Little, Brown.

Dentan, R. K. (1987). "Entropic consideration of the cross-cultural study of dreams." In

J. Gackenbach (Ed.). *Sleep and Dreams: A Source Book.* New York: Garland.

DeValious, K. K., DeValious & Yund, W. W. (1979). "Responses of striate cortex cell to grating and checkerboard patterns." *Journal of Physiology* 291, 483–505.

Donald, M. (1991). *Origins of the Modern Mind: Three Stages in the Evolution of Culture and Cognition.* Cambridge, MA: Harvard University Press.

Dossey, L. (1993). *Healing Words.* San Francisco: Harper.

Eccles, J. C. (1994). *How the Self Controls the Brain.* Berlin: Springer-Verlag.

Edelman, G. M. (1992). *Bright Air Brilliant Fire: On the Matter of the Mind.* New York: Basic Books.

Einstein, A., Podelsky, P., & Rosen, N. (1935). "Can quantum-mechanical description of physical reality be considered complete?" In J. Wheller & W. H. Zurek (Eds.) *Quantum Theory.* Princeton, NJ: Princeton University Press. Original in *Physics Review* 47, 777–80.

Eisler, R. (1987). *The Chalice and the Blade: Our History Our Future.* San Francisco: Harper & Row.

Ekeh, P. P. (1970). "Dreams and society: a sociological analysis of Nigerian dreams." Ph.D. dissertation, Colombia University. (*Dissertation Abstracts.* International, 30 [10-B, 4790, 1970]).

Eldredge, N. & Gould, S. (1972). "Punctuated equilibria: An alternative to phyletic gradualism." In T. Schopf (Ed.). *Models in Paleobiology.* San Francisco: Freeman.

Elson, J., Harris, P., & Cunis, D. (1977). "Physiological changes in yoga meditation." *Psychophysiology* 14(1), 52–57.

Fagen, B. M. (1990). *The Peopling of Our World.* London: Thames & Hudson.

Falk, D. (1983). "Cerebral cortices of East African early hominids." *Science* 222, 1072–74.

Feigenbaum, M. (1980). "Universal behavior in nonlinear systems." *Los Alamos Science* 1, 4.

Fisher, C., Gross, J., & Zuch, J. (1955). "Cycle of penile erections synchronous with dreaming (REM) sleep." *Archives of General Psychiatry* 12, 29–45.

Foulkes, D. (1967). "Dreams of the male child: Four case studies." *Journal of Psychology and Psychiatry* 8, 81–97.

———. (1972). *Theories of Dream Formation and Recent Studies of Sleep Consciousness.* New York: Doubleday.

———. (1982). *Children's Dreams: Longitudinal Studies.* New York: Wiley.

———. (1985). "Dreaming and consciousness." *European Journal of Cognitive Psychology* 2, 39–55.

Foulkes, D., & Vogal, G. (1965). "Mental activity at sleep onset." *Journal of Abnormal Psychology* 70, 231–43.

Freeman, W. (1983). "Physiological basis of mental images." *Biological Psychiatry* 18 (10), 1107.

———. (1991). "The physiology of perception; the brain transforms sensory messages into consciousness perception instantly." *Scientific American* Feb. 264 (2) 78.

Freeman, W., & Skarda, C. (1985). "Spatial EGG pattern, nonlinear dynamics and perception: The neo-Sherrington view." *Brain Research Review,* 10, 147.

Freud, S. (1953). "Dreams and telepathy." In G. Devereux (Ed.) *Psychoanalysis and the Occult.* New York: International Universities Press.

———. (1961). *The Future of the Illusion.* New York: Anchor Doubleday. (original published in 1927.)

Friedman, W. J. (1990). *About Time, Inventing the Fourth Dimension.* Cambridge, MA: MIT Press.

Gabor, D. (1948). "A new microscopic principle." *Nature* 161, 777–78.

Gackenbush, J. (1990). "Women meditators as gifted lucid dreamers." In S. Krippner (Ed.). *Dreamtime and Dreamwork.* Los Angeles: Tarcher, 244–51.

Gackenbush, J., & Bosveld, J. (1989). *Control Your Dreams.* New York: Harper & Row.

Gallup, G. G. Jr. (1970). "Chimpanzees: Self recognition." *Science* 167, 86–87.

———. (1977). "Self recognition in primates: A comparative approach to bidirectional properties of consciousness." *American Psychologist* 32, 329–38.

———. (1982). "Self-awareness and the emergence of mind in primates." *American Journal of Primatology* 2, 237–48.

Galvin, F. (1989). "The boundary characteristics of lucid dreamers." Paper presented at the Annual Conference of the Association for the Study of Dreams, London.

Gazzaniga, M. S. (1992). *Nature's Mind: The Biological Roots of Thinking, Emotions, Sexuality, Language and Intelligence.* New York: Basic Books.

Gell-Mann, M. (1994). *The Quark and the Jaguar.* New York: W. H. Freeman.

Gimbutas, M. (1977). "The first wave of eurasian steppe pastoralists into copper age europe," *Journal of Indo-European Studies* 5 (Winter), 277.

———. (1982). *The Goddesses of Old Europe 7000–3500 B.C.* Berkeley: University of California Press.

Glantz, K., & Pearce, J. (1984). *Exiles from Eden: Psychotherapy from an Evolutionary Perspective.* New York: W.W. Norton.

Gleick, J. (1987). *Chaos: Making a New Science.* New York: Penguin.

Gödel, K. (1931). "Uber formal unentscheidbare staze per Principia mathematics und Verwandter system I." *Monatsheft fur Mathematik und Physik* 38, 178–98.

Goodfriend, M., & Wolpert, E. (1971). "Death from fright: Report of a case and literature review." *Psychosomatic Medicine* 38, 348.

Goodwin, B. (1994). *How the Leopard Changed Its Spots: The Evolution of Complexity.* New York: Scribner's.

Gould, S. J. (1982). "Is a new and general theory of evolution emerging?" In J. M. Smith (Ed). *Now, a Century after Darwin.* San Francisco: W.H. Freeman, 129–95.

Gould, S. J., & Marler, P. (1987). "Learning by instinct." *Scientific American* 256, 62–73.

Grant, M. (1977). *Jesus: An Historian's Review of the Gospel.* New York: Scribner's.

Greenberg, J. R., & Mitchell, S. A. (1983). *Object Relations in Psychoanalytic Theory,* Cambridge, MA: Harvard University Press.

Griffin, D. R. (1986). *Physics and the Ultimate Significance of Time, Bohm, Prigogine and Process Philosophy.* Albany: State University of New York Press.

Griffith, R., Miyagi, O., & Tago, A. (1958). "The univerisality of typical dreams: Japanese vs. American." *American Anthropologist* 60, 1173–79.

Grof, S. (1985). *Beyond the Brain: Birth, Death and Transcendence in Psychotherapy.* Albany: State University of New York Press.

Hall, C., & Domhoff, (1963). "Aggression in dreams." *International Journal of Social Psychology* 9, 259–67.

Hall, C., & Van de Castle, R. L. (1966). *The Content Analysis of Dreams.* New York: Appleton-Century-Crofts.

Hameroff, S. (1987). *Ultimate Computing: Biochemical Consciousness and Nantechnology.* Amsterdam: North Holland.

Hartse, K. M., Roth, T., & Zorick, F. J. (1982). "Day time sleepiness and daytime wakefulness: The effect of instruction." *Sleep* 5 (Suppl. 2), 107–18.

Hauri, P. (1976). "Dreams in patients readmitted from reactive depression." *Journal of Abnormal Psychology* 85, 1–10.

Hebb, D. D. (1949). *The Organization of Behavior: A Neuropsychological Theory.* New

York: Wiley.

Hegel, G. W. F. (1837, 1992). Quoted in Levin (1992). *Theories of the Self.* Washington, DC: Hemisphere Publishing Corporation.

Heidegger, M. (1927/1968). *Being and Time.* New York: Harper & Row.

Heisenberg, W. (1958). *Physics and Philosophy: The Revolution in Modern Science.* New York: Harper & Row.

———. (1984). "The debate between Plato and Democrius." In K. Wilber (Ed.). *Quantum Questions: The Mystical Writings of the Great Physicists.* Boston: Shambhala New Science Press.

Hiley, B. (1994). Personal communication.

Hobson, J. A. (1988). *The Dreaming Brain: How the Brain Creates Both the Sense of and Nonsense of Dreams.* New York: Basic Books.

Hobson, J. A., & McCarley, R. W. (1977). "The brain as a dream state generator: An activation-synthesis hypothesis of the dream process." *American Journal of Psychiatry* 136(3), 1335–47.

Honorton, C. (1991). "Summarizing research findings: Metaanalysis methods and their use in parapsychology." In L. Coly (Ed.). *PSI Research Methodology: A Reexamination.* New York: Parapsychology Foundation.

Honorton, C., Berger, R. E., Varvoglis, Quant, Deer, P., Scheuhter, E. & Ferrari, D. L. (1990). "Psi communication in the ganzfeld: Experiments with an automated testing system and comparison with a meta-analysis of earlier studes." *Journal of Parapsychology* 54, 99–140.

Honorton, C. & Schechner, E. (1986). "Ganzfeld target retrieval with an automated testing system: A model for initial ganzfeld success." In D. Weiner & R. D. Nelson (Eds.). *Research in Parapsychology.* Meteuchen, NJ: Scarecrow Press.

Hunt, H. (1989). *The Multiplicity of Dreams: Memory, Imagination and Consciousness.* New Haven, CT: Yale University Press.

———. (1995). *On the Nature of Human Consciousness.* New Haven, CT: Yale University Press.

Husserl, E. (1931/1962). *Ideas.* New York: Collier Books.

Huxley, A. (1948). *The Perennial Philosophy.* New York: Harper & Row.

Hyland, D. A. (1973). *The Origins of Philosophy: From Myth to Meaning.* New York: Putnam.

Hyman, R. (1994). "Anomaly or artifact? Comment on Bem and Honorton." *Psychological Bulletin* 115, 19–24.

Ingles, J., & Lawson, J. (1981). "Sex differences in the effects of unilateral brain damage on intelligence." *Science* 2(2).

Irwin, H. (1989). *An Introduction to Parapsychology.* Jefferson, NC: McFarland.

Jackson, D. (1957). "The question of family homeostasis." *Psychiatric Quarterly Supplement* 31, 79–90.

Jahn R. (1990). Paper presented at the Science and Consciousness Conference, San Francisco, 1990.

Jahn, R. J., & Dunne, B. J. (1987). *Margin of Reality: The Role of Consciousness in the Physical World.* New York: Harcourt Brace Jovanovich.

James, W. (1890/1950). *Principles of Psychology* . New York: Dover Publications.

Jantsch, E. (1980). *The Self Organizing Universe.* Oxford: Pergamon Press.

Jerison, H. (1973). *Evolution of Brain and Intelligence.* New York: Academic Press.

Jiayin, M. (1992). "Transformations in the Chinese cognitive map." In E. Laszlo, I. Masulli, R. Artigiani, & V. Csanyi (Eds.). *The Evolution of Cognitive Maps: New Paradigms for the Twenth-First Century,* 221–37.

Johanson, D. C., & Edey, M. (1981). *Lucy, the Beginning of Mankind.* New York: Warner Books.

Jung, C. G. (1955). "Synchronicity: An acausal connecting principle." In C. G. Jung & W. Pauli (Ed.). *The Interpretation of Nature and the Psyche*. New York: Pantheon Books.

———. (1958) *Psyche and Symbol*. Garden City, NY: Doubleday.

———. (1964). *Man and His Symbols*. New York: Dell.

Kauffman, S. (1993). *The Origins of Order: Self-organization and Selection in Evolution*. New York: Oxford University Press.

Kimura, D. (1979). "Neuromotor mechanisms in the evolution of human communication. In H. D. Steklis and M. J. Raleigh (Eds.). *Neurobiology of Social Communication in Primates*. New York: Academic Press, 197–219.

———. (1992). "Sex differences in the brain." *Scientific American* Sept.

Kobasa, S. C. (1990). "Stress-resistant personality." In R. Ornstein & C. Swencious (Eds.). *The Healing Brain, a Scientific Reader*. New York: Guilford Press.

Kohut, H. (1977). *The Restoration of the Self*. New York: International Universities Press.

Korzybski, A. (1925–26). *Time-Binding: The General Theory, Two Papers*. Lakeville, CO: Institute of General Semantics.

———. (1958). *Science and Society*, 4th ed Lakeville, CT: International Non-Aristotelian Library Publishing Co.

Krack, W. (1992). "Myths in dreams, thought in images: An amazonian contribution to the psychoanalytic theory of primary process." In B. Tedlock (Ed.). *Dreaming: Anthropological and Psychological Interpretations*. Santa Fe, NM: School of American Research Press.

Kramer, M. (1990). "Nightmares (dream disturbances) in post traumatic stress disorder, implications for a theory of dreaming." In R. Bootzin, J. Kihlstrom, & D. Schacter, (Eds.). *Sleep and Cognition*. Washington, DC: American Psychological Association.

Kramer, M., Kinney, L., & Scharf, M. (1983). "Sex differences in dreams." *Psychiatric Journal of the University of Ottawa* 8, 1–4.

Kramer, M., Trinder, J., Whitman, R. M., & Baldridge, B. J. (1969). "The incidence of 'masochistic' dreams in the night collected dreams of depressed subjects." *Psychophysiology* 6, 250 (APSS Abstracts).

Krippner, S. (1974). "Induction of psychotronic effects in altered states of consciousness." *Impact of Science on Society* 24, 339–46.

———. (1990). "Tribal shamans and their travels in dreamtime: Decoding the language of the night." In S. Krippner (Ed.). *Dreamtime and Dreamwork*. Los Angeles: Tarcher/Perigee Books.

Krippner, S., & Rubenstein, K. (1990). "Gender differences in dream content." *A.S.D. Newsletter* 125, 405–6.

Krippner, S., & Ullman, M. (1959). "Telepathic perception in the dream state." *Perception and Motor Skills* 29, 915–18.

Krippner, S., et al. (1974). "Content analysis of 30 dreams from 10 pre-operative male transsexuals." *Journal of the American Society of Psychosomatic Dentistry and Medicine*, monograph suppliment no. 2, 3–23.

———. (1996). "Psi research and brain 'resevere capacities.'" In B. Goertzel & A. Combs (Eds.). *Dynamical Psychology, an International Journal*. Availiable on the World Wide Web at: http://godel.uwa.edu.

Kroger, W. S. (1976). *Clinical and Experimental Hypnosis: In Medicine, Dentistry, and Psychology*. Philadelphia: J.B. Lippincott.

Kubler-Ross, E. (1991). *On Life after Death*. New York: Quality Paperback Book Club.

Kuhn, T. (1967). *The Structure of Scientific Revolutions.* 2nd ed. (1st ed. 1962). Chicago: University of Chicago Press.

Kuku, M. (1994). *Hyperspace.* New York: Oxford University Press.

LaBerge, S. (1990). "Lucid dreaming, psychophysiological studies of consciousness during REM sleep." In R. Bootzin, J. Kihlstrom, & D. Schacter (Eds.). *Cognition in Sleep.* Washington, DC: American Psychological Association, 109–26.

LaBerge, S., & Rheingold (1990). *Exploring the World of Lucid Dreaming.* New York: Ballantine Books.

Laszlo, E. (1987). *Evolution: The Grand Synthesis.* Boston and London: New Science Library, Shambala.

———. (1993). *The Creative Cosmos.* Edinburgh: Floris Books.

Leakey, R. E., & Lewin, R. (1977). *Origins.* New York: Dutton.

———. (1992) *Origins: Reconsidered.* New York: Doubleday.

Levin, J. D. (1991). *Theories of the Self.* Washington, DC.: Hemisphere Publishing Corporation.

Levi-Strauss, C. (1963). *Structural Anthropology.* New York: Basic Books.

Lewin, I., & Senger, J. (1991). "Psychological Effects of REM ('Dream') deprivation upon waking mentation." In S. Ellman & J. Antrobus (Eds.). *The Mind in Sleep, Psychology and Psychophysiology.* New York: Wiley, 396–412.

Lewin, R. (1992). *Complexity: Life at the Edge of Chaos.* New York: Macmillan.

Lieberman, P. (1991). *Uniquely Human: The Evolution of Speech, Thought, and Selfless Behavior,* Cambridge, MA: Harvard University Press.

Locke, S. E., & Kraus, L. (1982). "Modulation of natural killer cell activity by life stress and coping ability. In S. M. Levy (Ed.). *Biological Mediators in Behavior and Disease: Neoplasm.* New York: Elsevier Biomedical.

Lorenz, E. (1963). "Deterministic non periodic flow." *Journal of Atmospheric Science* 2, 130–41.

———. (1984). "Irregularity: A fundamental property of the atmosphere." *Tellus* 36A, 98–110.

Lortie-Lussier, M., Schwab, C., & DeKornick, J. (1985). "Working mothers vs. homemakers: Do dreams reflect the changing roles of women?" *Sex Roles* 12, 1009–12.

Lovejoy, O. C. (1981). "The origin of man." *Science* 221, 341–50.

Luria, A. R. (1966). *Higher Cortical Functions in Man.* New York: Basic Books.

———. (1973). *The Working Brain, an Introduction to Neuropsychology.* (B. Haigh, trans.). New York: Basic Books.

———. (1976). *Cognitive Development.* Cambridge, MA: Harvard University Press.

Mahoney, M. J. (1991). *Human Change Processes: The Scientific Foundations of Psychotherapy.* New York: Basic Books.

Malenoski, B. (1961). *The Dynamics of Culture Change.* New Haven, CT: Yale University Press.

Mallory, J. P. (1989). *In Search of the Indo-Europeans.* New York: Thames & Hudson.

Mamelak, A. N., & Hobson, J. A. (1989). "Dream bizarreness as the cognitive correlate of altered neuronal behavior in REM sleep." *Journal of Cognitive Neuroscience* 1, 201–22.

Marshack, A. (1991). T*he Roots of Civilization: Cognitive Beings of Man's First Art, Symbol and Notation.* Mt. Kicao, NY: Moyer Bell.

Maslow, A. (1968). *Motivation and Personality.* New York: Harper & Row.

Maturana, H. (1970). *Biology of Cognition.* Biological Computer Laboratory 9.0. Urbana, Ill: University of Illinois.

Maturana, H. R., & Varela, F. (1987). *The Tree of Knowledge: The Biological Roots of*

Human Understanding. Boston: New Science Library, Shambala.

McCarley, R. W., & Massaquoi, S. (1985). "The REM sleep ultradian rhythm: A limit cycle mathematical model." *Experimental Brain Research* Suppl. 12, 288–308.

Milgram, S. (1963). "Behavioral study of obedience." *Journal of Abnormal and Social Psychology* 67, 371–78.

Minsky, M. (1987). *The Society of Mind*. New York: Simon & Schuster.

Monroe, L., Rechtschaffen, A., Foulkes, D., & Jensen, J. (1965). "Discriminality of REM and NREM reports." *Journal of Personality and Social Psychology* 2, 456–60.

Morrison, A. R. (1983). "Paradoxical sleep and alert wakefulness: Variations on a theme. In M. Chase & E. Weitzman (Eds.). *Sleep Disorders: Basic and Clinical Research*. New York: SP Medical and Scientific Books, 95–122.

Murphy, J. (1976). "Psychiatric Labeling in Cross-Cultural Perspectives (Yoruba and Eskimo)." *Science* 191, 1019–28.

Murphy, M. (1992). *The Future of the Body: Explorations into the Further Evolution of Human Nature*. Los Angeles: Jeremy P. Tarcher.

Orne, M. (1986). "The validity of memories retrieved in hypnosis." In B. Zilbergeld, M. Edelstein, & D. Arnoz (Eds.). *Hypnosis: Questions and Answers*. New York: W. W. Norton.

Parrich, W., & Stevenson, I. (1986). "Near-death experience in India." *Journal of Nervous and Mental Disease* 174, 165–70.

Parrinder, G. (1971). *World Religions, from Ancient History to the Present*. New York: The Hamoly Publishing Group Limited.

Peat, F. D. (1987). *Synchronicity: The Bridge Between Matter and Mind*. New York: Bantam Books.

———. (1990). *Einstein's Moon: Bell's Theorem and the Curious Quest for Quantum Reality*. Chicago: Contemporary Books.

———. (1991). *The Philosophers Stone: Chaos, Synchronicity and the Hidden Order of the World*. New York: Bantam Books.

Penrose, R. (1989). *The Emperor's New Mind: Concerning Computers, Minds and the Laws of Physics*. New York: Oxford University Press.

———. (1994). *The Shadows of the Mind*. New York: Oxford University Press.

Perry, C., Laurence, J. R., Nadon, R., & Labelle, L. (1986). "Past life regression." In B. Zilbergeld, M. G. Edestein, and D. Araoz (Eds.). *Hypnosis: Questions and Answers* New York: Norton, 50–61.

Pert, C. (1990). "The wisdom of receptors: neuropeptides, the emotions and body-mind." In R. Ornstein & C. Swencionis (Eds.). *The Healing Brain: A Scientific Reader*. New York: Guilford Press.

Piaget, J. (1981). *Intelligence and Affectivity: Their Relationship During Child Development*. Palo Alto, CA: Annual Reviews.

Popper, K. (1982). *The Open Universe: An Argument for Indeterminism*. London: Hutchison.

Povinelli, D. J. (1993). "Reconstructing the evolution of the mind." *American Psychologist* May, 493–509.

Pribram, K. H. (1971). *Languages of the Brain: Experimental Paradoxes and Principles in Neuropsychology*. Englewood Cliffs, NJ: Prentice-Hall.

———. (1982). "Localization and distribution of function in the brain." In J. Orbach (Ed.). *Neuropsychology after Lashley*. New York: Lawrence Erlbaum Associates, 273–96.

———. (1991). *Brain and Perception: Holonomy and Structure in Figural Processing*. Hillsdale, NJ: Lawrence Erlbaum Associates.

Prigogine, I., & Stengers, I. (1984). *Order Out of Chaos: Man's Dialogue with Nature*.

New York: Bantam Books.

———. (1988). *Entbele te L'etermete*. Paris: Fayard.

Radin, D., & Nelson, D. (1989). "Consciousness-related effects in random physical systems," *Foundations of Physics*, 19, 1499–514.

Rhine, J. (1947). *The Reach of the Mind*. New York: William Sloane Associates.

Rhine, J., McDougall, W., & Prince, J. W. (1964). *Extrasensory Perception*. Boston Society for Psychic Research. Boston: Bruce Humphries.

Rhine, L. (1961). *Hidden Channels of the Mind*. New York: William Sloane Associates.

Ring, K. (1980). *The Ring of Death*, New York: Quill.

———. (1985). *Heading towards Omega: In Search of the Meaning of the Near-Death Experience*. New York: Quill.

Rogers, C. R. (1980). *A Way of Being*. Boston: Houghton Mifflin.

Roschke, J., & Aldenhoff, J. B. (1991). "A Nonlinear approach to brain function: Deterministic chaos and sleep EEG." *Sleep* 15 (2) 95–101.

Rosenbaum, R., & Dyckman, J. (1995). "Integrating self and system: An empty intersection?" *Family Process* 34, 21–44.

Ryle, G. (1949). *The Concept of the Mind*. London: Hutchison.

Sabini, M. (1981). "Dreams as an aid in determining diagnosis, prognosis and attitude towards treatment." *Psychotherapy and Psychosomatics* 36, 24–36.

Sabom, M. (1982). *Reflections on Death*. New York: Harper & Row.

Sargent, C. (1981). "Extraversion and performance in 'extra-sensory' perception tasks." *Personality and Individual Differences* 2, 137–43.

Sassin, J. F. (1969). "Human growth hormone release: Relation to slow wave sleep and sleep cycles." *Science* 32–41.

Savich, V. M. (1980). "Molecular clocks and hominid evolution after twelve years." *American Journal of Physical Anthropology* Feb., 52, 275–76.

Savich, V. M. & Wilson, A. C. (1967). "Immunological time scale for hominid evolution." *Science*, 158, 1200–1203.

Schauss, H. (1938, 1974). *The Jewish Festivals: History and Observerance*. New York: Schocken Books.

Schleifer, S. J., Keller, S. J. Camerino, M., Thornton, J. C., & Stein, M. (1983). "Suppression of lymphocyte stimulation following bereavement." *Journal of the American Medical Association* 250, 374–77.

Schneider, D., & Sharp, L. (1969). "The dream life of primitive people: The dreams of the Yir Yoront of Australia." *Anthropological Studies* 1, American Anthropological Association. Ann Arbor, MI: University Microfilms.

Schultz, K. L. & Koulack, D. (1980). "Dream affect and the menstrual cycle." *Journal of Nervous and Mental Disease* 168, 436–38.

Segal, J. (1975). "Biofeedback as a medical treatment." *Journal of the American Medical Association* 232, 172.

Shatz, C. (1992). "The developing brain." *Scientific American* Sept., 267 (3), 60–67.

Sheldrake, R. (1988). *The Presence of the Past: Morphic Resonance and the Habits of Nature*. New York: Vintage Books.

Shipman, P. (1986). "Scavenging or hunting in early homonids: Theoretical framework and tests." *American Anthropologist* 88, 27–47.

Singer, J. (1981). *Day Dreaming and Fantasy*. New York: Oxford University Press.

———. (1988). "Sampling ongoing consciousness and emotional experience: Implications for health." In M. Horowitz, (Ed.). *Psychodynamics and Cognition*. Chicago: University of Chicago Press 297–347.

Slife, B. D. (1993). *Time and Psychological Explanation*. Albany: State University of New York Press.

Smith, H. (1987). "Is there a perennial philosophy?" *Journal of the American Academy of Religion*, 553–66.

Solecki, R. S. (1977). "The implications of the Shanidar Cave Neanderthal floor burial." *Annals of the New York Academy of Sciences* 293, 114–24.

Solomon, G. (1990a). "The emerging field of psychoneuroimmunology, with a special note on AIDS." In R. Ornstein & C. Swencious, (Eds.). *The Healing Brain: A Scientific Reader*. New York: Guilford Press.

———. (1990b). "Emotions, Stress and Immunity." In R. Ornstein, & C. Swencious (Eds.). *The Healing Brain: A Scientific Reader*. New York: Guilford Press.

———. (1991). Personal communication.

Speer, D. C. (1970). "Family systems: Morphostasis and morphogenesis or is homeostasis enough?" *Family Process* 9, 259–78.

Sperry, R. (1976). "Changing concepts of consciousness and free will." *Perspectives in Biology and Medicine* 20, 9–19.

———. (1987). "Structure and significance of the consciousness revolution." *Journal of Mind and Behavior* 8, 37–66.

———. (1988). "Psychology's mentalist paradigm and the religion/science tension." *American Psychologist* 43 (No. 8), 607–13.

Spindler, G. D. (1978). *The Making of Psychological Anthropology*. Berkeley: University of California Press.

Stern, D. (1985). *The Interpersonal World of the Infant*. New York: Basic Books.

Stoyva, J. (1965). "Posthypnotically suggested dreams and sleep cycles." *Archives of General Psychiatry* 12, 287–94.

Suppe, F. (1977). *The Structure of Scientic Theories*, 2nd ed. Chicago: University of Illinois Press.

Suzuki, D. T. (1969). *The Field of Zen*. New York: Perennial Library.

Szentagothai, J., & Erdi, P. (1989). "Self-organization in the nervous system." *Journal of Socal and Biological Structures* 12, 367–84.

Tart, C. (1964). "A comparison of suggested dreams occurring in hypnosis and sleep." *International Journal of Clinical and Experimental Hypnosis* 12, 263–89.

———. (1965). "Toward experimental control of dreaming: A review of the literature." *Psychological Bulletin* 64, 81–91.

———. (1969). *Altered States of Consciousness*. New York: Doubleday.

———. (1970). "A comparison of suggested dreams occurring in hypnosis and sleep." *International Journal of Clinical and Experimental Hypnosis* 12, 263–89.

———. (1975). *States of Consciousness*. New York: Dutton.

———. (1976). *Learning to Use ESP*. Chicago: University of Chicago Press.

———. (1977). *PSI: Scientific Studies of the Psychic Realm*. New York: Dutton.

———. (1979). "From spontaneous event to lucity: A review of attempts to consciously control nocturnal dreaming." In B. Wolman (Ed.). *Handbook of Dreams*. New York: Van Nostrand Reinhold, 226–68.

———. (1991). *Open Mind, Discriminating Mind, Reflections on Human Potentialities*. San Francisco: Harper & Row.

Tedlock, B. (1987a). "Zuni and Quiche dream sharing." In B. Tedlock (Ed.). *Dreaming: Anthropological and Psychological Interpretations*. Santa Fe, NM: School of American Research Press.

———. (Ed.), (1987b). *Dreaming: Anthropological and Psychological Interpretations*. Santa Fe, NM: School of American Research Press.

Teilhard de Chardin, P. (1959/1961). *The Phenomenon of Man*. New York: Harper & Row (originally published in French in 1955).

Thom, R. (1972). *Structural Stability and Morphogenesis*. Reading, MA: Benjamin.

Thorne, K. (1994). *Black Holes and Time Warps.* New York: W. W. Norton.

Tomkins, S. (1962, 1963). *Affect, Imagery and Consciousness*, Vol. I and II. New York: Springer.

Ulman, M. (1987). "Wholeness and dreaming." In B. Hiley, & F. D. Peat (Eds.). *Quantum Implications.* New York: Routledge & Kegan Paul.

Ullman, M., & Krippner, S., with Vaughn, A. (1973). *Dream Telepathy.* Baltimore, MD: Penguin Books.

Valsiner, J. (1981). *Human Development and Culture, the Social Nature of Personality and Its Study.* Lexington, MA.: Lexington Books.

Van de Castle, R. L. (1968). "Differences in dream content among psychiatric inpatients with different MMPI profiles." *Psychophysiology* 4: 374 (APSS Abstracts).

———. (1974). *The Psychology of Dreaming.* Morristown, NJ: General Learning Press.

———. (1994). *Our Dreaming Mind.* New York: Ballantine Books.

Vandervert, L. (1990). "A measurable and testable brain-based emergent interactionalism: An alternative to Sperry's mentalist emergent interactionalism." *Journal of Mind and Behavior* 12, 201–20.

Varela, F. (1975). "A calculus of self-reference," *Journal of General Systems* 2, 5.

———. (1979). *Principles of Biological Autonomy.* New York: Elsevier/North-Holland.

Vico, G. (1744/1994). *The New Science of Giambattista Vico* (T. G. Bergin & M. H. Fisch, trans.). Ithaca, NY: Cornell University Press.

Vogel, G. W. (1979). "REM sleep and the prevention of endogenous depression." *Waking and Sleep* 3, 313–18.

Washburn, M. (1988). *The Ego and the Dynamic Ground: A Transpersonal Theory of Human Development.* Albany: State University of New York Press.

Watkins, K., & Fromm, D. (1984). "Labial coordination in children preliminary considerations." *Journal of Acoustical Society of America* 75, 629–32.

Watts, A. (1957). *The Way of Zen.* New York: Pantheon Books.

Webb, W. B. (1969). "Partial and differential sleep deprivation." In A. Kales (Ed.). *Sleep Physiology and Pathology: A Symposium.* Philadelphia: J.P. Lippincott.

Weinburg, S. (1977). "The search for unity: notes for a history of quantum field theory." *Daedalus Discoveries and Interpretations: Studies in Contemporary Scholarship* 11 Fall.

Weinstein, L., Schartz, D., & Arkin, A. (1991). "Qualitative aspects of sleep mentation." In S. Ellman & J. Antrobus (Eds.), *The Mind in Sleep Psychology and Psychophysiology*, 2nd ed. New York: Wiley 172–213.

Werntz, D., Bickford, R. Bloom, F., & Shannahoff, D. (1983). "Alternating cerebral hemisphere activity and lateralization of autonomic nervous system function." *Neurobiology* 4, 225–42.

Wetzenhoffer, A. (1986). "Scientific support for hypnosis and its effects." In B. Zilbergeld, M. Edelstein, & D. Araoz, (Eds.). *Hypnosis: Questions and Answers.* New York: W. W. Norton.

Whinney, J. (1996). "The induction of conciousness in ischemic brain." In S. Hameroff, A. Koszniak, and A. Scott, (Eds.). *Toward a Science of Consciousness.* Boston: MIT Press, 161–87.

White, J. (1996). *Toward a Transpersonal America.* Unpublished manuscript.

White, T.D. (1976). "Fossil hominids from the Laetolil beds." *Nature* August 262, 460–66.

Whitehead, A. N. (1925/1954). *Science and the Modern World* New York: Free Press. (original published in 1925 New York: Macmillan).

———. (1929/1957). *Process and Reality: An Essay in Cosmology.* New York: Harper & Row. (original published in 1929, New York: Macmillan).

Whiting, B. B., & Whiting, J. W. (1975). *Children of Six Cultures: A Psychological Analysis.* Cambridge, MA: Harvard University Press.

Wiener, N. (1948). *Cybernetics.* New York: Wiley.

Wilber, K. (1977). *The Spectrum of Consciousness.* Weaton, IL: Quest.

———. (1982). *The Holographic Paradigm and Other Paradoxes.* Boulder CO: Shambala Press.

———. (1983). *Up from Eden: A Transpersonal View of Human Evolution.* Boulder CO: Shambala Press.

———. (Ed.). (1984). *Quantum Questions: The Mystical Writings of the World's Great Physicists.* Boston: Shambala New Science Library.

———. (1995). *Sex, Ecology, and Spirituality: The Spirit of Evolution.* Boston: Shambala.

Wingett, C., Kramer, M., & Whitman, R. (1970). "Dreams and demography." Paper presented at the 13th annual meeting of a Group without a Name, Montreal. (reprinted in *Canadian Psychiatric Association Journal* 17, 203–8, 1972).

Winnicott, D. W. (1958). *Through Paeditrics to Psychoanalysis.* London: Hogarth Press.

Winson, J. (1991). "The meaning of dreams." *Scientific American* 263 (5), 86–96.

Wolkove, N., et al. (1984). "The effect of transcendental meditation on breathing and respiratory flow." *Journal of Applied Physiology* 56(3), 607–12.

Young-Eisendrath, P., & Hall, J. (1991). *Jung's Self Psychology: A Constructionvist Perspective.* New York: Guilford Press.

Index

About the Author

JOHN BOGHOSIAN ARDEN is the Chief Psychologist at the Kaiser Permanente Medical Center in Vallejo and Vacaville, California. Recently, he served as an Adjunct Research Faculty Member at the California School of Professional Psychology in Berkeley/Alameda, California. He is the author of *Consciousness, Dreams, and Self: A Transdisciplinary Approach*, among other works.

ISBN 0-275-96032-3

90000>

EAN

9 780275 960322

HARDCOVER BAR CODE